Archival Science Bibliography

Bibliographie en archivistique

1986-1988

Canadian Centre for Information and
Documentation on Archives

Centre canadien d'information et de
documentation en archivistique

 National Archives   Archives nationales
of Canada   du Canada

Canadian Cataloguing in Publication Data

Canadian Centre for Information and Documentation on Archives.

Archival science bibliography, 1986-1988 =
Bibliographie en archivistique, 1986-1988.

Text in English and French.
Includes index.
DSS Cat. no SA2-220/1988
ISBN 0-662-58342-6

1.   Archives — Bibliography — Catalogs.
2.   Records — Management — Bibliography — Catalogs.
3.   Canadian Centre for Information and Documentation on Archives — Catalogs.
I.   Title.
II. Title: Bibliographie en archivistique, 1986-1988.

Z5140.C35   1988

Données de catalogage avant publication (Canada)

Centre canadien d'information et de documentation en archivistique.

Archival science bibliography, 1986-1988 =
Bibliographie en archivistique, 1986-1988.

Texte en français et en anglais.
Comprend un index.
Cat. MAS n° SA2-220/1988
ISBN 0-662-58342-6

1.   Archives — Bibliographie — Catalogues.
2.   Archives — Gestion — Bibliographie — Catalogues.
3.   Centre canadien d'information et de documentation en archivistique — Catalogues.
I.   Titre.
II. Titre : Bibliographie en archivistique, 1986-1988.

Z5140.C35   1988

This publication is printed on alkaline paper.

National Archives of Canada
395 Wellington Street
Ottawa, Ontario
K1A 0N3
(613) 995-5138

© Minister of Supply and Services
Canada 1991
Cat. No: SA2-220/1988
ISBN: 0-662-58342-6

Le papier de cette publication est alcalin.

Archives nationales du Canada
395, rue Wellington
Ottawa (Ontario)
K1A 0N3
(613) 995-5138

© Ministre des Approvisionnements et
Services Canada 1991
N° de cat. : SA2-220/1988
ISBN 0-662-58342-6

Table of Contents/
Table des matières

Introduction

The **Canadian Centre for Information and Documentation on Archives** (CCIDA) is pleased to release the continuation of the retrospective bibliography published in the special June-September 1987 issue of the journal, *Archives*.

Like the previous bibliography, it consists mainly of the references given in the current bibliographies published in each issue of this journal, but also includes all those that we were unable to provide because of a lack of space.

In fact, the present bibliography completely reproduces the content of CCIDA's automated bibliographic data base known as **ARCHBIB.87**. It therefore comprises 2,066 references to publications dealing with all facets of archives administration, records management and their auxiliary techniques.

More than half of these references (1,550) refer researchers to articles or works published in English. French is, of course, the second most represented language with close to 400 titles. The rest refer to sources published in Russian (51), German (47), Dutch (9), Spanish (6) and Italian (4).

We hope that this bibliography, like its predecessors, will be of service to all members of the Canadian archival community.

In closing, we would like to inform interested individuals that publication of **ARCHBIB.89**, including references gathered during the past two years, is planned for 1991. It in turn will be followed by a complete review covering 1986 to 1991, which will appear under the auspices of the Association des archivistes du Québec, in anticipation of the XII International Council on Archives Congress in Montreal.

Acknowledgements

This bibliography would never have been possible without the co-operation and constant effort of many people. We would particularly like to thank all those who kindly assisted in the updating of our data base, namely:

Diane BEATTIE
Jim BOWMAN
Jim BURANT
Twila BUTTIMER
Victorin CHABOT
Denys CHOUINARD
Barbara CRAIG
Susan DUPUIS
Burt GLENDENNING
Brian HALLETT
Flora HAMILTON
Marcel LAROCQUE
Ruth MACEACHERN

Janine MCGEE
Yves MARCOUX
Diane MENARD
Jean-Paul MOREAU
Jeff MURRAY
Lise PERRON-CROTEAU
Denis PLANTE
Allan POULIN
Normand ST-PIERRE
Patricia SHOTTON
Auguste VACHON
Anne WHITEHURST
Ruth WILSON

And a very special thanks to Susan Dupuis, Judy Jean and Diane Ménard for their invaluable technical assistance. We would also like to acknowledge the services provided by the Public Programs Branch of the National Archives.

Introduction

Le **Centre canadien d'information et de documentation en archivistique** (CCIDA) est heureux de faire paraître la suite de la bibliographie rétrospective publiée dans le numéro spécial de la revue *Archives* de juin-septembre 1987.

Comme cette dernière, elle est constituée en majeure partie des références signalées dans les bibliographies courantes publiées dans chaque livraison de cette revue, mais comprend également toutes celles qu'il nous a été impossible d'y inclure, faute d'espace.

En fait, la présente bibliographie correspond intégralement au contenu de la base de données bibliographiques automatisée du CCIDA connue sous l'appellation **ARCHBIB.87**. Elle comprend donc 2 066 références à des publications touchant toutes les facettes de l'administration des archives, de la gestion des documents et de leurs techniques auxiliaires.

Plus de la moitié de ces références (1 550) renvoient à des articles ou à des ouvrages parus en anglais. Le français y est naturellement la deuxième langue la mieux représentée avec près de 400 titres. Le reste réfère à des sources publiées en russe (51), en allemand (47), en néerlandais (9), en espagnol (6) et en italien (4).

Nous espérons que cette bibliographie, comme les précédentes, rendra service à tous les membres de la communauté archivistique canadienne.

En terminant, nous tenons à signaler que la publication d'**ARCHBIB.89**, comprenant les références accumulées durant les deux dernières années, est prévue pour 1991. Elle sera elle-même suivie d'une refonte complète, couvrant les années 1986-1991, qui paraîtra sous les auspices de l'Association des archivistes du Québec, en prévision du XIIe Congrès du Conseil international des archives, à Montréal.

Remerciements

La présente bibliographie n'aurait jamais vu le jour sans le concours et les constants efforts d'un grand nombre de personnes. Nous tenons donc à particulièrement remercier tous ceux et celles qui nous ont assuré leur bienveillante collaboration pour la mise à jour de notre base de données :

Diane BEATTIE	Janine MCGEE
Jim BOWMAN	Yves MARCOUX
Jim BURANT	Diane MÉNARD
Twila BUTTIMER	Jean-Paul MOREAU
Victorin CHABOT	Jeff MURRAY
Denys CHOUINARD	Lise PERRON-CROTEAU
Barbara CRAIG	Denis PLANTE
Susan DUPUIS	Allan POULIN
Burt GLENDENNING	Normand ST-PIERRE
Brian HALLETT	Patricia SHOTTON
Flora HAMILTON	Auguste VACHON
Marcel LAROCQUE	Anne WHITEHURST
Ruth MACEACHERN	Ruth WILSON

Et un merci tout spécial s'adresse à Susan Dupuis, Judy Jean et Diane Ménard pour leur précieuse collaboration technique.

Nous aimerions également souligner la contribution de la Direction des programmes publics des Archives nationales du Canada.

Classification Code/
Cadre de classification

1. General / Généralités

BEARMAN, David, comp. Directory of software for archives and museums. *Archival Informatics Technical Report.* Spring 1988: 2(1), 100 p.

BEATON, Elizabeth. The Beaton Institute Steel Project. *Archivaria.* Winter 1988/89: 27, 194-198.

BRICHFORD, Maynard J. Margaret Cross Norton: a tribute. *Illinois Libraries.* October 1987: 69(8), 537-538.

BROOM, Andrew. Standards for archives: the work of the British Standards Institution related to archives. *Journal of the Society of Archivists.* April 1987: 8(3), 174-180.

COOK, Terry. ACA Conference overview. *ACA Bulletin.* July 1988: 12(6), 1-4.

FRANKLIN, Dorothy. Les Archives nationales du Canada fières de leur passé, confiantes pour l'avenir. *L'Archiviste.* Septembre/octobre 1987: 14(5), 12-13.

FRANKLIN, Dorothy. The National Archives of Canada new name, proud tradition. *The Archivist.* September/October 1987: 14(5), 12-13.

GAGNON-ARGUIN, Louise. Les archives au Canada: quelques références bibliographiques utiles aux études canadiennes. *Bulletin de l'AEC.* Hiver 1988/1989: 10(4), 31-32.

HÉON, Gilles. L'article dans les répertoires: élément de cotation ou élément de rangement? *La Gazette des archives.* 1987: (136), 5-16.

MITCHELL, Gary. "Archives have a future". IN Proceedings: Conference of the Association of Canadian Archivists (1987: McMaster University). Hamilton, Ont., 1987. 10 p.

POKROVSKI, M. L'importance politique des archives. *Sovietskje Arkhivy.* 1988: (3), 11-15.

RENÉ-BAZIN, Paule. *La création et la collecte des nouvelles archives.* Congrès international des archives (11ᵉ: 1988: Paris). Paris, 1988. 40 p.

SERJEANT, William. New lamps for old: some reflections on information. *Journal of the Society of Archivists.* October 1987: 8(4), 241-246.

SHELDON, Ted P. and Gordon O. HENDRICKSON. Emergency management and academic library resources. *Special Libraries.* Spring 1987: 78(2), 93-99.

TAYLOR, Hugh A. "My very act and deed": some reflections on the role of textual records in the conduct of affairs. *The American Archivist.* Fall 1988: 51(4), 456-469.

THIAM, Mbaye. Pour une approche globale de la fonction archives en Afrique de l'Ouest francophone. *La Gazette des archives.* 1988: (142-143), 18-24.

VAGANOV, F.M. La vitalité des principes léninistes de l'édification des archives. *Sovietskje Arkhivy.* 1988: (3), 3-10.

1.1 Bibliographies

AEBERSOLD, Rolf, Alexandre BAICOIANER et Barbara ROTH. Bibliographie archivistique 1983-1984. *Arbido-R.* 1986: 1(1), 16-25.

ARCHIVES PUBLIQUES CANADA. *Catalogues des fonds sur la société Radio-Canada déposés aux Archives publiques.* Préparé sous la direction de Ernest J. Dick. Ottawa: Archives publiques Canada, 1987. viii, 125, 141, viii p.

AUGER, Henriette et Carol COUTURE. Bibliographie commentée sur la formation en archivistique. *Archivum.* 1988: 34, 191-236.

BECHOR, Malvina B. Bibliographic access to archival literature. *The American Archivist.* May 1987: 50(2), 243-247.

BELOVA, T.V. et K.G. TCHERNENKOV. L'utilisation des documents des archives de la R.F.A.: critique et bibliographie. *Sovietskje Arkhivy.* 1988: (5), 99.

Bibliography on recent automation articles. *SAA Newsletter.* January 1988: 5.

BLUM, Sylvie. Télévision/spectacle/ politique. *Dossiers de l'audiovisuel.* Janvier/février 1988: 17, 61.

BOTTOMLEY, Michael. Microforms: an annotated bibliography. *Business Archives.* May 1988: (55), 61-64.

CHOUINARD, Denys, Jacques DUCHARME et Denis PLANTE. *Bibliographie des publications du Service des archives.* 5e éd., rev., corr. et augm. Montréal: Université de Montréal, Division des archives historiques, 1986. 17 p. (Publication n° 21)

COX, Richard J. American archival literature: expanding horizons and continuing needs, 1901-1987. *The American Archivist.* Summer 1987: 50(3), 306-323.

DIXON, Diana. Bibliography [business archives]. *Business Archives.* November 1988: (56), 45-58.

Electronic records policy: a bibliography. *Archival Informatics Newsletter.* Winter 1988/1989: 2(4), 76-79.

ELSHAMI, Ahmed M. *CD-ROM: an annotated bibliography.* Englewood, Colo.: Libraries Unlimited, 1988. xiv, 138 p.

FLAHERTY, David H. *Privacy and data protection: an international bibliography.* White Plains, N.Y.: Knowledge Industry Publications, 1984. xxvi, 276 p. (Professional librarian series)

GRIMSTED, Patricia Kennedy. *Archives and manuscript repositories in the USSR. Ukraine and Moldavia. Vol. 1: General bibliography and institutional directory.* Princeton, N.J.: Princeton University Press, 1988. liii, 1107 p.

GROUPE-CONSEIL LLP INC. ET IST-INFORMATHÈQUE. *La gestion de documents au Québec, 1987.* [Montréal]: ARMA-Montréal, 1987. 39, 379 p.

GUYOTJEANNIN, Olivier. Métrologie française d'ancien régime. Guide bibliographique sommaire. *La Gazette des archives.* 1987: (139), 233-247.

HARLOW, E. Lynn, comp. *Bibliography update to towards descriptive standards* (1986). [Toronto]: Archives of Ontario, Task Force on Intellectual Controls, 1988. ii, 32 p.

KAY, Terry. Helen M. Wallis: a bibliography of published works. *The Map Collector.* Autumn 1987: 40, 30-38.

KITCHING, Christopher. The history of record keeping in the United Kingdom to 1939: a select bibliography. *Journal of the Society of Archivists.* April 1988: 9(2), 88-100.

KOOBATIAN, James. *Faking it: an international bibliography of art and literary forgeries, 1949-1986.* 1st ed. Washington, D.C.: Special Libraries Association, c1987. x, 240 p.

LADEIRA, Caroline Durant and Maryellen TRAUTMAN. Writings on archives, historical manuscripts, and current records: 1984. *The American Archivist.* Fall 1986: 49(4), 425-454.

LEONARD, Kevin B. Writings on Illinois Archives, 1980-1987: a bibliography. *Illinois Libraries.* October 1987: 69(8), 549-565.

MERRILL-OLDHAM, Jan. A brief preservation bibliography. *Conservation Administration News.* July 1987: (30), 9.

MOREAU, Jean-Paul et Denis CARRIER. Bibliographie analytique d'Yves Thériault, 1940-1984. *Revue d'histoire littéraire du Québec et du Canada.* Hiver/printemps 1987: 13, 242-244.

MURRAY, Toby. Bibliography on disasters, disaster preparedness and disaster recovery. *Records Management Quarterly.* April 1987: 21(2), 18-24, 26-30, 41.

PADFIELD, Tim. Further readings [disaster planning]. *Business Archives.* May 1988: (55), 45-47.

PENNIX, Gail B. and Marti FISCHER. Cumulative index to the Records Management Quarterly 1967-1987. *Records Management Quarterly.* January 1988: 22(1), 27-122.

PERKINS, C.R. Map libraries [bibliographical essay]. IN British librarianship and information work, 1981-1985. London: Library Association, 1988: 116-131.

PIEJUT, Geneviève. Feuilletons et séries. *Dossiers de l'audiovisuel.* Novembre/décembre 1987: 16, 51.

POSTLES, D. Archives [bibliographical essay]. IN British librarianship and information work, 1981-1985. 1988: 294-302.

PRESLOCK, Karen. Publications. *Conservation Administration News.* July 1987: (30), 16-17.

PRESLOCK, Karen. Publications. *Conservation Administration News.* October 1987: (31), 18-19.

PRESLOCK, Karen. Publications. *Conservation Administration News.* January 1988: (32), 17.

PRESLOCK, Karen. Publications. *Conservation Administration News.* April 1988: (33), 18, 21.

PRESLOCK, Karen. Publications. *Conservation Administration News.* July 1988: (34), 14, 22.

PRESLOCK, Karen. Publications. *Conservation Administration News.* October 1988: (35), 20.

PUBLIC ARCHIVES CANADA. *Guide to CBC sources at the Public Archives.* Compiled under the direction of Ernest J. Dick. Ottawa: Public Archives Canada, 1987. viii, 125, 141, viii p.

Religious archives in the United States and Canada: a bibliography. Compiled by the SAA Religious Archives Section. Chicago: Society of American Archivists, 1984. 17 p.

ROBERGE, Michel. *L'expertise québécoise en gestion des documents administratifs: bibliographie thématique et chronologique 1962-1987.* En collaboration avec Alban Boudreau et Elyse Tremblay. Saint-Augustin, Qué.: GESTAR, 1987. [env. 200 p.]

ROPER, Michael. *Directory of national standards relating to archives administration and records management: a RAMP study.* Paris: UNESCO, 1986. 59 p. (PGI-86/WS/16)

SABLE, Martin H. The Northwest ordinance of 1787: an interdisciplinary bibliography. *SLA. Geography & Map Division. Bulletin.* September 1987: 149, 16-43.

SALAUN, Jean-Michel. Sport et télévision. *Dossiers de l'audiovisuel.* Mars/avril 1988: 18, 11-55.

SCHNARE, Robert E. Publications. *Conservation Administration News.* July 1986: (26), 18-20.

SCHNARE, Robert E. Publications. *Conservation Administration News.* January 1987: (28), 18-21.

SCHNARE, Robert E. Publications. *Conservation Administration News.* April 1987: (29), 24-25, 28.

STARK, Peter L. A cartobibliography of separately published USGS Special Maps of Alaska. *Western Association of Map Libraries. Information Bulletin.* June 1987: 18(3), 195-220.

THOMAS, John B. III. Standards and guidelines prepared by the Rare Books and Manuscripts Section of the Association of College and Research Libraries. *Rare Books & Manuscripts Librarianship.* Fall 1987: 2(2), 109-112.

TURNER, D. John and Micheline MORISSET. *Canadian feature film index, 1913-1985.* Ottawa: Public Archives Canada, National Film, Television and Sound Archives, 1987. xx, 816 p.

TURNER, D. John et Micheline MORISSET. *Index des films canadiens de long métrage, 1913-1985.* Ottawa: Archives publiques Canada, Archives nationales du film, de la télévision et de l'enregistrement sonore, 1987. xx, 816 p.

TURTON, Alison. Business archives principles and practice, a select bibliography. *Business Archives.* May 1987: (53), 51-57.

WOLF, Eric W. Toward a bibliography of cartobibliographies. *SLA. Geography & Map Division. Bulletin.* September 1987: 149, 12-15.

YOUNG, Rod. Labour archives: an annotated bibliography. *Archivaria.* Winter 1988/89: 27, 97-110.

1.2 Manuals and general works / Manuels et ouvrages généraux

ANDERSON, Hazel and John E. MCINTYRE. *Planning manual for disaster control in Scottish libraries and records offices.* Edinburgh: National Library of Scotland, 1985. 75 p.

ARCHIVES NATIONALES DU CANADA. *Au-delà de l'écrit: actualités filmées et reportages radio et télé diffusés au Canada.* Ottawa: Les Archives, 1988. 348 p.

ARMSTRONG, John and Stephanie JONES. *Business documents: their origins, sources and uses in historical research.* London: Mansell, 1987. xvi, 251 p.

ASSOCIATION OF BRITISH COLUMBIA ARCHIVISTS. SMALL ARCHIVES COMMITTEE, Donald Alexander BAIRD and Laura M. COLES. *A manual for small archives.* Vancouver: Association of British Columbia Archivists, 1988. [10], iii, 213, [9] p. (Publications; no. 1)

BARR, Debra. The Fonds Concept in the Working Group on Archival Descriptive Standards Report. *Archivaria.* Winter 1987-1988: (25), 163-170.

BRADSHER, James Gregory. *Managing archives and archival institutions.* Chicago: University of Chicago Press, 1988.

BRICHFORD, Maynard J. A brief history of the physical protection of archives. *Conservation Administration News.* October 1987: (31), 10, 21.

BURWASSER, Suzanne M. *Files management handbook for managers and librarians.* Studio City, Calif.: Pacific Information, 1986. 165 p.

COOK, Michael and Margaret PROCTER. *A manual of archival description.* 2nd ed. rev. London: Society of Archivists, 1988. 1v. (various pagings) (British Library R & D Report)

COUTURE, Carol and Jean-Yves ROUSSEAU. *The life of a document: a global approach to archives and records management.* Translated by David Homel. Montréal: Véhicule Press, 1987. 357 p.

COX, Richard J. Fund raising for historical records programs: an underdeveloped archival function. *Provenance.* Fall 1988: 6(2), 1-19.

DAWE, Claire. Management of archives in the organisation. *Archifacts.* 1988: (3), 6-16.

ENGLAND, Claire and Karen EVANS. *Disaster management for libraries planning and process.* [Ottawa]: Canadian Library Association, 1988. xi, 207 p.

KENWORTHY, Mary Anne, [et al.]. *Preserving field records: archival techniques for archaeologists and anthropologists.* Philadelphia: University Museum, University of Pennsylvania, 1985. x, 102 p.

KETELAAR, Éric. Muller, Feith and Fruin. *Archives et bibliothèques de Belgique.* 1986: 57(1/2), 255-268.

Manual de levantamento da produçao documental. Rio de Janeiro: Arquivo Nacional, 1986. 34 p. (Publicaçoes técnicas; 44)

MORDDEL, Anne, [et al.]. *Records management handbook.* Aldershot: Gower, 1988. 200 p.

NATIONAL ARCHIVES OF CANADA. *Beyond the printed word: newsreel and broadcast reporting in Canada.* Ottawa: The Archives, 1988. 348 p.

NEAL, Donn C. Archives. IN The ALA yearbook of library and information services. 1988: 47-49.

PAES, Marilena Leite. *Arquivo: teoria e pratica.* Rio de Janeiro: Instituto de Documentacao, 1986. 162 p.

Parish archives handbook: guidelines for the care and preservation of parochial records. Auckland: Provincial Archives Committee of the Anglican Church in New Zealand, 1986. 42 p.

PEDERSON, Ann, ed. *Keeping archives.* Sydney: Australian Society of Archivists, 1987. vii, 374 p.

POSTLES, D. Archives [bibliographical essay]. IN British librarianship and information work, 1981-1985. 1988: 294-302.

RAFAEL, R.K., [et al.]. *Western Jewish History Center: guide to archival and oral history collections.* Berkeley, Calif.: Western Jewish History Center, 1987. 207 p.

RHODES, Barbara J. *Hell and high water: a disaster information sourcebook.* New York: METRO, 1988. 58 p.

ROBEK, Mary F., Gerald F. BROWN and Wilmer O. MAEDKE. *Information and records management.* 3rd ed. Encino, Calif.: Glencoe Publishing, 1987. vi, 580 p.

STIELOW, Frederick J. *The management of oral history sound archives.* New York: Greenwood Press, 1986. 158 p.

SYLVESTRE, Guy. *Guidelines for national libraries.* Paris: United Nations Educational, Scientific and Cultural Organization, 1987. 108 p.

UNESCO. GENERAL INFORMATION PROGRAMME. *Guide des archives des organisations internationales: troisième partie: autres organisations internationales, intergouvernementales et non gouvernementales.* Paris: UNESCO, 1986. 41 p. (PGI-85/WS/19)

UNION OF SOVIET SOCIALIST REPUBLICS. MAIN ARCHIVAL ADMINISTRATION. *Basic rules for the work of the USSR State Archives.* Moscow: Main Archival Administration at the USSR, Council of Ministers, 1984. xv, 352 p.

VERDERY, John D. *Dear Chris: advice to a volunteer fund raiser.* Washington, D.C.: Taft Group, 1986. x, 105 p.

WALLACE, Patricia E., [et al]. *Records management: integrated information systems.* 2nd ed. New York: Wiley, 1987. x, 500 p.

WEINBERG, Gerhard L. Proposed goals for the National Archives. *OAH Newsletter (Organization of American Historians).* November 1987: 15(4), 17.

WRIGHT, Sandra. New conservation policy. *The Archivist.* November/December 1988: 15(6), 18.

WRIGHT, Sandra. La politique de conservation des Archives nationales du Canada. *L'Archiviste.* Novembre/décembre 1988: 15(6), 18.

WYTHE, Deborah. A case study in museum archives: the Brooklyn Museum and its Master Plan Competition. *Museum Archivist.* September 1988: 2(2), 8-11.

1.3 Terminology / Terminologie

BARR, Debra. The Fonds Concept in the Working Group on Archival Descriptive Standards Report. *Archivaria.* Winter 1987-1988: (25), 163-170.

CHARTRAND, Robert Lee. Glossary of selected terms of key information technologies. *Special Libraries.* Spring 1987: 78(2), 86-87.

DELAGE, Gisèle. *Vocabulaire de la gestion des documents administratifs: français-anglais.* Montréal: Office de la langue française, 1986. 91 p.

DELMAS, Bruno. *Les nouvelles archives: problèmes de définitions.* Congrès national des archivistes français (28ᵉ: 1986: Paris, France). Paris, 1987: 178-183.

DENEL, Francis. *Les archives et l'audiovisuel: les archives audiovisuelles, définition des concepts.* Congrès national des archivistes français (28ᵉ: 1986: Paris, France). Paris, 1987: 63-68.

DRYDEN, Jean E. Subject headings: the PAASH experience. *Archivaria.* Summer 1987: (24), 173-180.

Glossary of basic archival and library conservation terms: English with equiva-

lents in Spanish, German, Italian, French and Russian. München: Saur, 1988. 151 p. (ICA handbooks series; v. 4)

GRAY, David P. *Records management for parishes and schools.* Richardton, N.D.: Diocesen of Bismarck, 1985. 44 p.

HÉON, Gilles. L'article dans les répertoires: élément de cotation ou élément de rangement? *La Gazette des archives.* 1987: (136), 5-16.

LOVE, J.H. What are records? *Archives and Manuscripts.* May 1986: 14(1), 54-60.

TATEM, Jill M. and Jeffrey ROLLISON. *Thesaurus of university terms developed at Case Western Reserve University Archives.* Chicago: Society of American Archivists, 1986. 46 p.

Vocabulaire de la documentation. 2ᵉ éd. Paris: Afnor, 1987. 159 p.

Vocabulaire des archives: archivistique et diplomatique contemporaines. Paris: Afnor, 1986. 118 p.

WILLIAMS, Anne E. *Termau Archifau — Archive terms.* Caernarfon: Gwasanaeth Archifau Gwynedd, Cyngor Sir Gwynedd, 1986. iv, 55 p.

YEE, Martha M. *Moving image materials: genre terms.* Washington, D.C.: Cataloging Distribution Service, Library of Congress, 1988. 108 p.

1.4 Laws, decrees and constitutions / Lois, décrets et constitutions

ACA brief to the legislative committee on Bill C-95. *ACA Bulletin.* March 1987: 11(4), [3-5].

ALSBERG, P.A. The Israel Archives Law: a retrospect after 30 years. *Archives et bibliothèques de Belgique.* 1986: 57(1/2), 13-49.

ARNOLD III, Robert W. The Albany Answer: pragmatic and tactical considerations in local records legislative efforts. *The American Archivist.* Fall 1988: 51(4), 475-479.

AUER, Leopold. Staatennachfolge bei archiven. *Archives et bibliothèques de Belgique.* 1986: 57(1/2), 51-68.

BERRY, E.K. The Local Government Act 1985 and the archive services of the Greater London Council and the metropolitan county councils. *Journal of the Society of Archivists.* April 1988: 9(2), 119-147.

Bill C-95 Archives of Canada Act. *ABCA Newsletter.* Summer 1986: 12(3), 10.

BOURDON, Jérôme. L'esprit des lois ou comment réformer l'audiovisuel (1917-1988). *Dossiers de l'audiovisuel.* Juillet/août 1988: 20, 9-52.

BRADSHER, James Gregory. Privacy Act expungements: a reconsideration. *Provenance.* Spring 1988: 6(1), 1-25.

BROWN, Thomas Elton. Archives law and machine-readable data files: a look at the United States. *ADPA.* 1986: 5(2), 37-42.

CALAS, Marie-France. *Problèmes juridiques posés par la consultation et la reproduction des documents sonores: critères de sélection des documents sonores dans une phonothèque.* Congrès national des archivistes français (28ᵉ: 1986: Paris, France). Paris, 1987: 218-225.

Canadian Council of Archives. *ABCA Newsletter.* Spring 1986: 12(2), 8.

CHESTERMAN, John and Andy LIPMAN. *The electronic pirates: DIY crime of the century.* London: Routledge, 1988. x, 224 p. (A Comedia book)

CLARK, Ian Christie. The protection of cultural property: illicit traffic in cultural property: Canada seeks a bilateral agreement with the United States. *Museum.* 1986: (151), 182-187.

Copyright Act Amendments. *ACA Bulletin.* July 1987: 11(6), 10.

DESLONGCHAMPS, Denis. La loi sur les archives. *Le Bureau.* Juillet/août 1986: 12.

DIEUZEDE, Geneviève. *Repérage des collections photographiques à l'échelon national et problèmes juridiques posés lors de la collecte*. Congrès national des archivistes français (28e: 1986: Paris, France). Paris, 1987: 49-53.

DORAY, Raymond. *Loi sur l'accès aux documents des organismes publics et sur la protection des renseignements personnels, texte annoté*. Montréal: Société québécoise d'information juridique, 1988. 565 p.

DUCHEIN, Michel. Législation et structures administratives des Archives de France, 1970-1988. *La Gazette des archives*. 1988: (141), 7-18.

DUPUIS, Yvon. *Accès à l'information: loi sur l'accès aux documents des organismes publics et sur la protection des renseignements personnels*. Indexée, annotée et commentée (feuilles mobiles). Cowansville: Éditions Yvon Blais, 1988. 1 vol. (reliure mobile)

EASTWOOD, Terry and Robin G. KEIRSTEAD. Editorial/Project Pride. *ABCA Newsletter*. Summer 1987: 13(1), 1-2.

FLINT, Michael F. *A user's guide to copyright*. 2nd ed. London: Butterworths, 1985. xvii, 289 p.

FRANKLIN, Dorothy. Les Archives nationales du Canada fières de leur passé, confiantes pour l'avenir. *L'Archiviste*. Septembre/octobre 1987: 14(5), 12-13.

FRANKLIN, Dorothy. The National Archives of Canada new name, proud tradition. *The Archivist*. September/October 1987: 14(5), 12-13.

Freedom of information act: accuracy of the state department's automated case tracking system. Washington, D.C.: General Accounting Office, General Government Division, 1987. 14 p.

La gestion de l'information gouvernementale. IN Traité de droit administratif, tome II, par René Dussault et Louis Borgeat. 2e éd. Québec: Presses de l'Université Laval, 1986: 769-1160.

GILLIS, Peter. "Revamping information policies: a Federal approach". IN Proceedings: Conference of the Association of Canadian Archivists (1987: McMaster University). Hamilton, Ont., 1987. 7 p.

HYAM, Grace Maurice. Copyright revision: awaiting the second stage. *Archivaria*. Winter 1988/89: 27, 175-177.

KAMBA, Angeline S. Archives and national development in the Third World. *Information Development*. April 1987: 3(2), 108-113.

KAMBA, Angeline S. The impact of the National Archives of Zimbabwe Act 1986 on records management in Zimbabwe. *Commonwealth Archivists Association Newsletter*. November 1987: (5), 10-13.

KETELAAR, Éric. *Législation et réglementation en matière d'archives et de gestion des documents: étude RAMP, accompagnée des principes directeurs*. Paris: UNESCO, 1986. 83 p. (PGI-85/WS/9)

LABERGE, Danielle. Information, knowledge and rights: the preservation of archives as a political and social issue. *Archivaria*. Winter 1987-1988: (25), 44-50.

Local archives: current statutory provisions. *Archifacts*. 1986: (3), 12-13.

La loi sur l'accès aux documents des organismes publics et sur la protection des renseignements. *Le Bureau*. Juillet/août 1986: 23.

Loi sur les Archives nationales du Canada — Résumé. *Archives nationales du Canada. Bulletin des documents gouvernementaux*. Janvier/septembre 1987: 2.

MITCHELL, Gary. I wonder... [editorial]. *ABCA Newsletter*. Fall 1986: 12(4), 1.

MITCHELL, Gary. Rocky road ahead [editorial]. *ABCA Newsletter*. Summer 1986: 12(3), 1, 5.

National Archives of Canada Act — Summary. *National Archives of Canada. Government Records Bulletin*. January/September 1987: 3(1), 2.

National policy statement on our documentary heritage [draft statement]. *SAA Newsletter*. January 1987: 6.

New Archives Act for Canada. *ACA Bulletin*. July 1987: 11(6), 1.

1987 Local Government Records Bill [state of New York]. *Record*. Spring 1987: 5(1), 1, 4.

NIVERD, Frédéric. *État de la loi sur l'audiovisuel*. Congrès national des archivistes français (28e: 1986: Paris, France). Paris, 1987: 69-73.

NORTHWEST DISTRICT COUNCIL OF CARPENTERS. Brief to project pride. *ABCA Newsletter*. Fall 1987: 13(2), 1-2.

ORDRE DES INFIRMIÈRES ET INFIRMIERS DU QUÉBEC. *Recommandations de l'Ordre des infirmières et infirmiers du Québec relativement au document de consultation concernant les dispositions inconciliables avec la loi sur l'accès (secteur santé et services sociaux)*. [Montréal]: L'Ordre, 1986. 10 f.

Perspectives on the National Archives of Canada Act. *National Archives of Canada. Government Records Bulletin*. January/September 1987: 3(1), 1.

Perspectives sur la Loi sur les Archives nationales du Canada. *Archives nationales du Canada. Bulletin des documents gouvernementaux*. Janvier/septembre 1987: 3(1), 1.

PIEYNS-RIGO, Paulette. *Les conséquences juridiques de la production des documents informatiques par les administrations publiques: une étude RAMP*. Paris: Unesco, 1988. 78 p.

PINKERTON, Linda F. Preventive legal audits for museums. *Museum News*. October 1987: 66(1), 36-39.

Privacy Act: privacy act system notices. Washington, D.C.: General Accounting Office, General Government Div., 1987. 17 p.

QUETIN, Michel. *Législation française concernant la sauvegarde de la mémoire audiovisuelle de la France*. Congrès natio-

nal des archivistes français (27e: 1985: Limoges, France). Paris, 1986: 45-48.

SARNIA, Lazar. *Authors and publishers: agreements and legal aspects of publishing*. 2nd ed. Toronto: Butterworths, 1987. xiv, 216 p.

SIBLEY, Kathryn. Enchanted evenings — without the morning — after headaches. *Museum News*. October 1987: 66(1), 59-68.

SKUPSKY, Donald S. Legal requirements for computer records containing federal tax information: an update. *Records Management Quarterly*. July 1988: 22(3), 32-35.

STRACHAN, S.R. The protection of local archives notice. *Archifacts*. 1986: (3), 14-18.

WEBER, Dieter and Margaret POELLEN. Gesetzliche Bestimmungen und Verwaltungsvorschriften fuer das staatliche Archivwesen und zur Archivpflege in der Bundesrepublik Deutschland [Legal restrictions and administrative requirements for state archive work and archive care in West Germany]. *Archivar*. May 1986: 39(2), 187-196.

WEIL, Stephen E. A checklist of legal considerations for museums (1987). *Museum News*. October 1987: 66(1), 40-42.

1.5 Organization and administration of archives / Organisation et administration des archives

Addresses given at archivist Wilson's swearing-in ceremony. *SAA Newsletter*. May 1988: 7-8.

AMBROSIO, Johanna. Micrographics remains a viable medium. *Government Computer News*. March 27, 1987: 6(6), 40.

Archivists' resource allocators: the next step. *SAA Newsletter*. January 1987: 8-9.

BEARMAN, David. Functional requirements for collections management systems. *Archival Informatics Technical Report*. Fall 1987: 1(3), 1-87.

BERCHE, Claire. *Les implications sur le plan du fonctionnement et du personnel.* Congrès national des archivistes français (27ᵉ: 1985: Limoges, France). Paris, 1986: 33-34.

BERNIER, Hélène et Guy DINEL. Le réseau des archives du Québec. *Archives (Revue de l'Association des archivistes du Québec).* Décembre 1986: 18(3), 26-34.

BEYEA, Marion et Marcel CAYA. Les associations professionnelles et le développement du système archivistique canadien. *Janus.* 1987: (2), 20-28.

BEYEA, Marion and Marcel CAYA. The professional associations and the formation of the Canadian archival system. *Janus.* 1987: (2), 18-25.

BILDFELL, Laurie. Border skirmish: National Library and Archives. *Quill & Quire.* June 1986: 52(6), 9-10.

BOATRIGH, John and G. Donald ADAMS. The selling of the museum 1986. *Museum News.* April 1986: 64(4), 16-21.

BOGGE, Alfonso. Histoire et informatique. *ADPA.* 1986: 5(2), 79-89.

BOUDANOV, O.A., V.R. KLEIN et V.V. TSAPLINE. Sur le perfectionnement des formes d'organisation des activités des Archives centrales d'État de l'économie nationale de l'URSS et des Archives centrales d'État de la documentation scientifique et technique de l'URSS. *Sovietskje Arkhivy.* 1987: (4), 52-54.

BRADSHER, James Gregory. *Managing archives and archival institutions.* Chicago: University of Chicago Press, 1988.

BRADSHER, James Gregory. A brief history of the growth of Federal Government records, archives and information 1789-1985. *Government Publications Review.* July/August 1986: 13, 491-505.

BURKE, Frank G. You don't have to live in Washington to visit the National Archives. *Prologue: Journal of the National Archives.* Winter 1986: 18(4), 220-221.

BUTCHER-YOUNGHANS, Sherry. Using volunteers in history. *History News.* July/August 1988: 43(4), 11-14.

CAMPBELL, T.M. "Archives and Information Management — Ships passing in the right". IN Proceedings: Conference of the Association of Canadian Archivists (1987: McMaster University). Hamilton, Ont., 1987. 5 p.

CANAVAGGIO, Perrine. La conservation des archives présidentielles aux États-Unis. *La Gazette des archives.* 1986: (133), 123-142.

CAVALCANTI, C.R. Arquivos e bibliotecas: semelhanças e diferenças [Archives and libraries: similarities and differences]. *Revista de Biblioteconomia de Brasilia.* January 1988: 16, 5-17.

CLOUD, Patricia D. The cost of converting to MARC AMC: some early observations. *Library Trends.* Winter 1988: 36(3), 573-583.

COLLOQUE ENAP/IIAP (6ᵉ: 1985: QUÉBEC, QUÉBEC). *La protection des renseignements personnels et l'accès aux documents administratifs: actes du colloque ENAP/IIAP tenu du 7 au 10 octobre 1985 au Château Frontenac.* Sainte-Foy: Centre d'études politiques et administratives du Québec, École nationale d'administration publique, 1986. iii, 255 p. (Collections Bilans et perspectives)

CONWAY, Paul. Perspectives on archival resources: the 1985 census of archival institutions. *The American Archivist.* Spring 1987: 50(2), 174-191.

COOK, Michael. International survey of automated applications in archival management. *ADPA.* 1986: 5(2), 53-67.

COOPER, Sarah. The politics of protest collections: developing social action archives. *Provenance.* Spring 1987: 5(1), 8-16.

COX, Richard J. and Anne S.K. TURKOS. Establishing public library archives. *Journal of Library History.* Summer 1986: 21, 574-584.

COX, Richard J. Fund raising for historical records programs: an underdeveloped archival function. *Provenance.* Fall 1988: 6(2), 1-19.

DANIELLS, Laurenda. *Grantsmanship and the archivist.* Vancouver: Association of British Columbia Archivists, 1988. 10 p. (A.B.C.A. publications; no. 4)

DANILOV, Victor J. Promoting museums through advertising. *Museum News.* August/September 1986: 64(6), 33-39.

DAVIS, Susan E. Development of managerial training for archivist. *The American Archivist.* Summer 1988: 51(3), 278-285.

DAWE, Claire. Management of archives in the organisation. *Archifacts.* 1988: (3), 6-16.

DUFFY, Mark J. The archival bridge: history, administration, and the building of church tradition. *Historical Magazine of the Protestant Episcopal Church.* December 1986: 55, 275-287.

DUMONT, Jacques. Les techniques de la télévision. *Dossiers de l'audiovisuel.* Mars/avril 1987: 12, 13-54.

EASTWOOD, Terry. Attempts at national planning for archives in Canada, 1975-1985. *The Public Historian.* Summer 1986: 8(3), 74-91.

EASTWOOD, Terry. A small world expands. *Archivaria.* Summer 1987: (24), 129-136.

ESO, Elizabeth. *Promotion and outreach in a community archives.* [Vancouver]: Association of British Columbia Archivists, c1988. 7 p. (A.B.C.A. publications; no. 2)

FINLAY, Douglas. Archives: old records meet new technologies. *Administrative Management.* December 1986: 37-40.

FRIESEN, Paul T. Automation of a map library. *Association of Canadian Map Libraries and Archives. Bulletin.* June 1988: 67, 2-16.

GAVREL, Katharine. National Archives of Canada: Machine Readable Records Program. *Reference Services Review.* 1988: 16(1), 25-29.

GILDEMEISTER, Glen A. Automation, reference, and the small repository, 1967-1997. *The Midwestern Archivist.* 1988: 13(1), 5-15.

GILLILAND, Anne J. The development of automated archival systems: planning and managing change. *Library Trends.* Winter 1988: 36(3), 519-537.

The Guelph Collegiate and Vocational Institute Archives: statement of policy and procedures. *Emergency Librarian.* May/June 1988: 15, 22-23.

HACKMAN, Larry J. Cuomo transfers record management to New York State Archives. *SAA Newsletter.* March 1987: 8.

HACKMAN, Larry J. A perspective on American archives. *The Public Historian.* Summer 1986: 8(3), 10-28.

HARTMAN, Hedy A. *Fund raising for museums: the essential book for staff and trustees.* Bellevue, Washington: The Hartman Planning and Development Group, Ltd, 1986. 529 p.

HEFNER, Loretta L. The change masters: organizational development in a State Archives. *The American Archivist.* Fall 1988: 51(4), 440-454.

HOHMANN, Judy and Richard J. COX. Private sector fund raising and historical record program: learning in New York. *SAA Newsletter.* September 1987: 6.

HUNTER, Gregory S. Filling the GAP: planning on the local and individual levels. *The American Archivist.* Winter 1987: 50(1), 110-115.

IOFFE, I.A. Sur l'efficacité de l'activité scientifique et d'information. *Sovietskje Arkhivy.* 1988: (2), 62-68.

JORGENSEN, Harold. Should the history of public administration be viewed exclusively as a support discipline to archival studies? *Archives et bibliothèques de Belgique.* 1986: 57(1/2), 207-220.

KER, Neil. Preparing your archives for the next 20,000 years. *International Journal of Micrographics and Video Technology.* 1986: 15(3/4), 223-226.

KETELAAR, Éric. Centralisation, décentralisation et les archives aux Pays-Bas. *Janus.* 1986: 3, 15-19.

KETELAAR, Eric. Centralization, decentralization and the archives in the Netherlands. *Janus.* 1986: 3, 16-25.

KIRK, Simon. The University of Leicester Archives Project. *Journal of the Society of Archivists.* October 1986: 8(2), 120-123.

KLAASSEN, David J. Archival word-processing operations. *MAC Newsletter.* January 1988: 15(3), 24-26.

KOLOTOV, O.B. La succession au travail et la collaboration des archives administratives et d'État [en russe]. *Sovietskje Arkhivy.* 1987: (1), 26-33.

KUYK, Robert Egeter van. La recommandation pour la sauvegarde et la conservation des images en mouvement, huit ans après. *Janus.* 1988: (3), 34-38.

KUYK, Robert Egeter van. Recommendations for the preservation and conservation of moving images, eight years on. *Janus.* 1988: (3), 31-34.

LOWELL, Howard P. Elements of a state archives and records management program. *Records Management Quarterly.* October 1987: 21(4), 3-14, 23.

MCCARTHY, Paul H. The management of archives: a research agenda. *The American Archivist.* Winter/Spring 1988: 51(1/2), 52-73.

MCCRANK, Lawrence J. *Archives and library administration: divergent traditions and common concerns.* New York: Haworth Press, 1986. 184 p.

MANASSE, P.M. and H.A. SANDERS. Conservering in het IISG: beleids-en organisatorische aspecten "Conservation at the International Institute for Social History: policy and organizational aspects". *Open.* April 1987: 19, 206-212.

MBAYE, Saliou. Archives et recherche au Sénégal (1976-1984). *Archives et bibliothèques de Belgique.* 1986: 57(1/2), 295-308.

MITCHELL, Gary. Editorial... 1986. *ABCA Newsletter.* Winter 1987: 12(5), 1-2.

MITCHELL, Gary. Rocky road ahead [editorial]. *ABCA Newsletter.* Summer 1986: 12(3), 1, 5.

NEAL, Donn C. (ed.). An action agenda for the archival profession: institutionalizing the planning process; a report to SAA Council by the Committee on Goals and Priorities. *The American Archivist.* Fall 1988: 51(4), 528-535.

NELSON, Anna Kasten. The 1985 report of the Committee on the Records of Government: an assessment. *Government Information Quarterly.* 1987: 4(2), 143-150.

NOKES, Jane. The value of archives: selling the program. *Archives and Manuscripts.* May 1988: (1), 31-41.

Normes et procédures archivistiques. 1ʳᵉ éd. Québec: Archives nationales du Québec, 1987. 124 p.

NORTHWEST DISTRICT COUNCIL OF CARPENTERS. Brief to project pride. *ABCA Newsletter.* Fall 1987: 13(2), 1-2.

O'BRIEN, A.P. Establishing local authority archives. *Archifacts.* 1986: (3), 7-9.

Optical disk may preserve millions of National Archives documents. *Infosystems.* July 1987: 34(7), 14.

OVERMIRE, Rozell. Functional requirements for exibit management systems. *Archival Informatics Technical Report.* Winter 1988/1989: 2(4), 1-127.

PAES, Marilena Leite. *Arquivo: teoria e pratica.* Rio de Janeiro: Instituto de Documentacao, 1986. 162 p.

PAUL, D. Archives in libraries. IN A Manual of local studies librarianship. Gower, 1987: 70-96.

PIEYNS, Jean. Le Comité de l'informatique du Conseil international des archives. *Information Development.* January 1987: 3(1), 20-22.

Princeton microform guide. Princeton, N.J.: Princeton Microfilm Corp., 1987-1988. 189 p.

ROBERGE, Michel. Manifeste pour une véritable approche globale, systématique et systémique de la gestion des documents administratifs et des archives. IN L'expertise québécoise en gestion des documents administratifs: bibliographie thématique et chronologique 1962-1987. Saint-Augustin, Qué.: GESTAR, 1987: 2-6.

ROBERTS, David. "In the agora". *Archives and Manuscripts.* May 1988: (1), 42-44.

ROLON, Rosalind de. Getting the world out: a practical approach to museum print media plans. *Museum News.* August/September 1986: 64(6), 25-31.

SAVARD, Réjean. L'enseignement du marketing aux spécialistes de l'information documentaire. *Arbido-R.* 1987: 2(2), 26-31.

SELMER, Marsha L. Standards for university map collections: the rationale, history, and method. *SLA. Geography & Map Division. Bulletin.* June 1988: (152), 10-18.

SHEPPARD, John. Creating a public image. *Museum News.* August/September 1986: 64(6), 5-13.

SMITH, Brian S. Archives and government policy. *Journal of the Society of Archivists.* October 1988: 9(4), 181-184.

SMITH, George D. Managing the corporate memory. *INFORM: the Magazine of Information and Image Management.* June 1988: 2(6), 8.

SMITH, Wilfred I. "Total archives": the Canadian experience. *Archives et bibliothèques de Belgique.* 1986: 57(1/2), 323-346.

STRACHAN, S.R. Establishing an archive. *Archifacts.* 1986: (3), 2-6.

STREIT, Samuel Allen. All that glitters: fund raising for special collections in academic libraries. *Rare Books & Manuscripts Librarianship.* Spring 1988: 3(1), 31-41.

Surveying your arts audience. Washington, D.C.: National Endowment for the Arts, 1985. 77 p.

SWEENEY, Shelley. Sheep that have gone astray? Church record keeping and the Canadian archival system. *Archivaria.* Winter 1986-87: (23), 54-68.

TAYLOR, Hugh A. Strategies for the future: the preservation of archival materials in Canada. *Conservation Administration News.* April 1987: (29), 1-3.

TENER, Jean. "Automation and small archives". IN Proceedings: Conference of the Association of Canadian Archivists (1987: McMaster University). Hamilton, Ont., 1987. 5 p.

THIAM, Mbaye. Pour une approche globale de la fonction archives en Afrique de l'Ouest francophone. *La Gazette des archives.* 1988: (142-143), 18-24.

TOURTIER-BONAZZI, Chantal de. La commission pour la sauvegarde des archives privées contemporaines. *La Gazette des archives.* 1986: (133), 157-161.

VERDERY, John D. *Dear Chris: advice to a volunteer fund raiser.* Washington, D.C.: Taft Group, 1986. x, 105 p.

WALLOT, Jean-Pierre. *Intégration des nouvelles archives dans les services d'archives existants ou création d'institutions spécifiques?* Congrès international des archives (11e: 1988: Paris). Paris, 1988: 11, 4 p.

WARNER, Alice Sizer. Making money: fees for information service. *Special Libraries.* Fall 1987: 78(4), 277-280.

WOLFSHOERNDL, Vladimir. Povercnictvo poohospodarstva 1945-1960 [Commissionary of Agriculture 1945-1960]. *Slovenska Archivistika.* 1986: 21(1), 31-53.

WRIGHT, Sandra and Peter YURKIW. The collections survey in the Federal Archives and Manuscript Divisions of the Public Archives of Canada: a progress report on conservation programme planning. *Archivaria*. Summer 1986: (22), 58-74.

1.6 The profession / La profession d'archiviste

Addresses given at archivist Wilson's swearing-in ceremony. *SAA Newsletter*. May 1988: 7-8.

AEBERSOLD, Rolf. Jahresbericht des VSA-Bilkdungsausschusses 1984/1985 [Annual report of the Association of Swiss Archivists Training Committee 1984/1985]. *Arbido-B*. 1986: 1(1), 8-10.

AFANASYEV, Y.N. Professional training of archivists in U.S.S.R. *Archivum*. 1988: 34, 1-11.

ALMEIDA CAMARGO, Ana Maria de. *La formation des archivistes*. Congrès international des archives (11e: 1988: Paris). Paris, 1988. 3 p.

ALONSO, Vicenta Cortez. Archival education in Spain. *The American Archivist*. Summer 1988: 51(3), 330-335.

ARES, Florence, Carol COUTURE et Louise GAGNON-ARGUIN. L'archivistique à l'École de bibliothéconomie et des sciences de l'information. *Argus*. Mars 1987: 16(1), 9-11.

ARONSSON, Patricia and Thomas Elton BROWN. Information automation changes role of archivist. *Government Computer News*. 9 October 1987: 6(20), 40-43.

ART task force: learning objectives. *Archival Informatics Newsletter*. Spring 1987: 1(1), 7.

Assemblée générale de l'Association des archivistes français. Paris, 8-10 décembre 1986. *La Gazette des archives*. 1987: (136), 53-75.

ASSOCIATION OF BRITISH COLUMBIA ARCHIVISTS. MEMBERSHIP COMMITTEE. Editorial: your associa-tion wants you. *ABCA Newsletter*. Spring 1987: 12(6), 1-2.

BANSA, Helmut. IFLA principles on conservation and preservation. *Restaurator*. December 1986: 7(4), 202-206.

BARLEE, Kathleen. Presidential message. *ABCA Newsletter*. Spring 1987: 12(6), 4-5.

BARRITT, Marjorie Rabe. Archival training in the land of Muller, Feith, and Fruin: the Dutch National Archives School. *The American Archivist*. Summer 1988: 51(3), 336-344.

BARTELS, Kerry. The Northwest Archivists, Incorporated. *SAA Newsletter*. May 1988: 13.

BATY, Laurie. The NHPRC Archival Administration Fellowship Program. *SAA Newsletter*. November 1987: 6-7.

BAYNES-COPE, A.D. Ethics and the conservation of archival documents. *Journal of the Society of Archivists*. October 1988: 9(4), 185-187.

BECHOR, Malvina B. Bibliographic access to archival literature. *The American Archivist*. May 1987: 50(2), 243-247.

BELANGER, Terry. Standards for ethical conduct for rare book, manuscript, and special collections libraries. *College and Research Libraries News*. March 1987: 48(3), 134-135.

Berichte der Fachgruppen der Verein deutscher Archivare ueber ihre Arbeitssitzungen auf dem 58 Deutschen Archivtag [Reports of the various sections of the Association of German Archivists on their meetings at the 58th Congress of German Archivists]. *Archivar*. February 1987: 40(1), 77-88.

BERNER, R.C. Archival management and librarianship: an exploration of prospects for their integration. IN Advances in librarianship, vol. 14. New York: Academic Press, 1986: 253-283.

BEYEA, Marion et Marcel CAYA. Les associations professionnelles et le développement du système archivistique canadien. *Janus*. 1987: (2), 20-28.

BEYEA, Marion and Marcel CAYA. The professional associations and the formation of the Canadian archival system. *Janus*. 1987: (2), 18-25.

BLOUIN, Francis X., Jr. Moscow State Historico-Archival Institute and archival education in USSR. *The American Archivist*. Fall 1988: 51(4), 501-511.

BOLOTENKO, George. Professional convergence: new bindings, old pages. *Archivaria*. Winter 1988/89: 27, 133-142.

BOWDEN, Russell. Colloquium on the Harmonization of Education and Training Programmes for Library, Information and Archival Personnel. *Education for Information*. September 1987: 5(2/3), 207-233.

BRANDAK, George. British Columbia Archives Council: funding for an archival system in Canada — a move in the right direction. *BCLA Reporter*. January 1987: 31(1), 18-19.

BRAZIER, Jan. The archivist: scholar or administrator? *Archives and Manuscripts*. May 1988: (1), [9]-14.

BRICHFORD, Maynard J. Margaret Cross Norton: a tribute. *Illinois Libraries*. October 1987: 69(8), 537-538.

BRICHFORD, Maynard J. Who are the archivists and what do they do? *The American Archivist*. Winter/Spring 1988: 51(1/2), 106-110.

A Brief introduction of the Chinese Archives Society. *Janus*. 1986: 3, 14-15.

BROOM, Andrew. The ICA Committee on Conservation and Restoration. *IFLA Journal*. 1986: 12(4), 314-316.

BRYANS, Victoria. [Letter to the editor concerning certification of archivists]. *ABCA Newsletter*. Fall 1987: 13(2), 4-5.

CAIN, Virginia J.H. Featured regional: the Society of Georgia Archivists. *SAA Newsletter*. July 1987: 14.

CAMPBELL, T.M. "Archives and Information Management — Ships passing in the right". IN Proceedings: Conference of the Association of Canadian Archivists (1987: McMaster University). Hamilton, Ont., 1987. 5 p.

Canadian Centre for Information and Documentation on Archives. *ACA Bulletin*. March 1988: 12(4), 10.

CANTIN, Claude. L'Association des archivistes du Québec. *Bulletin de l'AEC*. Hiver 1988/1989: 10(4), 18-19.

Careers in records management. *Records and Retrieval Report*. December 1986: 2(10), 1-10.

CARLISLE, Diane. Gaining credibility. *Records Management Quarterly*. January 1987: 21(1), 29-31.

Le Centre de formation de l'Association des archivistes français. *Janus*. 1987: (1), 13-16.

Certification? *ACA Bulletin*. September 1987: 12(1), 1-4.

Certification: dissatisfaction South of the Border? *ABCA Newsletter*. Fall 1988: 14(2), 2, 9.

Certification response. *ACA Bulletin*. July 1988: 12(6), 16-18.

CHABIN, Marie-Anne. Les Capétiens en Île-de-France. Un jeu-concours organisé par le groupe Île-de-France de l'Association des archivistes français. *La Gazette des archives*. 1988: (140), 75-79.

CHABIN, Michel. La formation permanente des archivistes communaux: une collaboration entre l'Association des archivistes français et les centres de formation du personnel communal. *La Gazette des archives*. 1986: (133), 165-167.

CHEN ZHAO, Wu. An introduction to archives education in China. *Archivum*. 1988: 34, 13-16.

CHESTNUT, Paul. Certification update. *SAA Newsletter*. November 1988: 6-7.

CHMIDT, S.O. Sur la formation des historiens-archivistes à l'Institut d'État d'histoire et des archives de Moscou (réflexions à l'occasion de la Réforme de l'école supérieure); le point de vue de la section du personnel de la Direction générale des Archives de l'URSS [en russe]. *Sovietskje Arkhivy*. 1987: (4), 55-62.

Code de déontologie et guide du praticien à l'intention des personnes œuvrant dans le domaine de la conservation des biens culturels au Canada. Ottawa: Institut international pour la conservation — Groupe canadien (IIC-GC): Association canadienne des restaurateurs professionnels (ACRP), 1986. 18, 18 p.

Code of ethics and guidance for practice for those involved in the conservation of cultural property in Canada. Ottawa: International Institute for Conservation — Canadian Group (IIC-CG): Canadian Association of Professional Conservators (CAPC), 1986. 18, 18 p.

COLLIER, Rosemary. Ten years on: the Archives and Records Association of New Zealand. *Archifacts*. 1987: (2), 10-14.

Comparison of archivists certification programmes in the UK and US. *ACA Bulletin*. May 1988: 12(5), 1-2.

Consulting in records management. *Records and Retrieval Report*. June 1986: 2(6), 1-6.

CONWAY, Paul. Archival education and the need for full-time faculty. *The American Archivist*. Summer 1988: 51(3), 254-265.

CONWAY, Paul. Perspectives on archival resources: the 1985 census of archival institutions. *The American Archivist*. Spring 1987: 50(2), 174-191.

COOK, J. Frank. Academic archivists and the SAA, 1938-1979: from Arcana Siwash to the C&U PAG. *The American Archivist*. Fall 1988: 51(4), 428-439.

COOK, Michael. Information technology: a challenge to training. *Archivum*. 1988: 34, 17-33.

COOK, Terry. ACA Conference overview. *ACA Bulletin*. July 1988: 12(6), 1-4.

COOK, Terry. Shadows in the Canadian archival zeitgeist: the jeremiad of Terry Eastwood considered. *Archivaria*. Summer 1986: (22), 156-162.

COOKE, Anne. A code of ethics for archivists: some points for discussion. *Archives and Manuscripts*. November 1987: 15(2), 95-104.

COUTURE, Carol. La formation en archivistique: évolution, contexte et contenu. *Archivum*. 1988: 34, 35-59.

COX, Richard J. American archival literature: expanding horizons and continuing needs, 1901-1987. *The American Archivist*. Summer 1987: 50(3), 306-323.

COX, Richard J. Council revises its priorities. *SAA Newsletter*. September 1988: 4-5.

COX, Richard J. Educating archivists: speculations on the past, present and future. *Journal of the American Society for Information Science*. Summer 1988: 39, 340-343.

CRAIG, Barbara L. Meeting the future by returning to the past: a commentary on Hugh Taylor's transformations. *Archivaria*. Winter 1987-1988: (25), 7-11.

CRUSH, Peter. Archives and historians. *Archives and Manuscripts*. May 1988: (1), 15-24.

DAVIS, Susan E. Development of managerial training for archivist. *The American Archivist*. Summer 1988: 51(3), 278-285.

DELMAS, Bruno. Origine et développement de l'enseignement de l'archivistique. *Archivum*. 1988: 34, 61-73.

DELMAS, Bruno. Trente ans d'enseignement de l'archivistique en France. *La Gazette des archives*. 1988: (141), 19-32.

DELOTTINVILLE, Peter. Life in an age of restraint: recent developments in labour union archives in English Canada. *Archivaria*. Winter 1988/89: 27, 8-24.

DEMPSEY, Colleen. [Letter to the editor concerning certification of archivists]. *ABCA Newsletter*. Winter 1987: 13(3), 4-5.

DEMPSEY, Colleen. Summary BCA needs assessment survey. *ACA Bulletin.* May 1988: 12(5), 7-8.

Der 58 Deutsche Archivtag 1986 in Muenchen. Vortraege, Berichte, Referate [The 58th Congress of German Archivists 1986 in Munich. Reports, Lectures, Seminar papers. *Archivar.* February 1987: 40(1), 1-22.

DURANTI, Luciana. Education and the role of the archivist in Italy. *The American Archivist.* Summer 1988: 51(3), 346-355.

EASTWOOD, Terry. The education of archivists and Canadian studies. *ACS Newsletter.* Winter 1988/1989: 10(4), 27.

EASTWOOD, Terry. Nurturing archival education in the university. *The American Archivist.* Summer 1988: 51(3), 228-252.

EASTWOOD, Terry. A small world expands. *Archivaria.* Summer 1987: (24), 129-136.

EELES, Graham and Jill KINNEAR. Archivists and oral historians: friends, strangers or enemies? *Journal of the Society of Archivists.* October 1988: 9(4), 188-189.

ELDER, Sean. Just the facts, Ma'am: San Francisco's archivist, Gladys Hansen, debunks myths and resurrect buried thruth. *Image.* September 28, 1986: 15-16.

ENDELMAN, Judith E. and Joel WURL. The NHPRC/Mellon Foundation fellowship in archives administration: structured training on the job. *The American Archivist.* Summer 1988: 51(3), 286-297.

ENGLERT, Marianne. Berfusbild "Pressearchivar": Grundsaetze und Veraenderungen [The "Press archivist" and his professional image: principles and changes]. *Archivar.* July 1986: 39(3), 323-334.

ERICSON, Timothy L. Professional associations and archival education: a different role, or a different theater? *The American Archivist.* Summer 1988: 51(3), 298-311.

EVANS, Frank B. The organization and status of archival training: an historical perspective. *Archivum.* 1988: 34, 75-91.

FLECKNER, John A. CGAP and the future of the archival profession. *SAA Newsletter.* July 1988: 6-8.

FLECKNER, John A. The SAA Committee on Goals and Priorities: a report to the profession: June 1987. *SAA Newsletter.* July 1987: 6-8.

FRANZ, Eckhart G. *Archives and education: a RAMP study with guidelines.* Paris: Unesco, 1986. 59 p. (PGI-86/WS/18)

FRANZ, Eckhart G. Zwischen Tradition und Innovation: die Arbeit des Archivars heuteund morgen [Between tradition and innovation: the archivist's work today and tomorrow]. *Archivar.* February 1986: 39(1), 19-26.

FUGATE, R.L. Records management: a global perspective to information. IN Intellectual foundations for information professionals. Boulder: Social Science Monographs, 1987: 97-111.

GAGNON-ARGUIN, Louise. L'enseignement de l'archivistique à l'École de bibliothéconomie et des sciences de l'information de l'Université de Montréal. *Bulletin de l'AEC.* Hiver 1988/1989: 10(4), 28-29.

GELLER, L.D. In-house conservation and the general practice of archival science. *Archivaria.* Summer 1986: (22), 163-167.

GOESSI, Anton. Bericht des VSA-Praesidenten ueber das vereinsjahr 1984/1985 [Report from the President of the Association of Swiss Archivists for the year 1984/1985]. *Arbido-B.* 1986: 1(1), 6-8.

GRACE, Michael J. The Chicago Area Archivists. *Illinois Libraries.* October 1987: 69(8), 546-547.

GRACY, David B. II. Is there a future in the use of archives? *Archivaria.* Summer 1987: (24), 3-9.

GROVER, Ray. Archives education in New Zealand. *Archifacts.* 1987: (2), 35-37.

Guidelines for ACA Special Interest Sections. *ACA Bulletin.* March 1988: 12(4), 8-9.

Guidelines for the granting of awards. *ACA Bulletin*. March 1988: 12(4), 7.

Guidelines for the granting of awards. *ACA Bulletin*. September 1988: 13(1), [5].

HACKMAN, Larry J. and Joan WARNOW-BLEWETT. The documentation strategy process: a model and case study. *The American Archivist*. Winter 1987: 50(1), 12-47.

HARRISON, Donald Fisher. Computers, electronic data and the Vietnam War. *Archivaria*. Summer 1988: (26), 18-32.

HAWORTH, Kent M. [Letter to the editor concerning certification of archivists]. *ABCA Newsletter*. Winter 1987: 13(3), 4.

HAYWARD, Robert J. Working in thin air: of archives and the Deschênes Commission. *Archivaria*. Summer 1988: (26), 122-136.

HEALY, S. The Society's chronicle: Annual Conference, 1988. *Journal of the Society of Archivists*. October 1988: 9(4), 227-229.

HEDLIN, Edie. Update on the certification initiative. *SAA Newsletter*. September 1988: 6.

HENDERSON, Cathy. Curator or conservator: who decides on what treatment? *Rare Books & Manuscripts Librarianship*. Fall 1987: 2(2), 103-107.

HILLER, Marc. L'archiviste de référence: instrument de recherche ultime? IN Couture, Carol. Réflexions archivistiques. Montréal: Université de Montréal, École de bibliothéconomie et des sciences de l'information, 1987: 11-24.

HOLBERT, Sue E. Open letter to the SAA membership on certification. *SAA Newsletter*. May 1988: 10-11.

HOLDEN, Jill R.J. *Opportunities in the United States for Education in Book and Paper Conservation and Preservation*. January 1988. 25 p.

HOPKINS, Mark. Computerizing a government records archives — The FED-DOC Experience. *Records Management Quarterly*. July 1986: 20(3), 36-39.

HOWE, Richard D. and Allen ANTONE. *Salary-trend study of faculty in library and archival sciences for the years 1983-84 and 1986-87*. Boone, N.C.: Appalachian State University, 1987. 16 p.

HUNTER, Gregory S. Filling the GAP: planning on the local and individual levels. *The American Archivist*. Winter 1987: 50(1), 110-115.

HYAM, Grace Maurice. Copyright revision: awaiting the second stage. *Archivaria*. Winter 1988/89: 27, 175-177.

Information and image management industry: job descriptions. Silver Spring, M.D.: Association for Information and Image Management, 1987. 30 p.

INSTITUTE OF CERTIFIED RECORDS MANAGERS. Outline for Certified Records Manager Examination. *Records Management Quarterly*. January 1988: 22(1), 136-144.

JANUSZONOK, Teresa. The Society of Archivists' training scheme for archive conservators. *Conservation Administration News*. April 1987: (29), 9.

JANZEN, Mary E. Featured regional: Midwest Archives Conference. *SAA Newsletter*. November 1987: 10-11.

JANZEN, Mary E. The Midwest Archives Conference. *Illinois Libraries*. October 1987: 69(8), 542.

JAROSCHKA, Walter. Dic Aufgaben der Archive in unscrer Zeit. Vortrag zur Eroeffnung des 58 Deutschen Archivtages [Archival tasks in our time. Opening lecture at the 58th Congress of German Archivists]. *Archivar*. February 1987: 40(1), 19-26.

JOHNSON, Nikki. Further thoughts on a code of practice. *Journal of the Society of Archivists*. 1986: 8(2), 93-94.

JOYCE, William L. Archival education: two fables. *The American Archivist*. Winter/Spring 1988: 51(1/2), 16-22.

JOYCE, William L. The SAA certification program: a report to the profession. *SAA Newsletter*. May 1987: 8.

JOYCE, William L. An uneasy balance: voluntarism and professionalism. *The American Archivist*. Winter 1987: 50(1), 7-11.

KATHPALIA, Y.P. Training in conservation. *Archivum*. 1988: 34, 105-112.

KECSKEMETI, Charles. Contrastes et nuances: réflexions sur la formation des archivistes. *Archives et bibliothèques de Belgique*. 1986: 57(1/2), 245-253.

KECSKEMETI, Charles. The professional culture of the archivist. *The American Archivist*. Summer 1987: 50(3), 408-413.

KENNEY, Anne R. SAA Council priorities modified. *SAA Newsletter*. September 1987: 7.

KESNER, Richard M. A room with a view: the 1987 ACA Conference in Hamilton, Ontario. *Archivaria*. Winter 1987-1988: (25), 155-162.

KETELAAR, Éric. Une brève introduction à la Société des archives en Chine. *Janus*. 1986: 3, 13-14.

KETELAAR, Éric. Muller, Feith and Fruin. *Archives et bibliothèques de Belgique*. 1986: 57(1/2), 255-268.

KGABI, D.K. The role of the archivist in oral traditions — the Botswana Case. *Commonwealth Archivists Association Newsletter*. November 1987: (5), 4-6.

KLAASSEN, David J. The American Archivist in transition. *SAA Newsletter*. November 1988: 12-13.

KLAUDA, Mary. The Twin Cities Archives Round Table. *ACA Bulletin*. May 1988: 14.

KLAUE, Wolfgang. New media require specialized archivists: training and education for audiovisual archives. *Archivum*. 1988: 34, 113-123.

KOUZNETSOVA, T.V. La chaire de la documentation et de l'organisation de la gestion d'État des dossiers à MGIAI (l'Institut de Moscou d'État de l'histoire et des archives) [en russe]. *Sovietskje Arkhivy*. 1987: (1), 57-60.

LACHOWSKI, Michel. La formation professionnelle aux métiers de l'audiovisuel. *Problèmes audiovisuels*. Janvier 1985: 23, 1-48.

LAJEUNESSE, Marcel. L'archivistique: une science de l'information à la recherche d'un milieu de formation. *Archives (Revue de l'Association des archivistes du Québec)*. Décembre 1986: 18(3), 35-47.

LEESCH, Wolfgang. Zur Geschichte der Archivarsausbildung [On the history of training archivists]. *Archivar*. May 1986: 39(2), 149-156.

LODOLINI, Elio. La Guerra di Indipendenza Degli Archivisti. *Archives et bibliothèques de Belgique*. 1986: 57(1/2), 269-293.

LODOLINI, Elio. L'insegnamento della teoria archivistica nella formazione degli archivisti. *Archivum*. 1988: 34, 125-166.

MCMILLEN, Liz. New professionalism and surging interest boost the academic credibility of "public" historians. *Chronicle of Higher Education*. May 20, 1987: 33(36), 13, 15.

MCTIERNAN, Miriam. The Canadian Council of Archives. *ACS Newsletter*. Winter 1988/1989: 10(4), 12-13.

MAHER, William J. Contexts for understanding professional certification: opening Pandora's box? *The American Archivist*. Fall 1988: 51(4), 408-427.

MILLER, Page Putnam. Fighting for a qualified, nonpartisan U.S. archivist: what we learned. *SAA Newsletter*. September 1988: 12.

MITCHELL, Ann M. and Colin SMITH. "...in the Agora". *Archives and Manuscripts*. November 1988: 16(2), 129-132.

MITCHELL, Gary. Ask yourself [editorial]. *ABCA Newsletter*. Spring 1986: 12(2), 1.

MITCHELL, Gary. Crossroads [editorial]. *ABCA Newsletter*. Winter 1986: 12(1), 1.

MITCHELL, Gary. Editorial... 1986. *ABCA Newsletter*. Winter 1987: 12(5), 1-2.

MITCHELL, Gary. Editorial: who speaks for us? *ABCA Newsletter*. Winter 1987: 13(3), 1.

MITCHELL, Gary. I wonder... [editorial]. *ABCA Newsletter*. Fall 1986: 12(4), 1.

[MITCHELL, Gary]. A moment please [editorial]. *ABCA Newsletter*. [Spring 1988]: [13(4)], 1.

MONTEIRO, Norma de Goes. Réflexions sur l'enseignement de l'archivistique au Brésil. *Archivum*. 1988: 34, 93-103.

MORGAN, Dennis F. Personnel selection and interviewing: professional and personnal perspectives. *Records Management Quarterly*. July 1986: 20(3), 20-24.

MWIYERIWA, Steve. Archive training in developing countries: Africa. *Archivum*. 1988: 34, 167-182.

NEAL, Donn C. (ed.). An action agenda for the archival profession: institutionalizing the planning process; a report to SAA Council by the Committee on Goals and Priorities. *The American Archivist*. Fall 1988: 51(4), 528-535.

NEAL, Donn C. The Society of American Archivists. *Illinois Libraries*. October 1987: 69(8), 538-542.

NJOVANA, Samuel. Cours de gestion des documents au Zimbabwe. *Janus*. 1988: (2), 31-32.

NJOVANA, Samuel. Zimbabwe, national certificate in records management. *Janus*. 1988: (2), 14-15.

O'BRIEN, J.W. Only time will tell. *The Archivist*. July/August 1986: 13(4), 3.

O'BRIEN, J.W. Qui vivra verra. *L'Archiviste*. Juillet/août 1986: 13(4), 8-9.

PACIFICO, Michele F. Founding mothers: women in the Society of American Archivists, 1936-1972. *The American Archivist*. Summer 1987: 50(3), 370-389.

PATTERSON, Brad. The Saunders Report. *Archifacts*. 1988: (1), 34-37.

PERTI, R.K. *Le recrutement des spécialistes*. Congrès international des archives (11e: 1988: Paris). Paris, 1988. 5 p.

PHILLIPS, Faye. Harper's Ferry revisited: the role of congressional staff archivists in implementing the Congressional Papers Project Report. *Provenance*. Spring 1988: 6(1), 26-44.

POTIN, Monique. La relation entre les spécialistes de l'information documentaire et les utilisateurs: trois approches. *Documentation et bibliothèques*. Avril/juin 1987: 33(2), 39-44.

PROULX, Chantal. Le bibliothécaire-archiviste: un atout pour l'entreprise privée? IN Couture, Carol. Réflexions archivistiques. Montréal: Université de Montréal, École de bibliothéconomie et des sciences de l'information, 1987: 1-10.

QUINN, Patrick M. Archivists against the current: for a fair and truly representative record of our times. *Provenance*. Spring 1987: 5(1), 1-7.

RASTAS, Pirkko. Training of business archivists. *Archivum*. 1988: 34, 183-190.

Records management consultants. *Records and Retrieval Report*. June 1986: 2(6), 7-12.

REHKOPF, Charles F. Featured regional: the Association of St. Louis Area Archivists. *SAA Newsletter*. November 1988: 11.

RENÉ-BAZIN, Paule and Marie-Françoise TAMMARO. Le stage technique international d'archives: an historical overview and future prospects. *The American Archivist*. Summer 1988: 51(3), 356-362.

Report of the interim board for certification. *SAA Newsletter*. January 1988: 10-15.

Reports on archival education programs. *SAA Newsletter*. September 1987: 10-12.

RHOADS, Bert. Certification by examination. *SAA Newsletter*. November 1988: 7.

ROBERGE, Michel. Le certificat de premier cycle en gestion des documents administratifs et des archives de l'UQAM: un programme qui colle à la réalité québécoise. *Bulletin de l'AEC*. Hiver 1988/1989: 10(4), 28-29.

ROBERTS, John W. Archival theory: much ads about shelving. *The American Archivist*. Winter 1987: 50(1), 66-74.

ROPER, Michael. Archival education in Britain. *The American Archivist*. Fall 1987: 50(4), 586-590.

RUTH, Janice E. Educating the reference archivist. *The American Archivist*. Summer 1988: 51(3), 266-276.

SANTORO, Corrado A. "Continuing education for archivists: towards a revised professionalism in the information age". IN Proceedings: Conference of the Association of Canadian Archivists (1987: McMaster University). Hamilton, Ont., 1987. 10 p.

SCHOUPS, I.C. Wyffels, algemeen rijksarchivaris 1969-1987 " C. Wyffels, general archivist for Belgium, 1969-1987". *Bibliotheek-en Archiefgids*. January 1987: (63), 3-7.

SCHREYER, Alice. RBMS at 30: growing along with the profession. *Rare Books & Manuscripts Librarianship*. Spring 1988: 3(1), 3-18.

SCHULZ, Constance B. Analysis of the marketplace for educated archivists: state archives as a case study. *The American Archivist*. Summer 1988: 51(3), 320-329.

SEIBEL, C. Sheldon. Records management in its intellectual context: experience at the University of Texas at Austin. *Records Management Quarterly*. July 1987: 21(3), 3-14, 42, 59.

SMART, John. "The leadership record and potential of Canada's provincial and regional archivists associations in the information age". IN Proceedings: Conference of the Association of Canadian Archivists (1987: McMaster University). Hamilton, Ont., 1987. 11 p.

SMITH, Kenneth E. Vale David MacMillan (1925-1987). *Archives and Manuscripts*. November 1988: 16(2), 87-89.

SOCIETY OF AMERICAN ARCHIVISTS. COMMITTEE ON EDUCATION AND PROFESSIONAL DEVELOPMENT. Society of American Archivists guidelines for graduate archival education programs. *The American Archivist*. Summer 1988: 51(3), 380-389.

SPEIRS, Brian. Development of Alberta's archival community. *ACS Newsletter*. Winter 1988/1989: 10(4), 25-26.

STERN, Teena. The Society of California Archivists. *SAA Newsletter*. September 1988: 18.

STUART, Elizabeth A. A question of culture: the usefulness of study tours. *Journal of the Society of Archivists*. April 1988: 9(2), 84-87.

TAYLOR, Hugh A. From dust to ashes: burnout at the Archives. *The Midwestern Archivist*. 1987: 12(2), 73-82.

TAYLOR, Hugh A. Transformations in the archives: technological adjustment or paradigm shift. *Archivaria*. Winter 1987-1988: (25), 12-28.

TCHIRKOV, S.V. L'historiographie et la science des sources de l'archivistique en URSS. Annotations [en russe]. *Sovietskje Arkhivy*. 1987: (1), 103-104.

THOMPSON, Terry. Archivaria: a brief introduction to the journal of the Association of Canadian Archivists. *The American Archivist*. Winter/Spring 1988: 51(1/2), 132-134.

The Training Centre of the French Association of Archivists. *Janus*. 1987: (1), 9-12.

TRAUE, J.E. Training needs and career structure. *Archifacts*. 1987: (2), 32-33.

TRUFFER, Bernard. 62. Jahresversammlung der Vereinigung schweizerischer archivare [62nd Annual General Meeting of the Swiss Society of Archivists]. *Arbido-B*. 1986: 1(1), 3-6.

WALCH, Victoria Irons. *Conference on information resources for archivists and records administrators. Final report. Summary of proceedings (Washington, D.C., June 19-20, 1987)*. Albany, N.Y.: National Association of Government Archives and Records Administrators, 1987. 11 p.

WALCH, Victoria Irons. *Information resources for archivists and records administrators. A report and recommendations.* Albany, N.Y.: National Association of Government Archives and Records Administrators, 1987. 46 p.

WARNER, R.M. Archives and the new information age: a reluctant partnership. IN Intellectual foundations for information professionals. Boulder: Social Science Monographs, 1987: 69-80.

WEBER, Lisa B. Educating archivists for automation. *Library Trends*. Winter 1988: 36(3), 501-518.

WELFELE, Odile. Information et formation du personnel des administrations centrales et des établissements publics nationaux. *La Gazette des archives*. 1987: (137-138), 162-164.

What the blazes is an archivist IPA? (And what is one doing in NEH?) *SAA Newsletter*. January 1988: 6-9.

WHITTICK, Christopher and Margaret WHITTICK. Anglo-Dutch exchange visits. *Janus*. 1987: (2), 26-28.

WHITTICK, Christopher et Margaret WHITTICK. Visites d'échanges anglo-hollandaises. *Janus*. 1987: (2), 29-31.

WOELDERINK, Bernard. Esquisse du temps passé et du temps présent de l'Association des archivistes aux Pays-Bas. *Janus*. 1987: (1), 20-23.

WOELDERINK, Bernard. Times past and present: a profile of the Dutch Association of Archivists. *Janus*. 1987: (1), 17-19.

1.7 Archives history / Histoire des archives

AGAFONOVA, E.A. et G.E. SOMINITCH. Les documents des Archives centrales historiques d'État de l'URSS sur l'activité des institutions d'archives en 1918-1922. *Sovietskje Arkhivy*. 1988: (3), 44-47.

ALEGBELEYE, G.B.O. Archival development in Nigeria. *Janus*. 1988: (2), 9-11.

ALEGBELEYE, G.B.O. Archives administration and records management in Nigeria: up the decades from amalgamation. *Records Management Quarterly*. July 1988: 22(3), 26-30.

ALEGBELEYE, G.B.O. Le développement des archives au Nigeria. *Janus*. 1988: (2), 26-28.

ALEXANDER, Philip N. and Elizabeth PESSEK. Archives in emerging nations: the Anglophone experience. *The American Archivist*. Winter/Spring 1988: 51(1/2), 120-131.

ARCHIVES NATIONALES DU CANADA. *Au-delà de l'écrit: actualités filmées et reportages radio et télé diffusés au Canada*. Ottawa: Les Archives, 1988. 348 p.

BABELON, Jean-Pierre. Le Musée de l'histoire de France aux Archives nationales à Paris. *La Gazette des archives*. 1987: (139), 260-265.

BABICKA, Vacslav. Archiv ministerstva unitra a archivy na slovensku 1918-1938 [Archives of the Ministry of Interior and archives in Slovakia]. *Slovenska Archivistika*. 1986: 21(1), 54-72.

BARTELS, Kerry. The Northwest Archivists, Incorporated. *SAA Newsletter*. May 1988: 13.

BAUMANN, Roland M. Oberlin College and the movement to establish an archives, 1920-1966. *The Midwestern Archivist*. 1988: 13(1), 27-38.

BERTRAND, Jean-Wilfrid. Les Archives nationales d'Haiti: près de deux siècles d'histoire, un nouveau départ. *La Gazette des archives.* 1988: (142-143), 25-35.

BLUM, Sylvie. Télévision/spectacle/politique. *Dossiers de l'audiovisuel.* Janvier/février 1988: 17, 61.

BRACHMANN-TEUBNER, Elisabeth and Wolfgang MERKER. 40 Jahre Zentrales Staatsarchiv: Archivarbeit im Dienste des Friedens und des Sozialismus [40 years of a Central State Archive: archive work in the service of peace and socialism]. *Archiv Mitteilungen.* 1986: 36(2), 44-51.

BRADSHER, James Gregory. A brief history of the growth of Federal Government records, archives and information 1789-1985. *Government Publications Review.* July/August 1986: 13, 491-505.

BRADSHER, James Gregory. Federal field archives: past, present, and future. *Government Information Quarterly.* 1987: 4(2), 151-166.

COUTURE, Carol. La formation en archivistique: évolution, contexte et contenu. *Archivum.* 1988: 34, 35-59.

COX, Richard J. American archival literature: expanding horizons and continuing needs, 1901-1987. *The American Archivist.* Summer 1987: 50(3), 306-323.

COX, Richard J. On the value of archival history in the United States. *Libraries and Culture.* Spring 1988: 23, 135-151.

Les chroniques de l'édification archivistique en URSS [1962-1979]. *Sovietskje Arkhivy.* 1988: (1), 45-48.

Les chroniques de l'édification archivistique en URSS [1980-1987]. *Sovietskje Arkhivy.* 1988: (2), 48-51.

DANIELS, Maygene. The Genesis and structure of the International Council on Archives: an American view. *The American Archivist.* Summer 1987: 50(3), 414-419.

Le Décret du Conseil des Commissaires du peuple de la R.S.F.S.R. « Sur la conservation et la destruction des archives ». *Sovietskje Arkhivy.* 1988: (1), 41-44.

DELOTTINVILLE, Peter. Life in an age of restraint: recent developments in labour union archives in English Canada. *Archivaria.* Winter 1988/89: 27, 8-24.

EVANS, Frank B. The organization and status of archival training: an historical perspective. *Archivum.* 1988: 34, 75-91.

FRANKLIN, Dorothy. Les Archives nationales du Canada fières de leur passé, confiantes pour l'avenir. *L'Archiviste.* Septembre/octobre 1987: 14(5), 12-13.

FRANKLIN, Dorothy. The National Archives of Canada new name, proud tradition. *The Archivist.* September/October 1987: 14(5), 12-13.

FRANZ, Eckhart G. Archival development: the last decade. *ACA Bulletin.* September 1988: 13(1), [1-2].

GAGNON-ARGUIN, Louise. Les 20 ans de la revue Archives. Analyse des articles et des auteurs de 1969 à 1988. *Archives (Revue de l'Association des archivistes du Québec).* Été 1988: 20(1), 3-29.

HACKMAN, Larry J. A perspective on American archives. *The Public Historian.* Summer 1986: 8(3), 10-28.

HIVES, Christopher L. History, business records, and corporate archives in North America. *Archivaria.* Summer 1986: (22), 40-57.

HOLMAN, H.T. Having no entries, keeping no books: the records of the Prince Edward Island Fisheries Claims Commission, 1884-1888. *Archivaria.* Summer 1986: (22), 107-113.

KEIRSTEAD, Robin G. J.S. Matthews and an archives for Vancouver, 1951-1972. *Archivaria.* Winter 1986-87: (23), 86-106.

KHORKHORDINA, T.I. De l'histoire des Archives nationales de Cuba. *Sovietskje Arkhivy.* 1988: (5), 90-96.

KLAUDA, Mary. The Twin Cities Archives Round Table. *ACA Bulletin.* May 1988: 14.

KRAUSE, Eric. The Fortress of Louisbourg Archives: the first twenty-five years. *Archivaria*. Summer 1988: (26), 137-148.

LAINE, Edward W. Kallista Perintoa-Precious Legacy!: Finnish-Canadian archives, 1882-1985. *Archivaria*. Summer 1986: (22), 75-94.

LAPOINTE, Richard. « Petite histoire » et archives. La vie et l'œuvre de Pierre-Georges Roy. *Archives (Revue de l'Association des archivistes du Québec)*. Automne 1988: 20(2), 5-12.

LEBLANC, André. Tracking the worker's past in Quebec. *Archivaria*. Winter 1988/89: 27, 25-34.

MACE, Angela. *The Royal Institute of British Architects: a guide to its archive and history*. With an essay by Robert Thorne. London: New York: Mansell Publishing Limited, 1986. 378 p.

MACLEOD, Donald. Quaint specimens of the early days: priorities in collecting the Ontario archival record, 1872-1935. *Archivaria*. Summer 1986: (22), 12-39.

MENIER, Marie-Antoinette. Cent ans dans l'histoire des archives de la colonisation. *La Gazette des archives*. 1987: (139), 207-222.

MICHELSON, Avra. Introduction: descriptive standards and the archival profession. *Archival Informatics Technical Report*. Summer 1988: 2(2), 1-4.

MORELLE, Laurent. Qu'est-ce que les archives? Un débat insolite au sein des facultés parisiennes en 1878. *La Gazette des archives*. 1986: (134-135), 195-204.

NATIONAL ARCHIVES OF CANADA. *Beyond the printed word: newsreel and broadcast reporting in Canada*. Ottawa: The Archives, 1988. 348 p.

New facility recommended for the National Archives of Canada. *ACA Bulletin*. January 1988: 12(3), 1-2.

Obituary: Ainslie Helmcken, 1900-1987. *ABCA Newsletter*. Winter 1987: 13(3), 9.

PAC reorganization. *ACA Bulletin*. July 1987: 11(6), 10-11.

PCHENITCHNYI, A.P. De l'histoire de la gestion des archives en URSS 1918-1941. *Sovietskje Arkhivy*. 1988: (3), 18-26.

PIEJUT, Geneviève. Feuilletons et séries. *Dossiers de l'audiovisuel*. Novembre/décembre 1987: 16, 51.

POTHIER, Bernard. Archival material at the Canadian War Museum. *Archivaria*. Summer 1988: (26), 149-153.

Pour le 70e anniversaire du décret de V.I. Lénine sur les archives: l'arrêté du Conseil des Commissaires du peuple de la R.S.F.S.R. du 27 mars 1919. *Sovietskje Arkhivy*. 1987: (5), 46.

Pour le 70e anniversaire du décret de V.I. Lénine sur les archives: les chroniques de l'édification archivistique en URSS [1930-1941]. *Sovietskje Arkhivy*. 1987: (5), 47-49.

QUINN, Patrick M. Archives in Illinois, 1981-1987. *Illinois Libraries*. October 1987: 69(8), 534.

ROBERTS-MOORE, Judith. The Office of the Custodian of Enemy Property: an overview of the office and its records, 1920-1952. *Archivaria*. Summer 1986: (22), 95-106.

ROBERTSON, Peter, ed. But we are fortunately able to carry on: letters from PAC's London Office, 1940. *Archivaria*. Summer 1988: (26), 176-177.

ROSS, Alex. The records of the Hudson's Bay Company Land Department, 1879-1963. *Archivaria*. Summer 1986: (22), 114-119.

RUSSELL, Bill. D'hier à demain: le bureau de Londres. *L'Archiviste*. Novembre/décembre 1987: 14(6), 16-18.

RUSSELL, Bill. From the London Office. *The Archivist*. November/December 1987: 14(6), 16-18.

SALAUN, Jean-Michel. Sport et télévision. *Dossiers de l'audiovisuel*. Mars/avril 1988: 18, 11-55.

SMITH, Wilfred I. "Total archives": the Canadian experience. *Archives et bibliothèques de Belgique*. 1986: 57(1/2), 323-346.

70 ans du décret de Lénine du 1er juin 1918 sur les archives: la brochure de Petrograd sur les archives (1919). *Sovietskje Arkhivy*. 1988: (4), 27-30.

SPANG, Paul. Une page commune dans l'histoire des archives de la Belgique et du Luxembourg: le partage des archives du grand-duché de Luxembourg après le traité de Londres du 19 avril 1839. *Archives et bibliothèques de Belgique*. 1986: 57(1/2), 347-369.

TARANOV, I.T. Le développement ultérieur des Archives est le souci des Soviets des députés du peuple [en russe]. *Sovietskje Arkhivy*. 1987: (3), 40-46.

TESSIER, Marc et Pierre-Georges ROY. Pionnier des archives et de l'histoire du Canada. *Archives (Revue de l'Association des archivistes du Québec)*. Automne 1988: 20(2), 13-20.

THOMAS, Bettye Collier. Towards black feminism: the creation of the Bethune Museum-Archives. *Special Collections*. Spring/Summer 1986: 43-66.

Too close for comfort? A Reagan Library flap. *Newsweek*. February 23, 1987: 109(8), 30.

TURNER, Allan. Laurenda Daniells — A.B.C.A. honorary life member. *ABCA Newsletter*. Summer 1988: 14(1), 3 p.

UDINA, Federico. Espana y el consejo internacional de archivos (1950-1984). *Archives et bibliothèques de Belgique*. 1986: 57(1/2), 371-379.

VOSAHLIKOVA, Dana. Nas rozhovor s dr. Emmou Urbankovou o fondech oddeleni rukpoisu a vzacnych tisku Statni knihovny CSR [An interview with Dr. Emma Urbankova about the stock of the Department of Manuscripts and Rare Prints of the State Library of the Czech Socialist Republic]. *Ctenar*. 1986: 38(7), 215-218.

WALLOT, Jean-Pierre. Les archives, une voie vers l'avenir. *L'Archiviste*. Janvier/février 1988: 15(1), 2-3.

WALLOT, Jean-Pierre. What is an archives? *The Archivist*. January/February 1988: 15(1), 2-3.

WEILBRENNER, Bernard. Les Archives provinciales du Québec et leurs relations avec les Archives fédérales, 1867-1920. Troisième partie. *Archives (Revue de l'Association des archivistes du Québec)*. Décembre 1986: 18(3), 3-25.

WEILBRENNER, Bernard. Les Archives provinciales du Québec et leurs relations avec les Archives fédérales, 1867-1920. Quatrième partie: une longue torpeur, 1892-1920. *Archives (Revue de l'Association des archivistes du Québec)*. Mars 1987: 18(4), 3-21.

WEILBRENNER, Bernard. Au service du public vingt-quatre heures par jour. *Archives et bibliothèques de Belgique*. 1986: 57(1/2), 411-436.

WRIGHT, Glenn. Sir Arthur Doughty and the Archives: Stocking a treasure house. *The Archivist*. September/October 1987: 14(5), 14-15.

WRIGHT, Glenn. Sir Arthur Doughty archiviste national, 1904-1935. *L'Archiviste*. Septembre/octobre 1987: 14(5), 14-15.

YASUZAWA, Shuichi and M. ANDO. Japanese archives at the dawn of a new age. *Information Development*. January 1988: 4(1), 33-36.

1.8 International activities / Activités internationales

ALEXANDER, Philip N. and Elizabeth PESSEK. Archives in emerging nations: the Anglophone experience. *The American Archivist*. Winter/Spring 1988: 51(1/2), 120-131.

ARMA INTERNATIONAL CONFERENCE (32ND: 1987: ANAHEIM, CA.). *Proceedings of the ARMA International 32nd Annual Conference*. Prairie Village, KS.: Association of Records

Managers and Administrators, 1987. 482 p.

AUER, Leopold. Staatennachfolge bei archiven. *Archives et bibliothèques de Belgique*. 1986: 57(1/2), 51-68.

BROOM, Andrew. The ICA Committee on Conservation and Restoration. *IFLA Journal*. 1986: 12(4), 314-316.

BURKE, Frank G. Soviet-American Archival Exchange Meeting in Moscow. *The American Archivist*. May 1987: 50(2), 254-261.

CLAUZADE, Sophie de. Pour une archivistique audiovisuelle internationale. Analyse d'un ouvrage récent. *La Gazette des archives*. 1988: (140), 54-64.

CLEMENTS, D.W.G. *Preservation and conservation of library documents: a UNESCO/IFLA/ICA enquiry into the current state of the world's patrimony*. Paris: UNESCO, 1987. 32 p. (PGI-87/WS/15)

DANIELS, Maygene. The Genesis and structure of the International Council on Archives: an American view. *The American Archivist*. Summer 1987: 50(3), 414-419.

ELWOOD, Marie. The discovery and repatriation of the Lord Dalhousie Papers. *Archivaria*. Summer 1987: (24), 108-116.

EVANS, Frank B. Archives and research: a study in international cooperation between Unesco and ICA. *Archives et bibliothèques de Belgique*. 1986: 57(1/2), 127-158.

EVANS, Frank B. Promoting archives and research: a study in international cooperation. *The American Archivist*. Winter 1987: 50(1), 48-65.

FRANZ, Eckhart G. 23 Internationale Konferenz der "Table Ronde des Archives" in Austin (Texas). [23rd International Conference of the "Table Ronde des Archives" in Austin (Texas)]. *Archivar*. May 1986: 39(2), 195-198.

Intergovernmental Council for the General Information Programme. Final report of a session (6th, Paris, France, November 17-21, 1986). Paris: United Nations Educational, Scientific and Cultural Organization, 1987. 38 p.

JAITNER, K.J. The European Community Historical Archives in Florence. *Journal of the Society of Archivists*. October 1988: 9(4), 176-180.

KOJEVNIKOV, E.M. Les archives du Canada. *Sovietskje Arkhivy*. 1988: (4), 90-96.

LAROSE, Michèle. Colloque international sur la conservation. *L'Archiviste*. Novembre/décembre 1987: 14(6), 18.

LAROSE, Michèle. International Conservation Symposium in 1988. *The Archivist*. November/December 1987: 14(6), 18.

MORDDEL, Anne. Whatever happened to RAMP? *Records Management Quarterly*. January 1988: 22(1), 123, 147.

NDIAYE, Ahmeth. La coopération archivistique en Afrique noire. Le point sur la situation. *Archives (Revue de l'Association des archivistes du Québec)*. Automne 1988: 20(2), 45-51.

PIEYNS, Jean. Le Comité de l'informatique du Conseil international des archives. *Information Development*. January 1987: 3(1), 20-22.

RENÉ-BAZIN, Paule and Marie-Françoise TAMMARO. Le stage technique international d'archives: an historical overview and future prospects. *The American Archivist*. Summer 1988: 51(3), 356-362.

RHOADS, James B. North American contributions to international archival endeavors. *Archives et bibliothèques de Belgique*. 1986: 57(1/2), 309-322.

RINALDI MARIANI, Maria-Pia. *La coopération internationale dans le domaine technique*. Congrès international des archives (11ᵉ: 1988: Paris). Paris, 1988. 6 p.

ROBERTS, Kenneth S. Unesco's General Information Programme, 1977-1987: its characteristics, activities and accomplishments. *Information Development*. October 1988: 4(4), 208-238.

RUSSELL, Bill. D'hier à demain: le bureau de Londres. *L'Archiviste*. Novembre/décembre 1987: 14(6), 16-18.

RUSSELL, Bill. From the London Office. *The Archivist*. November/December 1987: 14(6), 16-18.

UDINA, Federico. Espana y el consejo internacional de archivos (1950-1984). *Archives et bibliothèques de Belgique*. 1986: 57(1/2), 371-379.

WALLOT, Jean-Pierre. A fascinating visit to the archives of the USSR. *The Archivist*. January/February 1987: 14(1), 14-15.

WALLOT, Jean-Pierre. Une visite fascinante des archives en URSS. *L'Archiviste*. Janvier/février 1987: 14(1), 14-15.

WEILL, Georges. La micrographie et l'archivistique dans la doctrine internationale (1950-1987). *Archives et bibliothèques de Belgique*. 1987: 58(1/2), 331-355.

2. Records management / Gestion des documents

ACTON, Patricia. Indexing is not classifying – and vice versa. *Records Management Quarterly*. July 1986: 20(3), 10-15.

ALEGBELEYE, G.B.O. Archives administration and records management in Nigeria: up the decades from amalgamation. *Records Management Quarterly*. July 1988: 22(3), 26-30.

ALLEN, Percy and Russell L. MOBLEY. A bank in search of good records management. *The Office*. October 1987: 106(4), 15, 18.

Archival management: the 1980's and beyond. *Records and Retrieval Report*. October 1986: 2(8), 9-14.

ARMA INTERNATIONAL CONFERENCE (32ND: 1987: ANAHEIM, CA.). *Proceedings of the ARMA International 32nd Annual Conference*. Prairie Village, KS.: Association of Records Managers and Administrators, 1987. 482 p.

ARONSSON, Patricia and Thomas Elton BROWN. Information automation changes role of archivist. *Government Computer News*. 9 October 1987: 6(20), 40-43.

Automation: the latest good idea at the U.S. Patent Office. *IMC Journal*. 1987: 23(5), 37-40.

BALON, Brett J. and H. Wayne GARDNER. Disaster contingency planning: the basic elements. *Records Management Quarterly*. January 1987: 21(1), 14-16.

BALON, Brett J. and H. Wayne GARDNER. Disaster planning for electronic records. *Records Management Quarterly*. July 1988: 22(3), 20-25, 30.

BALON, Brett J. and H. Wayne GARDNER. "It'll never happen here": disaster contingency planning in Canadian urban municipalities. *Records Management Quarterly*. July 1986: 20(3), 26-28.

BALON, Brett J. Microfilm systems: silver recovery is money recovery. *Records Management Quarterly*. April 1987: 21(2), 31-32.

BARR, Jean. Choosing a microfilm based technology. *Records Management Quarterly*. January 1987: 21(1), 32-37.

BAUTSCH, Gail. What you don't know can hurt you. *Records Management Quarterly*. October 1986: 20(4), 20-24.

BENDER, Avi. Full text search and image retrieval. *IMC Journal*. 1987: 23(4), 28-30.

BOZEVICH, Ken. Document management: business insurance that pays for itself. *IMC Journal*. January/February 1988: 24(1), 22-23.

BRAUNSTEIN, Yale M. The economics of information. *Records Management Quarterly*. January 1986: 20(1), 18-21.

BRIDGES, Edwin C. Can state archives meet the challenges of the eighties? *Records Management Quarterly*. April 1986: 20(2), 15-21, 52.

BROWN, Thomas Elton and William A. READER. Archival management of machine-readable records from database management systems: a technical leaflet. *Archival Informatics Newsletter.* Spring 1987: 1(1), 9-12.

BROWN, Thomas Elton. The evolution of an appraisal theory for automated records. *Archival Informatics Newsletter.* Fall 1987: 1(3), 49-51.

BULGAWICZ, Susan and Charles E. NOLAN. Disaster planning and recovery: a regional approach. *Records Management Quarterly.* January 1987: 21(1), 14-16.

BURWASSER, Suzanne M. *Files management handbook for managers and librarians.* Studio City, Calif.: Pacific Information, 1986. 165 p.

CALMES, Alan. *Preservation of permanently valuable information on paper, film, tape and disk.* Washington, D.C.: National Archives and Records Administration, 1987. 8 p.

CANADA. CONSUMER AND CORPORATE AFFAIRS CANADA. *FAAD internal review of records management.* [Hull]: Consumer and Corporate Affairs Canada, 1985. 1 v. (various pagings)

CANNING, Bonnie. Backup and redundancy for automated records systems. *Administrative Management.* September 1987: 48(9), 41.

CANNING, Bonnie. Les disques optiques au bureau. *IMC Journal.* 1987: 23(5), 11-12.

CANNING, Bonnie. Optical disk systems: pros and cons. *Administrative Management.* March 1987: 48(3), 51.

CANNING, Bonnie. Optical disks in the office. *IMC Journal.* 1987: 23(5), 9-10.

CANNING, Bonnie. Records automation: careers in records automation. *Administrative Management.* November 1987: 48(11), 39.

CANNING, Bonnie. Records automation: regulatory requirements for records. *Administrative Management.* February 1988: 49(1), 10.

CANNING, Bonnie. Technology marches on. *Administrative Management.* January 1987: 48(1), 55.

Careers in records management. *Records and Retrieval Report.* December 1986: 2(10), 1-10.

CARLISLE, Diane. Gaining credibility. *Records Management Quarterly.* January 1987: 21(1), 29-31.

CARLISLE, Van G. Avoiding electronic media disasters. *Records Management Quarterly.* January 1986: 20(1), 42-43.

CARLSON, Carol. How a young city solved its problems with filing. *The Office.* October 1987: 106(4), 106-107.

CARPENTIER, Louise. Quebec government publications in microform. *Microform Review.* December 1988: 17(5), 260-261.

CARSON, Eugene. Distributed access to administrative systems. *Cause/Effect.* September 1987: 10(5), 6-12.

CASURELLA, Joseph. Document management software. *AIIM Conference Daily.* April 28, 1987: 5, 20.

CHARMAN, Derek. *Recensement des archives courantes et tableaux de tri: une étude RAMP, accompagnée de principes directeurs.* Paris: UNESCO, 1986. 71 p. (PGI-84/WS/26)

CHIPPIE, Wendy L. A procedure for procedures. *Records Management Quarterly.* January 1986: 20(1), 36-40.

CITARELLA, Judith and Lynne LEAHY. Integrated CAR takes charge at Barclay's Bank. *INFORM: the Magazine of Information and Image Management.* July 1987: 1(7), 26-28.

CLITES, Lorraine and William TUTTLE. Industrial document management: an optical system. *INFORM: the Magazine of Information and Image Management.* August 1987: 1(8), 30-33.

Computer-assisted retrieval (CAR) systems. *Records and Retrieval Report.* December 1986: 1(10), 149-158.

Computer software for records management. *Records and Retrieval Report.* January 1986: 2(1), 1-14.

Computer software for records management — part II. *Records and Retrieval Report.* February 1986: 2(2), 1-6.

Computerized records management software. *Records and Retrieval Report.* May 1987: 3(6), 5-8.

Consulting in records management. *Records and Retrieval Report.* June 1986: 2(6), 1-6.

Converting to an automated system. *Records and Retrieval Report.* May 1987: 3(6), 5-8.

CORTISSOZ, Anne. Telco transition. *INFORM: the Magazine of Information and Image Management.* March 1987: 1(3), 14-18.

The Costs of creating and filing a letter. *Records and Retrieval Report.* June 1987: 3(6), 1-11.

CRAVEN, Paul Taylor. Optical records management: application development in action. *INFORM: the Magazine of Information and Image Management.* February 1987: 1(2), 35-39.

CREIGHTON, Ken. Using government records. *The Archivist.* July/August 1986: 13(4), 12-13.

CREIGHTON, Ken. Utilisation des documents du gouvernement. *L'Archiviste.* Juillet/août 1986: 13(4), 12-13.

CUNNINGHAM, Roger B. Microcomputer-based CAR system increases electronic filing flexibility. *Micro-notes.* Winter 1986: 15(1), 12, 22.

DAHL, Edward H. "The Veriest Rubbish": an example of cartographic records management at the Royal Engineers Office, Kingston, 1862. *Association of Canadian Map Libraries and Archives. Bulletin.* March 1988: 66, 9-10.

DAUM, Patricia B. Coordinating records management and the special library for effectiveness. *Records Management Quarterly.* April 1986: 20(2), 36-38.

DAVIS, Douglas L. Optical archiving: where are we now and where do we go from here? *Optical Information Systems.* January/February 1987: 7(1), 66-71.

DESMARAIS, Norman. CD/Private+: easy access to private company information. *Optical Information Systems.* September/October 1988: 8(5), 248-259.

DESMARAIS, Norman. Information management on a compact silver disc. *Optical Information Systems.* May/June 1987: 7(3), 193-204.

DIBBLE, Thomas G. *A guide to court records management.* Williamsburg, Va.: National Center for State Courts, 1986. xi, 94 p. (NCSC R-101)

DUKE, David. Electronic records: access documents instantly. *Administrative Management.* October 1987: 48(10), 28-32.

Electronic records policy: a bibliography. *Archival Informatics Newsletter.* Winter 1988/1989: 2(4), 76-79.

Financial markets: Filenet automates the flow. *INFORM: the Magazine of Information and Image Management.* July 1987: 1(7), 22-25.

FLEIG, Clare. "Managing records" has new meaning. *Government Computer News.* 9 October 1987: 6(20), 38.

FLUBACHER, F. Shirley. Old-line bank's approach to new records management. *The Office.* December 1987: 106(6), 15-19.

FLUTY, Steve. Growth management: American Express goes the distance. *INFORM: the Magazine of Information and Image Management.* January 1987: 1(1), 34-36.

FLUTY, Steve. Online reduction innovation at Chemical Bank. *INFORM: the Magazine of Information and Image Management.* July 1987: 1(7), 6-7.

FLUTY, Steve. Streamlining the flow: information management at CBS. *INFORM: the Magazine of Information and Image Management*. January 1987: 1(1), 32-33, 45-46.

FRANCIS, James, Cynthia L. SUTTON and Bill COX. New tools for the information manager. *Records Management Quarterly*. April 1987: 21(2), 3-8.

FRASE, H. Michael. Videomicrographics: multi-media image management. *INFORM: the Magazine of Information and Image Management*. April 1987: 1(4), 26-29.

FRUSCIONE, James J. A managerial framework for machine-readable data management. *Records Management Quarterly*. July 1986: 20(3), 3-9.

The Future is in automation. *Records and Retrieval Report*. May 1987: 3(6), 1-4.

La gestion des documents: trouver un chèque parmi tant d'autres [Recordak Reliant 550]. *Le Bureau*. Juillet/août 1986: 10-11.

GOMES, Winston A. À votre service: la Direction des documents gouvernementaux. *L'Archiviste*. Janvier/février 1988: 15(1), 15, 18.

GOMES, Winston A. The Government Records Branch at your service. *The Archivist*. January/February 1988: 15(1), 15, 18.

Grain inspection service simplifies records with fiche. *Government Computer News*. 9 October 1987: 6(20), 50.

GRAY, V. Information as a social need. The archivist's view. IN Information '85. Knowledge to Shape the Future. London: Aslib, 1986: 57-60.

GRIGSBY, Mason. Special report: the optical digital age. *INFORM: the Magazine of Information and Image Management*. September 1988: 2(8), 28-29.

GRIGSBY, Mason. Write-one optical disk systems in the automated office. *Records Management Quarterly*. July 1986: 20(3), 30-34.

GROUPE-CONSEIL LLP INC. ET IST-INFORMATHÈQUE. *La gestion de documents au Québec, 1987*. [Montréal]: ARMA-Montréal, 1987. 39, 379 p.

HAMILTON, Angela. Solving a diskette dilemna. *Records Management Quarterly*. April 1986: 20(2), 28-29, 52.

HAYES, Kenneth V. Are you too small for records management? *Records Management Quarterly*. January 1987: 21(1), 22-28, 44.

HAYWARD, Robert J. Working in thin air: of archives and the Deschênes Commission. *Archivaria*. Summer 1988: (26), 122-136.

HELGERSON, Linda W. *Introduction to scanning technology*. Silver Spring, M.D.: Association for Information and Image Management, 1987. 36 p.

HELGERSON, Linda W. Optical storage peripherals: the right format. *INFORM: the Magazine of Information and Image Management*. February 1987: 1(2), 14-16, 18-19.

HIGGINS, Kevin B. Optical disk and micrographic document management system. *Micro-notes*. September 1986: 14(3), 5-6.

HIVES, Christopher L. Records, information and archives management in business. *Records Management Quarterly*. January 1986: 20(1), 3-8, 17.

HOFFMAN, Annie and Bryan BAUMANN. Disaster recovery: a prevention plan for NWNL. *Records Management Quarterly*. April 1986: 20(2), 40-44.

HOLDER, Carol. Protecting your image: microform storage and security. *INFORM: the Magazine of Information and Image Management*. October 1987: 1(9), 18-21.

HOOTEN, Bill. Archiving the archives. *Computerworld*. 24 August 1987: 21(34), 63.

HUNTER, Gregory S. Microcomputing and micrographic control. *INFORM: the*

Magazine of Information and Image Management. October 1987: 1(10), 22-23.

Image computer enhances records management. *Modern Office Technology.* August 1987: 32(8), 28.

Information and image management industry: job descriptions. Silver Spring, M.D.: Association for Information and Image Management, 1987. 30 p.

Information management sourcebook. Silver Spring, M.D.: Association for Information and Image Management, 1987. 430 p.

INSTITUTE OF CERTIFIED RECORDS MANAGERS. Outline for Certified Records Manager Examination. *Records Management Quarterly.* January 1988: 22(1), 136-144.

JANELLI, Harvey. Evolving information management. *INFORM: the Magazine of Information and Image Management.* May 1987: 1(5), 28-31, 33.

JOHNSON, Don S. Creeping towards the paperless office. *Administrative Management.* October 1987: 48(10), 5.

JOHNSTON, R.E. (Bob). Standard threats. *Infosystems.* July 1987: 34(7), 35.

JONES, Virginia A. Retention schedules: at peace or in panic? *The Office.* October 1987: 106(4), 103-104.

KAEBNICK, Gregory. Engineering takes cautions steps to optical. *INFORM: the Magazine of Information and Image Management.* October 1988: 2(9), 15-17.

KALTHOFF, Robert J. 1987: industry leaders on the outlook for digital document automation (DDA) right decision. *IMC Journal.* 1987: 23(4), 15-19.

KATZ, Richard N. and Victoria A. DAVIS. The impact of automation on our corporate memory. *Records Management Quarterly.* January 1986: 20(1), 10-14.

KEANE, Edward T. The archiving microform. *Micro-notes.* Spring 1987: 15(2), 15.

LACY, John A. The future of document management: the "fourth stage" and beyond. *AIIM Conference Daily.* April 30, 1987: 5, 14, 16.

LANGEMO, Mark. Major trends in the managing of records. *Office.* January 1987: 105(1), 65.

Laser scanner inspection system. *Optical Information Systems.* September/October 1988: 8(5), 226-229.

LEA, Mary Ann. The records round up. *Management World.* September/October 1987: 16(5), 34-35.

The Leading edge of CALS. *INFORM: the Magazine of Information and Image Management.* September 1987: 1(9), 30.

LINDER, C.E. (Ted). COM services offer records-keeping alternative. *Micro-notes.* Spring 1987: 15(2), 13.

Listing of commercial off-site records centers. *Records and Retrieval Report.* September 1986: 2(7), 6-22.

LOWELL, Howard P. Elements of a state archives and records management program. *Records Management Quarterly.* October 1987: 21(4), 3-14, 23.

LUDWIG, Harry L. A corporate asset: records management. *Office.* January 1987: 105(1), 79-80.

LUEBBE, Mary. Update on Canadian government documents in microform. *Microform Review.* December 1988: 17(5), 254-259.

LUNDGREN, Terry D. and Carol A. LUNDGREN. Introduction to computer-based records management systems. *Records Management Quarterly.* July 1987: 21(3), 31-34.

LYNCH, Clifford A. Optical storage media, standards and technology life-cycle management. *Records Management Quarterly.* January 1986: 20(1), 44-54.

MACDONALD, R. Malcolm. Cooperation in local government: the Rome/Floyd Records Program. *Records Management Quarterly.* October 1986: 20(4), 12-14.

A Major utility builds automated records center. *Office*. March 1987: 105(3), 88-94.

Managing engineering drawings in the Department of National Defence. *Micronotes*. Winter 1986: 15(1), 10.

MARQUARDT, Leigh R. Priorities in bank document management. *INFORM: the Magazine of Information and Image Management*. July 1987: 1(7), 34-35.

MATTHEWS, Fred W. Sorting a mountain of books. *Library Resources and Technical Services*. January/March 1987: 31(1), 88, 94.

Media storage. *Information Center*. April 1987: 3(4), 7.

MENKUS, Belden. Records managers fail to meet MIS challenge. *Journal of Systems Management*. August 1987: 38(8), 36-37.

Microfilm or optical disc: choose the system. *The Office*. October 1987: 106(4), 130.

Micrographics at the Royal Bank. *Micronotes*. September 1986: 14(3), 10-11.

MIMS, Julian L. The politics of records management: your professional candidacy and steps toward personal success. *Records Management Quarterly*. October 1986: 20(4), 30-31, 38.

MOORE, Frank. Records management at IRS: the ultimate paper challenge. *INFORM: the Magazine of Information and Image Management*. November 1987: 1(11), 12-16.

MORDDEL, Anne. Data protection in the United Kingdom. *Records Management Quarterly*. October 1986: 20(4), 58-62.

MORDDEL, Anne, [et al.]. *Records management handbook*. Aldershot: Gower, 1988. 200 p.

MORDDEL, Anne. Records management in Switzerland. *Records Management Quarterly*. July 1988: 22(3), 36, 47.

MORGAN, Dennis F. Personnel selection and interviewing: professional and personnal perspectives. *Records Management Quarterly*. July 1986: 20(3), 20-24.

MOTZ, Arlene. Applying records management principles to magnetic media. *Records Management Quarterly*. April 1986: 20(2), 22-26.

MURRAY, Toby. Disaster planning and recovery: don't get caught with your plans down. *Records Management Quarterly*. April 1987: 21(2), 12-30, 41.

New document processing system boosting productivity at NEC American, Inc. *IMC Journal*. 1987: 23(3), 49-50.

NEWTON, Carl. Information or malformation. Records management in information systems. IN Information '85. Knowledge to Shape the Future. London: Aslib, 1986: 75-86.

NOVINGER, Walter B. Optical storage: a conversion perspective. *INFORM: the Magazine of Information and Image Management*. September 1987: 1(9), 22-23.

Off-site storage of records. *Records and Retrieval Report*. September 1986: 2(7), 1-5.

Optical character recognition. *Records and Retrieval Report*. February 1987: 3(2), 1-11.

An Optical disk primer. *Records and Retrieval Report*. October 1987: 3(8), 1-16.

OTTEN, Klaus. *Integrated document and image management*. Silver Spring, Md.: Association for Information and Image Management, 1987. 66 p.

PAUL, Karen Dawley. *Records management handbook for United States Senate Committees*. Prepared under the direction of Walter J. Stewart. Washington, D.C.: U.S. Senate, 1988. 170 p.

PENDERGRAFT, Lee. "I want to start a microfilm program". *Microfilm Services & Systems*. April/June 1987: 10-11.

PENNINGTON, Mike. Microfiche streams files at USDA. *INFORM: the Magazine of Information and Image Management*. November 1987: 1(11), 37-39.

PENNIX, Gail B. and Marti FISCHER. Cumulative index to the Records Management Quarterly 1967-1987. *Records Management Quarterly*. January 1988: 22(1), 27-122.

PENNIX, Gail B. Try a little TQC [Total Quality Control]. *Records Management Quarterly*. October 1987: 21(4), 24-30.

PFEIFFER, Ken. The paper challenge and progressive records management. *INFORM: the Magazine of Information and Image Management*. April 1987: 1(4), 18-20, 24, 44.

POPIUL, Jacklyn. The modern manager and the people/productivity balance. *INFORM: the Magazine of Information and Image Management*. April 1987: 1(4), 30-33.

POWER, William. Caseload automation with micrographics. *INFORM: the Magazine of Information and Image Management*. March 1988: 2(3), 8-9.

The Real revolution in office automation. *Records and Retrieval Report*. April 1987: 3(4), 1-3.

A Records management audit. *Records and Retrieval Report*. May 1986: 2(5), 1-12.

Records management consultants. *Records and Retrieval Report*. June 1986: 2(6), 7-12.

Records management, cost effective efficiency is here. *Modern Office Technology*. January 1987: 31(1), 100-110, 112-114.

Redefining records management. *Records and Retrieval Report*. April 1986: 2(4), 1-13.

Resources for records managers. *Records and Retrieval Report*. November 1986: 2(9), 10-17.

ROBERGE, Michel. Formation et perfectionnement des ressources humaines en gestion des documents. *Le Bureau*. Mars/avril 1988: 24(2), 32-33.

ROBERGE, Michel. Manifeste pour une véritable approche globale, systématique et systémique de la gestion des documents administratifs et des archives. IN L'exper-

tise québécoise en gestion des documents administratifs: bibliographie thématique et chronologique 1962-1987. Saint-Augustin, Qué.: GESTAR, 1987: 2-6.

ROBERGE, Michel. Plan directeur de conception et mise en œuvre d'un système de gestion des documents administratifs. *Le Bureau*. Mai/juin 1988: 24(3), 25, 34.

ROHM, Wendy Goldman. "That's all that's left!" *Infosystems*. February 1987: 34(2), 42, 45, 46, 48.

ROSENBERG, Norma V. Getting good mileage out of records management consultants. *Records Management Quarterly*. October 1986: 20(4), 16-18.

ROUSSEAU, Jean-Yves. La protection des archives essentielles. (Comment assurer la survie d'une organisation). *Archives (Revue de l'Association des archivistes du Québec)*. Été 1988: 20(1), 43-61.

ROWH, Mark C. Records management systems are better than ever before. *The Office*. October 1987: 106(4), 92-93.

SAFFADY, William. *Optical disks for data and document storage*. Westport, Ct.: Meckler, 1986. 94 p.

SAFFADY, William. Optical storage products at the 1988 AIIM Conference. *Optical Information Systems*. September/October 1988: 8(5), 233-241.

SANDERS, Robert L. The company index: information retrieval thesaurus for organizations and institutions. *Records Management Quarterly*. April 1986: 20(2), 3-14.

SANDERS, Robert L. The (ferocious) domestic paperwork kitten. *Records Management Quarterly*. January 1986: 20(1), 22-24, 40, 66.

SANDERS, Robert L. Records inventories and scheduling for small organizations: a case study. *Records Management Quarterly*. July 1987: 21(3), 24-30, 51-52, 58.

SANDERS, Robert L. Two suggestions for coping with the paperwork explosion. *Records Management Quarterly*. January 1987: 21(1), 3-9.

SCALA, Bea. Telco conversion: from paper records to online information system. *INFORM: the Magazine of Information and Image Management*. March 1987: 1(3), 20-23.

SCELI, W. Clair. Document management systems today and tomorrow. *AIIM Conference Daily*. April 28, 1987: 5, 20.

SCELI, W. Clair. Productivity: the promise of document management. *INFORM: the Magazine of Information and Image Management*. March 1987: 1(3), 6-7.

SCHOWEN, Jeffrey C. Information management: a matter of fact. *INFORM: the Magazine of Information and Image Management*. August 1987: 1(8), 18, 46.

SEIBEL, C. Sheldon. Records management in its intellectual context: experience at the University of Texas at Austin. *Records Management Quarterly*. July 1987: 21(3), 3-14, 42, 59.

SEIBEL, C. Sheldon. A superfund assessment from the records perspective. *Records Management Quarterly*. January 1986: 20(1), 28-34.

SEIGLE, David C. Document image processing: breaking the productivity barrier in today's office microfilm images of engineering drawings. *IMC Journal*. 1987: 23(4), 55-57.

SERGEEV, You V. et N. You GOUREEVA. La production automatisée des documents dans l'institution administrative. *Sovietskje Arkhivy*. 1988: (4), 85-86.

SETTANNI, Joseph Andrew. Information value: managing records as a viable resource. *JIIM: the Journal of Information and Image Management*. December 1986: 19(12), 10-13.

SHAW, Abigail. Integrating document storage: an end user's view. *INFORM: the Magazine of Information and Image Management*. May 1987: 1(5), 34-37.

SILBER, Sigmund. A case for electronic document interchange. *Infosystems*. January 1987: 34(1), 58.

SKUPSKY, Donald S. Admissibility of original records in evidence. *Records Management Quarterly*. April 1986: 20(2), 46-52.

SKUPSKY, Donald S. Determining litigation and statutes of limitation requirements for records retention requirements. *Records Management Quarterly*. July 1986: 20(3), 40-46.

SKUPSKY, Donald S. Legal liability of the records and information management professional. *Records Management Quarterly*. April 1987: 21(2), 36-39.

SKUPSKY, Donald S. The legal status of selected records. *Records Management Quarterly*. October 1986: 20(4), 32-35.

SKUPSKY, Donald S. *Recordkeeping requirements: the first practical guide to help you control your records... what you need to keep and what you can safely destroy*. Denver, Colo.: Information Requirements Clearinghouse, 1988. xviii, 323 p.

Solving the paper problem: an introduction to document processing. Sunnyvale, Calif.: Interfile, [1987?]. 8 p.

SPAULDING, George. An HMO chooses CAR. *IMC Journal*. 1987: 23(1), 31-33.

SPILKER, Chris. Medical imaging: merging picture archives and communications. *INFORM: the Magazine of Information and Image Management*. February 1987: 1(2), 24-27.

SPORCK, John H. Without a records recovery plan, start from square one. *Office*. June 1987: 105(6), 57-58.

Standards in records management. *Records and Retrieval Report*. October 1986: 2(8), 1-8.

Standards in records management — part II. *Records and Retrieval Report*. November 1986: 2(9), 1-9.

STANGE, Eric. Millions of books are turning to dust: can they be saved? *New York Times*. March 29, 1987: 3, 38.

STOCKSLAGER, Todd. Office automation: cost justification or management?

Records Management Quarterly. October 1987: 21(4), 15-19.

Storing paper. *Records and Retrieval Report*. September 1987: 3(7), 1-12.

STRATFORD, Juri. Public access to government document microforms. *Microform Review*. December 1988: 17(5), 292-294.

Third Expert Consultation on RAMP (RAMP III), Helsinki (Finland), 13, 15 and 20 September 1986: final report. Paris: UNESCO, 1987. 40 p. (PGI-87/WS/13)

THOMPSON, Robert J. Disaster recovery is silly! *Data Management*. February 1987: 46.

TIMBERS, Michael J. Microfilm: information management mainstay at IHS. *INFORM: the Magazine of Information and Image Management*. June 1987: 1(6), 30-31.

TIMBERS, Michael J. We are working to solve the problems of paper. *Office*. January 1987: 105(1), 122.

Vendors of CAR systems. *Records and Retrieval Report*. December 1986: 1(10), 159-165.

Vendors of computer software for records management. *Records and Retrieval Report*. February 1986: 2(2), 7-15.

VOSSLER, Janet L. The human element of disaster recovery. *Records Management Quarterly*. January 1987: 21(1), 10-12.

WEISE, Carl E. Records management: the management science too long ignored. *Records Management Quarterly*. April 1986: 20(2), 30-35.

WEISE, Carl E. Selling records management — do you know your product. *Records Management Quarterly*. July 1987: 21(3), 18-23, 58.

WHEALAN, Ronald E. Microfilmed records in the John Fitzgerald Kennedy Library. *Microform Review*. October 1988: 17(4), 197-201.

WILKINSON, David G. Where is hardware taking information management? *IMC Journal*. 1987: 23(4), 35-38.

WILLIAMS, Bernard. Optical disks at the Public Records Office. *Information Media & Technology*. September 1987: 20(5), 204-205.

WILLIAMS, Robert V. Records management education: an IRM perspective. *Records Management Quarterly*. October 1987: 21(4), 36-40.

WOLCHAK, William H. Conducting a systems analysis. *Records Management Quarterly*. July 1986: 20(3), 16-19.

ZAGAMI, Robert W. Record conversion to microfilm safe, stabilized procedure. *Administrative Management*. July 1987: 48(7), 48.

2.1 Organization and methods / Organisation et opérations

ACTON, Patricia. Indexing is not classifying — and vice versa. *Records Management Quarterly*. July 1986: 20(3), 10-15.

Approaches to problems in records management. Edited by Yvonne Buckland. London: Society of Archivist, Records Management Group, 1985. 57 p.

ARMSTRONG, John and Stephanie JONES. *Business documents: their origins, sources and uses in historical research*. London: Mansell, 1987. xvi, 251 p.

ASCHNER, Katherine. Computer strategies for records managers; cost effective solutions for computerized records management. *Office Systems Management*. Spring 1986: 5(2), 8-10.

ATHERTON, Jay. "Recent trends in the management of records". Proceedings: Conference of the Association of Canadian Archivists (1987: McMaster University). Hamilton, Ont., 1987. 8 p.

BARR, Robert D. Microfilm or optical disk: the choice is between systems, not media. *IMC Journal*. March/April 1988: 24(2), 7-8.

BELL, Steven J. Corporate change: impact on the corporate documents collection. *Special Libraries*. Fall 1988: 79(4), 265-270.

BENDER, Avi. Optical disc technology for records management: a user perspective. *The Electronic Library*. October 1987: 5, 276-281.

BENNICK, Ann. *Filing and records management fundamentals for the small business*. Prairie Village, Ks.: ARMA International, 1987. iv, 50 p.

BORDAS, Richard. The CAD-microfilm connection: linking for productivity. *INFORM: the Magazine of Information and Image Management*. January 1988: 2(1), 28-29.

BORDAS, Richard. Engineering document management systems: today's reality is becoming tomorrow's foundation. *IMC Journal*. March/April 1988: 24(2), 43-45.

BOZEVICH, Ken. Bar code technology: a basic glossary of terms. *IMC Journal*. November/December 1988: 24(6), 16-17.

BROWN, J.H.U., Carlos VALLBONA and H. KITASANONO. A new patient record system using the lasercard. *Optical Information Systems*. July/August 1988: 8(4), 156-161.

CANNING, Bonnie. Records automation: micrographics addresses records automation challenge. *Administrative Management*. April 1988: 49(3), 38.

CAR systems in records management — 1988. *Records and Retrieval Report*. September 1988: 4(7), 1-11.

CASTLE, Robert L. Document-image processing bringing productivity to the office. *Micro-notes*. Summer 1987: 15(3), 12-13.

CASTONGUAY, Russell. Maintenance and management of local government documents collections: survey findings. *Government Information Quarterly*. 1987: 4(2), 167-188.

CASURELLA, Joseph E. CAR versus paper files: hard facts about software driven systems. *IMC Journal*. January/February 1988: 24(1), 14.

CASURELLA, Joseph E. Document management software: new twist to a proven concept results in increased productivity. *JIIM: the Journal of Information and Image Management*. June 1986: 19(6), 26-29.

CHAPDELAINE, Susan A. The paperless office: hope for the future or a grand illusion? *Provenance*. Fall 1988: 6(2), 35-42.

CLARK, Steve. *Guidelines on computer-assisted records management*. Ottawa: National Archives of Canada, 1988. vii, 53, 60, vii p. (Management of Government Records)

CLARK, Steve. *Lignes directrices sur la gestion automatisée des documents*. Ottawa: Archives nationales du Canada, 1988. vii, 53, 60, vii p. (Gestion des documents gouvernementaux)

COKER, Kathy Roe. Lessons learned and to be learned in inter-governmental appraisal. *Provenance*. Fall 1987: 5(2), 1-13.

COLLIER, Rosemary. Will action follow Acton? *Archifacts*. 1986: (4), 14-16.

Court holds that Privacy Act requires federal agencies to maintain accurate records. *Information Hotline*. May 1986: 18(5), 1, 13-14.

COUVELIS, Joyce. Optimizing records management at Foodmaker, Inc. *INFORM: the Magazine of Information and Image Management*. January 1988: 2(1), 18-21.

CURRIE, Jack. International Development Research Centre (IDRC) assists government of Trinidad and Tobago to improve land registration information system. *Micro-notes*. Summer 1987: 15(3), 16-17, 20.

DAVIS, James V. Choosing records management software. *Records Management Quarterly*. July 1988: 22(3), 3-11.

DE BRUYN, Katherine Aschner. Effective management of case files. *IMC Journal*. March/April 1988: 24(2), 29-31.

DESLONGCHAMPS, Denis. La gestion des documents: on évalue à 90 dollars le coût moyen de recouvrer un document mal classé. *Le Bureau*. Juillet/août 1986: 24-25.

DICKINSON, A. Litchard. What are active files? Where and how should they be stored. *Office Systems Management*. Spring 1986: 5(2), 4-7, 13.

DIXON, Debra. Information salvage: the tobacco connection. *Records Management Quarterly*. January 1988: 22(1), 15-17, 132.

ENSMAN, Richard G. Paper free, not paperless. *Modern Office Technology*. April 1987: 32(4), 56, 58, 60.

FORBES, Jamie. *Records management and the Trail City Archives*. [Vancouver]: Association of British Columbia Archivists, c1988. 6 p. (A.B.C.A. publications; no. 5)

FRANKEL, Barry. Hypertext: a software solution. *INFORM: the Magazine of Information and Image Management*. March 1988: 2(3), 14-18.

FRASER, Alison. Records officers and the Acton Report, or, What's in it for me? *Archifacts*. 1986: (4), 13-14.

Gestion électronique des fichiers: les options se multiplient. *Le Bureau*. Juillet/août 1986: 26-27.

GOMES, Winston A. À votre service: la Direction des documents gouvernementaux. *L'Archiviste*. Janvier/février 1988: 15(1), 15, 18.

GOMES, Winston A. The Government Records Branch at your service. *The Archivist*. January/February 1988: 15(1), 15, 18.

GORBACH, Peter. Using client data. Using client data for planning service development. *BURISA*. July 1986: (74), 9-10.

GRAY, David P. *Records management for parishes and schools*. Richardton, N.D.: Diocesen of Bismarck, 1985. 44 p.

GRAY, David P. *Records management for parishes and schools*. San Diego: Association of Catholic Diocesan Archivists, 1987.

HACKMAN, Larry J. Cuomo transfers record management to New York State Archives. *SAA Newsletter*. March 1987: 8.

HALLEEN, Gary. Document retrieval for people who don't care. *IMC Journal*. September/October 1988: 24(5), 9-12.

HENDLEY, Anthony M. The development of microfilm in engineering applications. *IMC Journal*. March/April 1988: 24(2), 18-20.

HUDSON, B.J. *Electronic records administration at the Savannah River Plant, Department of Energy Automated Office Support System Conference, Denver, CO, USA, 1987*. Aiken, S.C.: Du Pont de Nemours (E.I.) and Co., 1987. 14 p.

Information security: actions taken to improve Lockheed's special access document accountability. Washington, D.C.: General Accounting Office, National Security and International Affairs Div., 1987. 17 p.

JAMES, Linda. *Standing the test of time: quality assurance for state and local government records microfilming*. St. Paul: Minnesota Historical Society, 1986. 70 p.

JANSEN, Chris F.M. Gestion des documents et conservation des documents d'archives de sociétés. *Conseil international des archives. Comité des archives d'entreprises. Bulletin*. 1988: (11), 17-21.

JANSEN, Chris F.M. Records management and preservation of business records. *International Council on Archives. Committee on Business Archives. Bulletin*. 1988: (11), 9-16.

JOHNSON, Mina M. and Norman F. KALLUS. *Records management*. 4th ed. Cincinnati, Ohio: South-Western Publishing Co., 1987. 405 p.

K Mart applies automation to information and product distribution. *IMC Journal*. January/February 1988: 24(1), 43-44.

KAMBA, Angeline S. The impact of the National Archives of Zimbabwe Act 1986 on records management in Zimbabwe. *Commonwealth Archivists Association Newsletter.* November 1987: (5), 10-13.

LARNED, Berle E. Putting a scanned document database to work. *INFORM: the Magazine of Information and Image Management.* May 1988: 2(5), 24-29.

Latest technology and beyond — sought as Caja Galicia improves information access. *IMC Journal.* March/April 1988: 24(2), 9-11.

LEE, F. Expanding your base: the law librarian as records manager. *The Law Library Journal.* Winter 1988: (80), 123-129.

MAKI, John. Automating image management: the software factor. *INFORM: the Magazine of Information and Image Management.* May 1988: 2(5), 33-34.

Manual de levantamento da produçao documental. Rio de Janeiro: Arquivo Nacional, 1986. 34 p. (Publicaçoes técnicas; 44)

MARR, Cathy. New Zealand government records management review: information can be managed, the Acton Report. *Archifacts.* 1986: (4), 11-12.

MENKUS, Belden. Electronic forms: document as image. *INFORM: the Magazine of Information and Image Management.* March 1988: 2(3), 11-12.

MENKUS, Belden. Image communications in electronic forms. *INFORM: the Magazine of Information and Image Management.* May 1988: 2(5), 31-32.

MIMS, Julian L. An outline for files control. *Records Management Quarterly.* January 1988: 22(1), 18-24.

MORLEY, Jeanine. Mobile storage systems glide toward greater efficiency. *Today's Office.* November 1988: 23(6), 16-23.

MUKHOPADHYAY, Uttam, [et al.]. An intelligent system for document retrieval in distributed office environment. *Journal of the American Society for Information Science.* May 1986: 37(3), 123-135.

NEWTON, Carl. Records management and business information systems. *Business Archives.* May 1988: (55), 1-15.

NIKOLAISON, Jeanne. Passport Services automates records process to provide rapid service to customers. *IMC Journal.* May/June 1988: 24(3), 33-36.

Oakville Fire Department computerizes microfiche. *Micro-notes.* Spring 1987: 15(2), 10, 23.

ORBELL, John. The introduction of a computer modern records control system at Barings Merchant Bank. *Business Archives.* May 1988: (55), 29-37.

PASS, Herman W. and Wayne W. WARTIAN. Automated document flow at McDonnell Douglas. *INFORM: the Magazine of Information and Image Management.* January 1988: 2(1), 23-27.

PAZNIK, Megan Jill. Optical disks vs. micrographics. *Administrative Management.* April 1988: 49(3), 18-23.

PEMBERTON, J. Michael. A video manual for disaster recovery and taking "AIIM" at a useful idea. *Records Management Quarterly.* January 1988: 22(1), 126-129.

PETILLAT, Christine et Anne-Claude LAMUR-DAUDREU. Le traitement des archives contemporaines dans les administrations centrales. *La Gazette des archives.* 1988: (141), 35-56.

PLUME, Terry. Optical disk systems-technology. *IMC Journal.* January/February 1988: 24(1), 29-32.

PTACEK, William P. Microfilm, microfilmers and the future. *INFORM: the Magazine of Information and Image Management.* July/August 1988: 2(7), 8-11.

The Quiet Revolution: managing New York's local government records in the information age. Albany: N.Y. State Archives and Records Administration, 1988.

RADICE, Michael D. Putting paper in its place. *INFORM: the Magazine of Information and Image Management*. January 1988: 2(1), 14-16.

RAIKHZAOUM, A.L. Les moyens contemporains de la technique pour la gestion des documents. *Sovietskje Arkhivy*. 1987: (5), 80-83.

RAMSAY, Nancy C. Using optical disk in non-image applications. *Optical Information Systems*. July/August 1988: 8(4), 164-168.

A Records management audit. *Records and Retrieval Report*. May 1986: 2(5), 1-12.

Records management for the 1990s. *Records and Retrieval Report*. October 1988: 4(8), 1-14.

RICHARDS, Carole. Color-coded filing in an innovative records center. *Office*. June 1987: 105(6), 84, 86.

RICKS, Betty R. and Kay F. GOW. *Information resource management: a records systems approach*. 2nd ed. Cincinnati: South-Western Pub. Co., 1988. xiii, 654 p.

ROBEK, Mary F., Gerald F. BROWN and Wilmer O. MAEDKE. *Information and records management*. 3rd ed. Encino, Calif.: Glencoe Publishing, 1987. vi, 580 p.

ROBERGE, Michel. La gestion des documents administratifs et archives. *Le Bureau*. Novembre/décembre 1987: 23(6), 22-23.

ROBERGE, Michel. Manifeste pour une véritable approche globale, systématique et systémique de la gestion des documents administratifs et des archives. IN L'expertise québécoise en gestion des documents administratifs: bibliographie thématique et chronologique 1962-1987. Saint-Augustin, Qué.: GESTAR, 1987: 2-6.

SAINT-PIERRE, Paul. La gestion des documents est souvent mal maîtrisée. *Le Bureau*. Juillet/août 1986: 20-22.

SAMUEL, Jean. The design of deposit documentation in a records centre. *Business Archives*. May 1988: (55), 17-28.

SANDERS, Robert L. The company index: information retrieval thesaurus for organizations and institutions. *Records Management Quarterly*. April 1986: 20(2), 3-14.

SANDERS, Robert L. Escape from the 4-D Monster (Dirty, disgusting document disposition). *Records Management Quarterly*. July 1988: 22(3), 12-16.

SCHOWEN, Jeffrey C. The information generalist: managing technology resources. *INFORM: the Magazine of Information and Image Management*. January 1988: 2(1), 13-14.

SEC and GAO at odds on a "paperless" system. *Office*. January 1987: 105(1), 50.

SEIGLE, David C. Office economics and document image processing. *INFORM: the Magazine of Information and Image Management*. January 1988: 2(1), 35-36.

SETTANNI, Joseph Andrew. Information management is a matter of records. *Office Systems*. January 1987: 4(1), 50, 52, 54, 57.

TEDDE, Pedro. La collecte des archives en regard des besoins des historiens d'entreprises. *Conseil international des archives. Comité des archives d'entreprises. Bulletin*. 1988: (11), 53.

TEDDE, Pedro. The ways we collect records — do they coincide with the needs of business historians? *International Council on Archives. Committee on Business Archives. Bulletin*. 1988: (11), 51-52.

ULFSPARRE, Anna Christina. Practical solutions for the preservation of business archives. *International Council on Archives. Committee on Business Archives. Bulletin*. 1988: (11), 37-40.

ULFSPARRE, Anna Christina. Solutions pratiques pour la préservation d'archives d'entreprises: quelques aspects. *Conseil international des archives. Comité des archives d'entreprises*. 1988: (11), 40-41.

U.S. OFFICE OF MANAGEMENT AND BUDGET. *Managing Federal Information Resources: Annual Report under the*

Paperwork Reduction Act of 1980. 6th ed. Washington, D.C.: The Office, July 1988. 63 p.

Update: health and records management. *Records and Retrieval Report.* September 1988: 4(7), 14-15.

VALIQUETTE, Diane. La gestion électronique des documents administratifs: une évolution ou une révolution? IN Couture, Carol. Réflexions archivistiques. Montréal: Université de Montréal, École de bibliothéconomie et des sciences de l'information, 1987: 67-81.

VASSILIEV, N.A. L'organisation du contrôle administratif sur la gestion des documents. *Sovietskje Arkhivy.* 1988: (5), 48-53.

WAEGEMANN, C. Peter, ed. Database management for records managers. *Records and Retrieval Report.* May 1988: 4(5), 1-16.

WAEGEMANN, C. Peter, ed. Integrating information carriers. *Records and Retrieval Report.* March 1988: 4(3), 1-16.

WAEGEMANN, C. Peter, ed. Microcomputers: filing and storage. *Records and Retrieval Report.* February 1988: 4(2), 1-16.

WAEGEMANN, C. Peter, ed. Portable records. *Records and Retrieval Report.* April 1988: 4(4), 1-16.

WAEGEMANN, C. Peter, ed. Software for records management. *Records and Retrieval Report.* December 1987: 3(10), 1-16.

WAEGEMANN, C. Peter, ed. Software for records management (Part 2). *Records and Retrieval Report.* January 1988: 4(1), 1-16.

WALKER, Cathy. "Automating the life cycle at Ontario Hydro". IN Proceedings: Conference of the Association of Canadian Archivists (1987: McMaster University). Hamilton, Ont., 1987. 5 p.

WALLACE, Patricia E., [et al]. *Records management: integrated information systems.* 2nd ed. New York: Wiley, 1987. x, 500 p.

WALLOT, Jean-Pierre. Gestion des documents fédéraux — défis et possibilités. *Bulletin de la gestion des documents.* Avril/juin 1986: 2(1), 1-3.

WALLOT, Jean-Pierre. Managing the federal government's records — current challenges and opportunities. *Records Management Bulletin.* April/June 1986: 2(1) 1-3.

WHITEHEAD, Janet C. and DiAnn CONYERS. Survival in a computer environment — the synergistic approach. *Records Management Quarterly.* January 1988: 22(1), 8-14.

2.2 Mail management / Gestion du courrier

BONVIE, Bill. Corporate mail rooms have become serious business. *The Office.* December 1987: 106(6), 56-60.

Corporate mailroom has sense of order and calm. *The Office.* December 1987: 106(6), 38.

SCHOULLER, Jacques, Sylvia FILLING et David BATAZZI. L'archivage sur microfilm à Codes-à-Barres au parlement européen: la Base ARCO (archives courrier officiel). *Archives et bibliothèques de Belgique.* 1987: 58(1/2), 313-330.

U.S. Postal Service stores constituent letter files on optical disk. *IMC Journal.* July/August 1988: 24(4), 43-44.

2.3 Records classification / Classification des documents

BUSSELS, N. Het beheer van het dynamisch en semi-statisch archief van de provincie Limburg [The management of dynamics in semi-static archives of Limburg province]. *Bibliotheek-en Archiefgids.* May 1987: (63), 127-135.

ÉCOLE DES HAUTES ÉTUDES COMMERCIALES. (MONTRÉAL, QUÉBEC) GESTION DES DOCUMENTS. *Guide de classification des documents.* Montréal: École des hautes études commerciales, Service des archives, 1988. 38 f.

LACROIX, Guylaine. Le classement des dossiers: une science. *Le Bureau.* Juillet/août 1987: 23(4), 28-29.

MIMS, Julian L. An outline for files control. *Records Management Quarterly.* January 1988: 22(1), 18-24.

UNIVERSITÉ DE MONTRÉAL. SERVICE DES ARCHIVES. *Le cadre de classement des archives de l'Université de Montréal.* Montréal: Les Archives, 1988. 72 p. (Publication; n° 3)

2.4 Scheduling and disposal / Délai de conservation et d'élimination

ARMA INTERNATIONAL CONFERENCE (32ND: 1987: ANAHEIM, CA.). *Proceedings of the ARMA International 32nd Annual Conference.* Prairie Village, KS.: Association of Records Managers and Administrators, 1987. 482 p.

BLOUNT, Gail and Peggy REID. Power packed records retention. *Modern Office Technology.* February 1986: 31(2), 62, 64, 66.

Books and records retention/destruction. *Micro-notes.* Winter 1986: 15(1), 20-21, 30.

BRIDGES, Edwin C. Retention schedules: the key to RM. *The Office.* September 1986: 104(3), 142-143.

CARLSON, Carol. How a young city solved its problems with filing. *The Office.* October 1987: 106(4), 106-107.

CHARLAND, Diane. Le traitement des dossiers administratifs à Ville de Saint-Laurent. *Archives (Revue de l'Association des archivistes du Québec).* Automne 1988: 20(2), 53-60.

CHARMAN, Derek. *Recensement des archives courantes et tableaux de tri: une étude RAMP, accompagnée de principes directeurs.* Paris: UNESCO, 1986. 71 p. (PGI-84/WS/26)

CHILD, M.S. Further thoughts on "Selection for preservation: a materialistic approach" [prepared for discussion at the 108th ARL meeting in Minneapolis]. *Library Resources and Technical Services.* October 1986: 30, 354-362.

DAUM, Patricia B. Coordinating records management and the special library for effectiveness. *Records Management Quarterly.* April 1986: 20(2), 36-38.

Le Décret du Conseil des Commissaires du peuple de la R.S.F.S.R. « Sur la conservation et la destruction des archives ». *Sovietskje Arkhivy.* 1988: (1), 41-44.

GRAY, David P. *Records management for parishes and schools.* Richardton, N.D.: Diocesen of Bismarck, 1985. 44 p.

Guide sur la conservation des documents essentiels. Ottawa: Publié conjointement par Protection civile Canada et Archives nationales du Canada, 1987. iii, 133, 123, iii p. (P.C.C. 12/87)

Guide to the preservation of essential records. Ottawa: Issued jointly by Emergency Preparedness Canada and National Archives of Canada, 1987. iii, 123, 133, iii p. (EPC 12/87)

HART, Beverly, Stephen ELLIS and Ian PRITCHARD. The appraisal and scheduling of government records: a new approach by the Australian Archives. *The American Archivist.* Fall 1987: 50(4), 591-597.

HAYES, Kenneth V. Are you too small for records management? *Records Management Quarterly.* January 1987: 21(1), 22-28, 44.

HAYWARD, Robert J. Working in thin air: of archives and the Deschênes Commission. *Archivaria.* Summer 1988: (26), 122-136.

HODGES, Anthony. 78-preservation or disposal? *Audiovisual Librarian.* February 1988: 14(1), 29-30.

HOPKINS, Mark. Computerizing a government records archives — The FEDDOC Experience. *Records Management Quarterly.* July 1986: 20(3), 36-39.

JONES, Virginia A. Retention schedules: at peace or in panic? *The Office*. October 1987: 106(4), 103-104.

KOPLOWITZ, Bradford. Scheduling the Governors' Papers. *The Midwestern Archivist*. 1987: 12(2), 105-109.

LEA, Mary Ann. The records round up. *Management World*. September/October 1987: 16(5), 34-35.

NATIONAL ARCHIVES AND RECORDS SERVICE. *Guide to records retention requirements*. Washington, D.C.: National Archives and Records Service, Office of the Federal Register, 1986. 355 p.

New IRS record retention requirements. *Modern Office Technology*. January 1987: 31(1), 33-34.

NORMANDEAU, Louis. Les calendriers de conservation: des acquis précaires, un avenir incertain. *Archives (Revue de l'Association des archivistes du Québec)*. Décembre 1987/mars 1988: 19(3/4), 23-27.

O'SHEA, Michael F. Classification, retention and automation: a case study. *Records and Retrieval Report*. June 1988: 4(6), 1-15.

Records retention and disposition schedule CO-1 for use by county governments. Albany, N.Y.: University of the State of New York, 1987. x, 89 p.

Records retention schedules. *Records and Retrieval Report*. April 1987: 3(4), 4-14.

RICHARDSON, Lee D. Retention of engineering documentation. *IMC Journal*. 1987: 23(3), 46-48.

ROUSSEAU, Jean-Yves et Madeleine ROY. *Calendrier de conservation des documents*. 5ᵉ éd. rev. et corr. Montréal: Université de Montréal, Service des Archives, 1986. 1 v. (pag. multiple) Collection Gestion des documents.

SANDERS, Robert L. Records inventories and scheduling for small organizations: a case study. *Records Management Quarterly*. July 1987: 21(3), 24-30, 51-52, 58.

SANDERS, Robert L. Two suggestions for coping with the paperwork explosion. *Records Management Quarterly*. January 1987: 21(1), 3-9.

SEHERMAN, Lloyd E. Records retention schedules: you start with an inventory. *Office*. March 1987: 105(3), 98-100.

SKUPSKY, Donald S. Determining litigation and statutes of limitation requirements for records retention requirements. *Records Management Quarterly*. July 1986: 20(3), 40-46.

SKUPSKY, Donald S. Legal and operational reasons for eliminating the "Authorization for destruction" form. *Records Management Quarterly*. January 1988: 22(1), 26, 124, 146.

SKUPSKY, Donald S. Legal liability of the records and information management professional. *Records Management Quarterly*. April 1987: 21(2), 36-39.

SKUPSKY, Donald S. Legal requirements for computer records containing federal tax information: an update. *Records Management Quarterly*. July 1988: 22(3), 32-35.

STEPHENS, David O. Making records retention decisions: practical and theoretical considerations. *Records Management Quarterly*. January 1988: 22(1), 3-7.

SYMONDSON, B. Records disposal schedules, Aukland City Council, an introductory statement. *Archifacts*. 1988: (3), 17-19.

TÉTREAULT, Marie-Josée. Le calendrier de conservation: au cœur d'une politique d'organisation des documents. IN Couture, Carol. Réflexions archivistiques. Montréal: Université de Montréal, École de bibliothéconomie et des sciences de l'information, 1987: 53-66.

UNIVERSITÉ DU QUÉBEC À MONTRÉAL. SERVICE DES ARCHIVES. *Calendrier de conservation des documents de l'UQAM. Montréal: Université du Québec à Montréal, Service des Archives, 1987. 1 v. (pag. multiple) (Publication; n° 28)*

2.5 Records centres / Dépôts de préarchivage

BAUTSCH, Gail. What you don't know can hurt you. *Records Management Quarterly*. October 1986: 20(4), 20-24.

BOAG, P.W. The state of NZ Archives in the 1980s — the administrative viewpoint. *Archifacts*. 1987: (2), 14-23.

COURTOT, Marilyn. Vaults of granite and steel: a journey through the genealogical storage complex of the Mormon Church. *INFORM: the Magazine of Information and Image Management*. July/August 1988: 2(7), 22-25.

DAVIS, James V. Computerized management of inactive record centers. *IMC Journal*. January/February 1988: 24(1), 16-18.

DICKINSON, A. Litchard. What are active files? Where and how should they be stored. *Office Systems Management*. Spring 1986: 5(2), 4-7, 13.

DOLLAR, Charles M. *Electronic records management and archives in international organizations: a RAMP study with guidelines*. Paris: UNESCO, 1986. 159 p. (PGI-86/WS/12)

DURANTI, Luciana. Records management in Italy. *The American Archivist*. Fall 1986: 49(4), 459-462.

JAMES, Linda. *Standing the test of time: quality assurance for state and local government records microfilming*. St. Paul: Minnesota Historical Society, 1986. 70 p.

MADDEN, Dennis D. *Offsite storage at the Nebraska State Archives: learning by strategy, trial, and error*. [Vancouver]: Association of British Columbia Archivists, [1988]. [7] p. (A.B.C.A. Publications; no. 6)

Off-site storage centers. *Records and Retrieval Report*. June 1987: 3(6), 11-15.

SETTANNI, Joseph Andrew. Special report: the records center. *INFORM: the Magazine of Information and Image Management*. November/December 1988: 2(10), 36-42, 47.

WRATTEN, Nigel. Setting up a records centre: some practical advice. *Business Archives*. May 1987: (53), 39-49.

3. Media archives / Supports d'archives

AHRENS, Gerhard. Hanseatische Archive und Geschichtswissenschaft in Vergangenheit und Gegenwart [Hanseatic archives and historical research-past and present]. *Archivar*. May 1986: 39(2), 171-178.

CORNISH, Graham P. *Archival collections of non-book materials*. London: British Library, 1986. 41 p.

DELMAS, Bruno. *Les nouvelles archives: problèmes de définitions*. Congrès national des archivistes français (28ᵉ: 1986: Paris, France). Paris, 1987: 178-183.

Electronic records policy: a bibliography. *Archival Informatics Newsletter*. Winter 1988/1989: 2(4), 76-79.

FRANZ, Eckhart G. 23 Internationale Konferenz der "Table Ronde des Archives" in Austin (Texas). [23rd International Conference of the "Table Ronde des Archives" in Austin (Texas)]. *Archivar*. May 1986: 39(2), 195-198.

KETELAAR, Éric. *La mise en œuvre des nouvelles archives*. Congrès international des archives (11ᵉ: 1988: Paris). Paris, 1988. 24 p.

MOSELEY, Eva. Sharing archives of women's organizations. *SAA Newsletter*. July 1988: 9.

PINEAU, Guy. L'Europe des programmes. *Dossiers de l'audiovisuel*. Mai/juin 1987: 13, 13-54.

RAFAJ, Pavel. Podil archivu na plncni volebnich programu Narodni fronty CSR [Sharing of archives in the implementation of the election programmes of the National Front of the Czech Socialist Republic]. *Archivni Casopis*. 1986: 36(2), 69-71.

TURNER, Éric. *Problèmes spéciaux dans les pays tropicaux*. Congrès international des archives (11ᵉ: 1988: Paris). Paris, 1988. 6 p.

UHL, Bodo, [et al.]. Berichte der Fachgruppen ueber ihre Arbeitssitzungen auf dem 57. Deutschen Archivtag [Reports from the specialist groups on their working sessions during the 57th German Archive Conference]. *Archivar*. February 1986: 39(1), 59-70.

VAGANOV, F.M. *La conservation des nouvelles archives*. Congrès international des archives (11e: 1988: Paris). Paris, 1988. 27 p.

ZIZHI, Feng. *Les choix technologiques des pays en voie de développement*. Congrès international des archives (11e: 1988: Paris). Paris, 1988. 4 p.

3.0 Media archives — general
Supports d'archives — généralités

BEARMAN, David. Functional requirements for collections management systems. *Archival Informatics Technical Report*. Fall 1987: 1(3), 1-87.

BOGGE, Alfonso. Histoire et informatique. *ADPA*. 1986: 5(2), 79-89.

COONEY, James P. What is information really worth? *Canadian Library Journal*. October 1987: 44(5), 293-297.

CORNISH, Graham P. Mixed-media publications: the Cinderella of the archive world. *Audiovisual Librarian*. August 1987 [Erratum Feb. 1988]: 13 [ERRATUM 14], 151-153.

HACKMAN, Larry J. A perspective on American archives. *The Public Historian*. Summer 1986: 8(3), 10-28.

MEYER ZU ERPEN, Walter V. Study of the archival record and its context: meaning and historical understanding. *ABCA Newsletter*. Summer 1986: 12(3), 6-7.

3.0.1 Acquisition, selection, appraisal and evaluation /
Acquisition, sélection et évaluation historique et monétaire

ADAMS, Patricia L. Assessing the historical value of the historical records survey. *The Midwestern Archivist*. 1987: 12(1), 5-12.

ALEXANDER, Philip N. and Helen Willa SAMUELS. The roots of 128: a hypothetical documentation strategy. *The American Archivist*. Fall 1987: 50(4), 518-531.

BASSETT, T.D. Seymour. Documenting recreation and tourism in New England. *The American Archivist*. Fall 1987: 50(4), 550-569.

BILDFELL, Laurie. Border skirmish: National Library and Archives. *Quill & Quire*. June 1986: 52(6), 9-10.

BLINKHORN, Victoria Kendall. Issues in the acquisition of artist's records. *ABCA Newsletter*. Fall 1988: 14(2), 6-8.

BOLES, Frank. Mix two parts interest to one part information and appraise until done: understanding contemporary record selection. *The American Archivist*. Summer 1987: 50(3), 356-368.

BRADSHER, James Gregory. Privacy Act expungements: a reconsideration. *Provenance*. Spring 1988: 6(1), 1-25.

BRETON, Arthur J. The critical first step: in situ handling of large collections. *The American Archivist*. Fall 1986: 49(4), 455-458.

BROWN, Lauren R. Present at the Tenth Hour: appraising and accessioning the papers of Congresswoman Marjorie S. Holt. *Rare Books & Manuscripts Librarianship*. Fall 1987: 2(2), 95-102.

BROWN, Thomas Elton. "Appraisal in the Information Age". IN Proceedings of the Conference of the Association of Canadian Archivists (1987: McMaster University). Hamilton, Ont., 1987. 8 p.

BUCHANAN, William, [et al.]. *Collection development policy*. Natchitoches, La.: Northwestern State University, 1987. 21 p.

CARLETON, Don E. "McCarthyism was more than McCarthy": Documenting the Red Scare at the state and local level. *The Midwestern Archivist*. 1987: 12(1), 13-19.

CHAMPAGNE, Michel et Denys CHOUINARD. *Le traitement d'un fonds d'archives: ses documents historiques.* La Pocatière, [Montréal]: Documentor [Université de Montréal, Secrétariat général, Service des archives], 1987. 176 p.

CHILD, M.S. Further thoughts on "Selection for preservation: a materialistic approach" [prepared for discussion at the 108th ARL meeting in Minneapolis]. *Library Resources and Technical Services.* October 1986: 30, 354-362.

COLMAN, Gould P. Documenting agriculture and rural life. *The Midwestern Archivist.* 1987: 12(1), 21-27.

COOK, Terry. Billions of records: What to keep? What to destroy? Archival appraisal and federal government records. *The Archivist.* March/April 1986: 13(2), 1-3.

COOK, Terry. Conserver ou détruire: comment évaluer les milliards de documents du gouvernement fédéral. *L'Archiviste.* Mars/avril 1986: 13(2), 1-4.

COOPER, Sarah. The politics of protest collections: developing social action archives. *Provenance.* Spring 1987: 5(1), 8-16.

COX, Richard J. and Helen Willa SAMUELS. The archivist's first responsibility: a research agenda to improve the identification and retention of records of enduring value. *The American Archivist.* Winter/Spring 1988: 51(1/2), 28-51.

CRAWFORD, Miriam I. *A model for donor organization and institutional repository relationships in the transfer of organizational archives.* Philadelphia: National Federation of Abstracting and Information Services, 1987. 25 p.

DAVIES, Stuart. Collecting and recalling the twentieth century. *Museums Journal.* June 1985: 85(1), 27-29.

ELWOOD, Marie. The discovery and repatriation of the Lord Dalhousie Papers. *Archivaria.* Summer 1987: (24), 108-116.

FISHBEIN, Meyer H. Reflections on appraising statistical records. *The American Archivist.* May 1987: 50(2), 226-234.

FITZGERALD, S.M.D. Botanical archives: notes for archive selection and classification. *Archives: the Journal of the British Records Association.* April 1988: 18(79), 144-152.

GRAHN, Gerlinde. Die Auswertung des Archivgutes beim Aufbau der Grundlagen des Sozialismus und im Kampf um den Sieg der sozialistischen Produktionsverhaeltnisse (1949-1961/62). [Appraisal of archive material in the development of the foundations of socialism and in the struggle for victory in socialist productivity quotas (1949-1961/62)]. *Archiv Mitteilungen.* 1986: 36(2), 52-5.

GUPTIL, Marilla B. *Évaluation et tri des documents d'archives dans les organisations internationales: une étude RAMP accompagnée de principes directeurs.* Paris: UNESCO, 1986. 66 p. (PGI-85/WS/4)

HAAS, Joan K., Helen Willa SAMUELS and Barbara Trippel SIMMONS. *Appraising the records of modern science and technology: a guide.* [Cambridge]: Massachusetts Institute of Technology, 1985. 96 p.

HACKMAN, Larry J. and Joan WARNOW-BLEWETT. The documentation strategy process: a model and case study. *The American Archivist.* Winter 1987: 50(1), 12-47.

HART, Beverly, Stephen ELLIS and Ian PRITCHARD. The appraisal and scheduling of government records: a new approach by the Australian Archives. *The American Archivist.* Fall 1987: 50(4), 591-597.

HYAM, Grace Maurice. Accès aux documents. *L'Archiviste.* Mars/avril 1986: 13(2), 1, 4.

HYAM, Grace Maurice. Access to records and manuscripts. *The Archivist.* March/April 1986: 13(2), 1, 3-4.

JOLY, Bertrand. Les archives contemporaines ont-elles un avenir? *La Gazette des archives*. 1986: (134-135), 185-194.

KAMBA, Angeline S. Archive repatriation in Southern Africa. *Information Development*. April 1988: 4(2), 79-85.

KARAPETIANTS, I.V. Sur le versement des microcopies des rapports scientifiques et de recherches dans les Archives centrales d'État de la documentation scientifique et technique de l'URSS. *Sovietskje Arkhivy*. 1988: (5), 44-48.

KATES, Christine J.N. The Osgoode Society: preservation of legal records. *Law Society Gazette*. March 1987: 21(1), 58-70.

KESWANI, Dhan. *Acquisition of archival materials in developing countries.* Paris: International Council on Archives, 1987. 2, 127 p. (Studies/International Council on Archives; 3)

KLAASSEN, David J. Achieving balanced documentation: social services from a consumer perspective. *The Midwestern Archivist.* 1986: 11(2), 111-124.

KNOWLTON, Elizabeth. Documenting the Gay Rights Movement. *Provenance.* Spring 1987: 5(1), 17-30.

KOHL, Margret. Erfahrungen aus der Bearbeitung eines Grossbestandes der sozialistischen Epoche im Zentralen Stattsarchiv, dargestellt am Beispiel Staatliche Plankommission [Experiences in processing a major collection from the socialist era in the Central State Archive, illustrated by the example of the State Planning Committee]. *Archiv Mitteilungen.* 1986: 36(3), 82-86.

KRESTOVSKAYA, K.V. Les problèmes de la garantie de l'intégrité des documents dans les archives de l'URSS. *Archives et bibliothèques de Belgique.* 1987: 58(1/2), 193-208.

LANDON, Richard. Embracing the flood: questions about collecting twentieth-century non-literary works. *Rare Books & Manuscripts Librarianship.* Fall 1987: 2(2), 81-93.

LIENERT, Marina. Gedanken zur archivwissenschaftlichen Berwertung der medizinischen Betreuungsdokumentation im Gesundheitswesen der DDR [Thoughts of the archival appraisal of medical care documentation within East Germany's health programme]. *Archiv Mitteilungen.* 1986: 36(2), 65-71.

MCINTYRE, Katherine. Preserving our paper heritage: evaluation and disposal of treasures — Part 2. *Canadian Collector.* January/February 1987: 22(1), 20-21.

MACLEOD, Donald. Quaint specimens of the early days: priorities in collecting the Ontario archival record, 1872-1935. *Archivaria.* Summer 1986: (22), 12-39.

MCREYNOLDS, Samuel A. Rural life in New England. *The American Archivist.* Fall 1987: 50(4), 532-548.

MILLER, Fredric. Use, appraisal, and research: a case study of social history. *The American Archivist.* Fall 1986: 49(4), 371-392.

Normes et procédures archivistiques. 1re éd. Québec: Archives nationales du Québec, 1987. 124 p.

O'TOOLE, James M. Things of the Spirit: documenting religion in New England. *The American Archivist.* Fall 1987: 50(4), 500-517.

Pourquoi conserver les archives des médias? Rapports et débats de la table ronde tenue en matinée. *La Gazette des archives.* 1988: (140), 9-37.

QUINN, Patrick M. Archivists against the current: for a fair and truly representative record of our times. *Provenance.* Spring 1987: 5(1), 1-7.

REMOND, René. Qu'est-ce qu'un homme politique? *La Gazette des archives.* 1986: (133), 115-122.

RENÉ-BAZIN, Paule. *La création et la collecte des nouvelles archives.* Congrès international des archives (11e: 1988: Paris). Paris, 1988. 40 p.

SCHAM, A.M. *Managing special collections.* New York: Neal-Schuman, 1987. 201 p.

SCHROCK, Nancy Carlson. Images of New England: documenting the built environment. *The American Archivist.* Fall 1987: 50(4), 474-498.

SLY, Margery N. Sampling in an archival framework: mathoms and manuscripts. *Provenance.* Spring 1987: 5(1), 55-75.

STURGES, P. Policies and criteria for the archiving of electronic publishing. *Journal of Librarianship.* July 1987: 19, 152-172.

TOURTIER-BONAZZI, Chantal de. La commission pour la sauvegarde des archives privées contemporaines. *La Gazette des archives.* 1986: (133), 157-161.

UNSWORTH, Michael E. Evaluating primary sources on microform. *Microform Review.* May 1988: 17(2), 76-79.

WHITTICK, Christopher and Margaret WHITTICK. CAS: a Dutch solution to records appraisal. *Journal of the Society of Archivists.* October 1986: 8(2), 111-116.

YATES, Nigel. The historical value of church building plans. *Archives: the Journal of the British Records Association.* October 1987: 78, 67-75.

3.0.2 Arrangement / Classement

BAKER, Ron. *Beulah Alliance Church Archives: a model for the arrangement and description of local church archives of the Christian and Missionary Alliance in Canada.* Edmonton: R. Baker, 1986. 1 v.

BOOKER, John. The historical records of Lloyds Bank: an exercise in classification. *Business Archives.* May 1987: (53), 9-19.

CHAMPAGNE, Michel et Denys CHOUINARD. *Le traitement d'un fonds d'archives: ses documents historiques.* La Pocatière, [Montréal]: Documentor [Université de Montréal, Secrétariat général, Service des archives], 1987. 176 p.

CRAWFORD, Miriam I. *A model for donor organization and institutional repository relationships in the transfer of organizational archives.* Philadelphia: National Federation of Abstracting and Information Services, 1987. 25 p.

GROHMANN, Ingrid. Zur Einfuehrung des Ordnungsmodells fuer das Archivgut des Bestandstyps "Kreistag und Rat des Kreises" in den Kreisarchiven der DDR [On the introduction of the arrangement for the archive class "Regional assemblies and regional councils" in East German regional archives]. *Archiv Mitteilungen.* 1986: 36(4), 116-118.

HÉON, Gilles. L'article dans les répertoires: élément de cotation ou élément de rangement? *La Gazette des archives.* 1987: (136), 5-16.

INTNER, Sheila S. and Richard P. SMIRAGLIA. *Policy and practice in bibliographic control of nonbook media.* Chicago: American Library Association, 1987. x, 197 p.

KOHL, Margret. Erfahrungen aus der Bearbeitung eines Grossbestandes der sozialistischen Epoche im Zentralen Stattsarchiv, dargestellt am Beispiel Staatliche Plankommission [Experiences in processing a major collection from the socialist era in the Central State Archive, illustrated by the example of the State Planning Committee]. *Archiv Mitteilungen.* 1986: 36(3), 82-86.

MATRAS, Hagit. Jewish collections in the Public Archives of Canada [in Hebrew]. *Yad La-Kore.* September 1986: 22(3/4), 118-127.

PIEYNS, Jean. *Méthodes de classement et nouvelles archives.* Congrès international des archives (11e: 1988: Paris). Paris, 1988. 6 p.

SCHAM, A.M. *Managing special collections.* New York: Neal-Schuman, 1987. 201 p.

SMITH, Colin. A case for abandonment of "Respect" part II. *Archives and Manuscripts.* May 1987: 15(1), 20-28.

SPEIDELSBACH, Annelie. Subgroup vs. series arrangement: the William Irvine Papers. *Archivaria*. Winter 1986-87: (23), 107-118.

STAROSTINE, E.V. La provenance d'un principe de fonds du classement des documents. *Sovietskje Arkhivy*. 1988: (6), 18-28.

UNIVERSITÉ DE MONTRÉAL. SERVICE DES ARCHIVES. *Le cadre de classement des archives de l'Université de Montréal*. Montréal: Les Archives, 1988. 72 p. (Publication; n° 3)

3.0.3 Description and finding aids / Description et instruments de recherche

ALA-SAA sponsors session on the use of the USMARC format. *Library of Congress Information Bulletin*. November 10, 1986: 45(45), 373-374.

ACTON, Patricia. "Indexing concepts for archives". IN Proceedings: Conference of the Association of Canadian Archivists (1987: McMaster University). Hamilton, Ont., 1987. 7 p.

BABICKA, Vacslav. Vyuziti pocitace pro zpracovani rejstriku k archivnim pomuckam [Use of computers in the working out of indexes on finding aids]. *Archivni Casopis*. 1986: 36(3), 133-140.

BAKER, Ron. *Beulah Alliance Church Archives: a model for the arrangement and description of local church archives of the Christian and Missionary Alliance in Canada*. Edmonton: R. Baker, 1986. 1 v.

BEARMAN, David and Peter SIGMOND. Explorations of form of material authority files by Dutch archivists. *The American Archivist*. May 1987: 50(2), 249-253.

BLACK, Jeremy. Archives and the problems of diplomatic research. *Journal of the Society of Archivists*. October 1986: 8(2), 104-110.

BUETTNER, Siegfried, Hanns Peter NEUHEUSER and Hubert COLLIN. Rationalisierung bei Erfassung, Archiviserung und Verwaltung des Archivgutes [Rationalisation in the listing, cataloguing and administration of archive material]. *Archivar*. February 1986: 39(1), 27-34.

CHAMPAGNE, Michel et Denys CHOUINARD. *Le traitement d'un fonds d'archives: ses documents historiques*. La Pocatière, [Montréal]: Documentor [Université de Montréal, Secrétariat général, Service des archives], 1987. 176 p.

CHESTAKOVA, I.S. Sur la possibilité du développement de l'instrument de recherche des archives en utilisant la langue formalisée [en russe]. *Sovietskje Arkhivy*. 1987: (1), 41-44.

CHOKHINE, L.I. La description des documents dans les Archives du Ministère de la Justice à Moscou dans la deuxième moitié du XIXe-le début du XXe siècle [en russe]. *Sovietskje Arkhivy*. 1987: (2), 53-57.

CHOUINARD, Denys. L'instrument de recherche à l'Université de Montréal: résultat d'une démarche globale dans l'acquisition et le traitement des archives. *Archives (Revue de l'Association des archivistes du Québec)*. Décembre 1987/mars 1988: 19(3/4), 3-9.

CLOUD, Patricia D. The cost of converting to MARC AMC: some early observations. *Library Trends. Winter 1988: 36(3), 573-583*.

COLES, Laura Millar. A.B.C.A. MARC workshop. *ABCA Newsletter*. Summer 1988: 14(1), 1, 5.

COOK, Michael. The move towards standards of description and what to do with them. *Janus*. 1987: (2), 29-32.

COOK, Michael. Les progrès des travaux sur les normes de répertoriage et les raisons d'être de celles-ci. *Janus*. 1987: (2), 32-36.

COOK, Michael. Standards of archival description. *Journal of the Society of Archivists*. April 1987: 8(3), 181-188.

CRAWFORD, Miriam I. *A model for donor organization and institutional repository relationships in the transfer of organizational archives*. Philadelphia:

National Federation of Abstracting and Information Services, 1987. 25 p.

DOOLEY, Jackie M. An introduction to authority control for archivists. *Archival Informatics Technical Report.* Summer 1988: 2(2), 5-20.

DOWLER, Lawrence. Descriptive standards for the archival profession. *SAA Newsletter.* November 1988: 13.

DRYDEN, Jean E. Descriptive standards for archives. *ACS Newsletter.* Winter 1988/1989: 10(4), 14-15.

DUCHEIN, Michel. La clef du trésor: l'évolution des instruments de recherche d'archives du Moyen Age à nos jours d'après des exemples français. *Archives et bibliothèques de Belgique.* 1986: 57(1/2), 109-126.

Een kritische doorlichting van de huidige methoden tot ontsluiting van archieven; handelingen van de studiedag ingericht door de Sectie Archief van de VVBAD te Brussel op 18 april 1986 [A critical view on actual finding aids at archives; proceedings of the colloquy of the Archives Section of the VVBAD, Brussels, April 18, 1986]. *Bibliotheek-en Archiefgids.* May 1987: (63), 101-144.

Finding aids on fiches. *The Archivist.* September/October 1988: 15(5), 9.

FISHBEIN, Meyer H. Reflections of the impact of automation on archives. *Archives et bibliothèques de Belgique.* 1986: 57(1/2), 159-172.

GARNETT, Thomas. Development of an authority control system for the Smithsonian Institution Libraries. *Archival Informatics Technical Report.* Summer 1988: 2(2), 21-28.

GARON, Louis. Normes et procédures en archivistique. Avantages scientifiques et administratifs des normes et procédures. *Archives (Revue de l'Association des archivistes du Québec).* Été 1988: 20(1), 31-41.

GILMORE, Matthew B. Increasing access to archival records in library online public access catalogs. *Library Trends.* Winter 1988: 36(3), 609-623.

GOSSI, Anton. Archivar und historische Ferschung [L'Archivistique et la recherche historique]. *Arbido-R.* 1988: 3(1), 2-5.

HALLER, Uli. Variations in the processing rates on the Magnuson and Jackson Senatorial Papers. *The American Archivist.* Winter 1987: 50(1), 100-109.

HARLOW, E. Lynn, comp. *Bibliography update to towards descriptive standards (1986).* [Toronto]: Archives of Ontario, Task Force on Intellectual Controls, 1988. ii, 32 p.

HAWORTH, Kent M. Putting the cart before the horse: automation and descriptive standards for archives. *ABCA Newsletter.* Winter 1987: 13(3), 6-7.

HENSEN, Steven L. Squaring the circle: the reformation of archival description in AACR2. *Library Trends.* Winter 1988: 36(3), 539-552.

HICKERSON, H. Thomas. Archival information exchange and the role of bibliographic networks. *Library Trends. Winter 1988: 36(3), 553-571.*

HONHART, Frederick L. The application of microcomputer-based local systems with the MARC AMC format. *Library Trends.* Winter 1988: 36(3), 585-592.

LANCASTER, Wilfrid. *Vocabulary control for information retrieval.* Arlington, Va.: Information Resources Press, 1986. 270 p.

LANGLOIS, Égide. L'accès-sujet en archivistique: vers une réforme en profondeur des instruments de recherche? IN Couture, Carol. Réflexions archivistiques. Montréal: Université de Montréal, École de bibliothéconomie et des sciences de l'information, 1987: 37-52.

MARTIN, Russell. "Archival indexing". IN Proceedings: Conference of the Association of Canadian Archivists (1987: McMaster University). Hamilton, Ont., 1987. 6 p.

MATRAS, Hagit. Jewish collections in the Public Archives of Canada [in Hebrew]. *Yad La-Kore.* September 1986: 22(3/4), 118-127.

MATTERS, Marion. Authority files in an archival setting. *Archival Informatics Technical Report.* Summer 1988: 2(2), 29-34.

MERRIN, Geneviève. L'indexation matières. *Arbido-R.* 1988: 3(2), 42-46.

MICHELS, Fredrick and Terry LOVE-GROVE. PC Corner: MicroMARC: AMC. *Library Hi Tech News.* March 1988: (47), 14-15.

MICHELSON, Avra, ed. Archives and authority control: proceeding of a seminar sponsored by the Smithsonian Institution, October 27, 1987. *Archival Informatics Technical Report.* Summer 1988: 2(2), ii, 63 p.

MICHELSON, Avra. Description and reference in the age of automation. *The American Archivist.* Spring 1987: 50(2), 192-208.

MICHELSON, Avra. Introduction: descriptive standards and the archival profession. *Archival Informatics Technical Report.* Summer 1988: 2(2), 1-4.

MicroMARC: AMC — Microcomputer bibliographic control for manuscripts and archives. *Information Intelligence Online Libraries and Microcomputers.* September 1986: 4(8-9), 11.

MOSELEY, Eva. Sharing archives of women's organizations. *SAA Newsletter.* July 1988: 9.

NOBLE, Richard A. The NHPRC Data Base Project: building the "Interstate Highway System". *The American Archivist.* Winter/Spring 1988: 51(1/2), 98-105.

Programme des instruments de recherche sur microfiches. *L'Archiviste.* Septembre/octobre 1988: 15(5), 12.

RICHEFORT, Isabelle. Les instruments de recherche élaborés par les missions. *La Gazette des archives.* 1987: (137-138), 165-177.

ROGERS, Dorothy. "Using MARC for online access". IN Proceedings: Conference of the Association of Canadian Archivists (1987: McMaster University). Hamilton, Ont., 1987. 9 p.

ROSCHLAU, Gertrud and Volker ERNST. Thematische Inventare im Militaerarchiv der DDR [Thematic inventories in the East German Military Archive]. *Archiv Mitteilungen.* 1986: 36(4), 130-131.

ROSSOL, Erika. Erfahrungen und Probleme bei der Erschliessung des Bestandes IG Farbeindustrie IG, Werk Premnitz, im Staatsarchiv Potsdam [Experiences and problems with the cataloguing of the collection for the IG Dyeing Works at Premnitz, in the Potsdam State Archive]. *Archiv Mitteilungen.* 1986: 36(4), 114-116.

SCHAM, A.M. *Managing special collections.* New York: Neal-Schuman, 1987. 201 p.

SERGEEVA, A.G. Voprosi katalogizatsii NTD v arkhivovyedchyeskoi lityeraturye [Questions of cataloguing scientific and technical documentation in archival management literature]. *Sovetskje Arkhivy. 1986: (1), 23-26.*

SLAVOVA-PETKOVA, S. L'État contemporain et les tendances du développement du système des instruments de recherche pour les documents d'archives. *Sovietskje Arkhivy.* 1988: (1), 96-101.

SMELTZER, Dennis K. Producing a computerized media catalog. *Small Computers in Libraries.* September 1987: 7(8), 19-25.

SZARY, Richard V. Technical requirements and prospects for authority control in the SIBIS — Archives databases. *Archival Informatics Technical Report.* Summer 1988: 2(2), 41-46.

TATEM, Jill M. and Jeffrey ROLLISON. *Thesaurus of university terms developed at Case Western Reserve University Archives.* Chicago: Society of American Archivists, 1986. 46 p.

VOLKOVA, I.V. et N.A. KARPOUNO-VA. Sur l'établissement des catalogues des documents dans les Archives d'État. *Sovietskje Arkhivy.* 1988: (5), 29-38.

WALFORD, John, Henry GILLETT and J.B. POST. Introducing computers to the record office: theory and practice. *Journal of the Society of Archivists.* January 1988: 9(1), 21-29.

WEBER, Lisa B. Archival automation: the MARC AMC format. *SAA Newsletter.* May 1987: 13.

WEBER, Lisa B. Describing microforms and the MARC formats. *Archival Informatics Newsletter.* Summer 1987: 1(2), 9-13.

WEBER, Lisa B. Development of authority control system within the archival profession. *Archival Informatics Technical Report.* Summer 1988: 2(2), 35-40.

WOOLGAR, C.M. The Wellington papers database: an interim report. *Journal of the Society of Archivists.* January 1988: 9(1), 1-20.

ZBORAY, Ronald J. dBASE III Plus and the MARC AMC format: problems and possibilities. *The American Archivist.* Spring 1987: 50(2), 210-225.

3.0.4 Public service / Service au public

BERZINS, Ina, [et al.]. *Research and Public Service Component Program Evaluation.* Ottawa: Public Archives Canada, 1985. 3 v.

BOWERS, Doris Roney. Genealogical research in the county courthouse. *Illinois Libraries.* September 1988: 70(7), 480-483.

CONWAY, Paul. Facts and frameworks: an approach to studying the users of archives. *The American Archivist.* Fall 1986: 49(4), 393-407.

DIAMOND, Sigmund. Archival adventure along the Freedom of Information Trail: what archival records reveal about the FBI and the universities in the McCar-

thy period. *The Midwestern Archivist.* 1987: 12(1), 29-42.

DOWLER, Lawrence. The role of use in defining archival practice and principles: a research agenda for the availability and use of records. *The American Archivist.* Winter/Spring 1988: 51(1/2), 74-95.

EASTWOOD, Terry and Robin G. KEIRSTEAD. Editorial/Project Pride. *ABCA Newsletter.* Summer 1987: 13(1), 1-2.

ERMISSE, Gérard. La communication. *La Gazette des archives.* 1988: (141), 201-217.

ESO, Elizabeth. *Promotion and outreach in a community archives.* [Vancouver]: Association of British Columbia Archivists, c1988. 7 p. (A.B.C.A. publications; no. 2)

FAGAN, Michele L. Practical aspects of conducting research in British libraries and archives. *RQ (Request Inquiries).* Spring 1987: 26(3), 370-376.

HODGSON, Judith. Teaching teachers: museums team up with schools and universities. *Museum News.* June 1986: 64(5), 28-35.

KARNS, Kermit B. The care and feeding of genealogists: or what every archivist should know about genealogy. *SAA Newsletter.* March 1987: 12.

KNOWLTON, Elizabeth. Documenting the Gay Rights Movement. *Provenance.* Spring 1987: 5(1), 17-30.

MACLEOD, A. and A.R. REUBER. The Array model: conceptual modeling approach to document retrieval. *Journal of the American Society for Information Science.* May 1987: 162-170.

MIREAULT, Manon. Les services éducatifs d'archives en Belgique wallonne. *Archives (Revue de l'Association des archivistes du Québec).* Décembre 1987/mars 1988: 19(3/4), 10-22.

OSBORNE, Ken. Archives in the classroom. *Archivaria.* Winter 1986-87: (23), 16-40.

PERRON-CROTEAU, Lise. Aide et entraide — Les Archives appuient de façon concrète la collectivité archivistique. *L'Archiviste*. Janvier/février 1988: 15(1), 16-17.

PERRON-CROTEAU, Lise. NA support to the Canadian Archival Community. *The Archivist*. January/February 1988: 15(1), 16-17.

PONOMAREVA, V.I. Les règles du travail des chercheurs dans les salles de lecture des Archives d'État [en russe]. *Sovietskje Arkhivy*. 1987: (3), 78-80.

POTIN, Monique. La relation entre les spécialistes de l'information documentaire et les utilisateurs: trois approches. *Documentation et bibliothèques*. Avril/juin 1987: 33(2), 39-44.

ROGERS, Dorothy. "Using MARC for online access". IN Proceedings: Conference of the Association of Canadian Archivists (1987: McMaster University). Hamilton, Ont., 1987. 9 p.

VSA-GILDUNGSAUSSCHUSS. Die Ausleihe von Archivalen für Ausstellungen, das Photokopieren und die Gebührenerhebung in den Archiven der Schweiz und des Fürstentums Liechtenstein. *Arbido-R*. 1987: 2(3), 74-79.

WARNER, Alice Sizer. Making money: fees for information service. *Special Libraries*. Fall 1987: 78(4), 277-280.

WEILBRENNER, Bernard. Au service du public vingt-quatre heures par jour. *Archives et bibliothèques de Belgique*. 1986: 57(1/2), 411-436.

3.0.4.1 Reference and research / Référence et recherche

ANDERSEN, Sven Aage. Salt and bread makes the cheeks red. *International Council on Archives. Committee on Business Archives. Bulletin*. 1987: (10), 23-29.

ARLETTAZ, Gérald. Une revue « Études et Sources ». *Arbido-R*. 1988: 3(1), 10-13.

BLACK, Jeremy. Archives and the problems of diplomatic research. *Journal of the Society of Archivists*. October 1986: 8(2), 104-110.

CRUSH, Peter. Archives and historians. *Archives and Manuscripts*. May 1988: (1), 15-24.

DASCHER, Ottfried. Social history. Recent developments and contemporary perspectives. *International Council on Archives. Committee on Business Archives. Bulletin*. 1987: (10), 1-4.

DEARSTYNE, Bruce W. What is the use of archives? A challenge for the profession. *The American Archivist*. Winter 1987: 50(1), 76-87.

EELES, Graham and Jill KINNEAR. Archivists and oral historians: friends, strangers or enemies? *Journal of the Society of Archivists*. October 1988: 9(4), 188-189.

FAGAN, Michele L. Practical aspects of conducting research in British libraries and archives. *RQ (Request Inquiries)*. Spring 1987: 26(3), 370-376.

GAGNON-ARGUIN, Louise. Les archives au Canada: quelques références bibliographiques utiles aux études canadiennes. *Bulletin de l'AEC*. Hiver 1988/1989: 10(4), 31-32.

HAMON, Maurice. Archives d'entreprises, histoire industrielle et histoire sociale. *Conseil international des archives. Comité des archives d'entreprises. Bulletin*. 1987: (10), 5-12.

HAWRY, David A. The research potential of religious archives: the Mennonite Experience. *The Midwestern Archivist*. 1986: 11(2), 135-140.

HEARN, Terry. Resources, institutions and economic change: Central Otago 1861-1921. *Archifacts*. 1988: (1), 25-34.

HICKERSON, H. Thomas. Archival information exchange and the role of bibliographic networks. *Library Trends*. Winter 1988: 36(3), 553-571.

HILLER, Marc. L'archiviste de référence: instrument de recherche ultime? IN Couture, Carol. Réflexions archivistiques.

Montréal: Université de Montréal, École de bibliothéconomie et des sciences de l'information, 1987: 11-24.

KOVAN, Allan. Helping friends: archives training for public historians. *The American Archivist.* Summer 1988: 51(3), 312-318.

MBAYE, Saliou. Archives et recherche au Sénégal (1976-1984). *Archives et bibliothèques de Belgique.* 1986: 57(1/2), 295-308.

MICHELSON, Avra. Description and reference in the age of automation. *The American Archivist.* Spring 1987: 50(2), 192-208.

MILLER, Fredric. Use, appraisal, and research: a case study of social history. *The American Archivist.* Fall 1986: 49(4), 371-392.

MORELLE, Laurent. Les missions et la recherche. *La Gazette des archives.* 1987: (137-138), 178-187.

MOTLEY, Archie. Opinion [Researcher access to unprocessed collections]. *ABCA Newsletter.* Spring 1986: 12(2), 2.

NOËL, Ginette. Les archives municipales et la recherche: la réalité à la Ville de Québec. *Archives (Revue de l'Association des archivistes du Québec).* Mars 1987: 18(4), 41-55.

POTIN, Monique. La relation entre les spécialistes de l'information documentaire et les utilisateurs: trois approches. *Documentation et bibliothèques.* Avril/juin 1987: 33(2), 39-44.

POTTER, Constance. Research at the National Archives [NARA]. *Perspectives [American Historical Association Newsletter].* March 1987: 25(3), 15-18.

RICHARDSON, Len. The playing fields of empire. *Archifacts.* 1988: (2), 12-16.

RIKHEIM, Brita. Business archives as source material to social history. *International Council on Archives. Committee on Business Archives. Bulletin.* 1987: (10), 13-16.

RUTH, Janice E. Educating the reference archivist. *The American Archivist.* Summer 1988: 51(3), 266-276.

SACLIER, Michael. Social history and business history in Australia. *International Council on Archives. Committee on Business Archives. Bulletin.* 1987: (10), 17-22.

WESSMAN, Lars. Archives and library of the Swedish Labour Movement. *International Council on Archives. Committee on Business Archives. Bulletin.* 1987: (10), 35-39.

YATES, Nigel. Marketing the record office: new directions in archival public relations. *Journal of the Society of Archivists.* April 1988: 9(2), 69-75.

3.0.4.2 Conferences, displays, diffusion and publications / Conférences, expositions, diffusion et publications

ACLAND, Glenda. The display's the thing... an exercise in archival exhibitionism. *Archives and Manuscripts.* May 1987: 15(1), 29-40.

ADAMS, Patricia L. Primary sources and senior citizens in the classroom. *The American Archivist.* May 1987: 50(2), 239-242.

ALLYN, Nancy, Aubits SHAWN and Gail F. STERN. Using archival materials effectively in museum exhibition. *The American Archivist.* Summer 1987: 50(3), 402-404.

BABELON, Jean-Pierre. Le Musée de l'histoire de France aux Archives nationales à Paris. *La Gazette des archives.* 1987: (139), 260-265.

BECKLEY, Susan. Archive therapy in Carmarthenshire: some further developments. *Journal of the Society of Archivists.* April 1987: 8(3), 199-201.

BOATRIGH, John and G. Donald ADAMS. The selling of the museum 1986. *Museum News.* April 1986: 64(4), 16-21.

BROCHU, Frédérick. La diffusion des archives historiques: un rôle éducatif et culturel à exercer dans une perspective mercatique. IN Couture, Carol. Réflexions archivistiques. Montréal: Université de Montréal, École de bibliothéconomie et des sciences de l'information, 1987: 25-36.

CHABIN, Marie-Anne. Les Capétiens en Île-de-France. Un jeu-concours organisé par le groupe Île-de-France de l'Association des archivistes français. La Gazette des archives. 1988: (140), 75-79.

COLES, Laura Millar. The decline of documentary publishing in Canadian archives, 1865-1984. Thesis (M.A.S.) — University of British Columbia, 1984. Ottawa: National Library of Canada, 1986. 3 microfiches.

COLES, Laura Millar. The decline of documentary publishing: the role of English-Canadian archives and historical societies in documentary publishing. Archivaria. Winter 1986-87: (23), 69-85.

COLES, Laura Millar. The role of archives in documentary publishing. ABCA Newsletter. Spring 1986: 12(2), 6-7.

DANILOV, Victor J. Promoting museums through advertising. Museum News. August/September 1986: 64(6), 33-39.

DAVID, Jonathan. Light in museums. Museums Journal. March 1986: 85(4), 203-215.

DEARSTYNE, Bruce W. What is the use of archives? A challenge for the profession. The American Archivist. Winter 1987: 50(1), 76-87.

DELSALLE, Paul. Les activités culturelles des archives municipales. La Gazette des archives. 1986: (133), 143-156.

FRANZ, Eckhart G. Archives and education: a RAMP study with guidelines. Paris: Unesco, 1986. 59 p. (PGI-86/WS/18)

GARRISON, Ellen. L'il Abner revisited: The Archives of Appalachia and regional multicultural education. The American Archivist. May 1987: 50(2), 236-238.

GAUTHIER-DESVAUX, Élisabeth. L'action culturelle aux archives. La Gazette des archives. 1988: (141), 218-236.

HODGSON, Judith. Teaching teachers: museums team up with schools and universities. Museum News. June 1986: 64(5), 28-35.

KARTOUS, Peter and Frantisek SEDLAK. Die methodologie des publizierens von Quellen aus dem 18-19. Jahrhundert. Archives et bibliothèques de Belgique. 1986: 57(1/2), 221-243.

KOZLOV, O.F. La littérature historique des années 1917-1940 sur le problème du tri des documents historiques pour leur édition [en russe]. Sovietskje Arkhivy. 1987: (1), 34-40.

KRIVENKO, M.V. L'utilisation des documents des Archives centrales d'État du Ministère de la Défense aux fins d'enseignement et d'éducation. Recherches et trouvailles aux archives [en russe]. Sovietskje Arkhivy. 1987: (1), 83.

NICHOLSON, Claudia J. Prologue portfolio: patriotic patents. Prologue: Quarterly of the National Archives. 1988: 20(3), 201-205.

OSBORNE, Ken. Archives in the classroom. Archivaria. Winter 1986-87: (23), 16-40.

PONOMAREVA, V.I. et L.I. SOLODOVNIKOVA. Sur l'activité d'information des institutions d'archives du pays. Sovietskje Arkhivy. 1988: (5), 21-29.

ROLON, Rosalind de. Getting the world out: a practical approach to museum print media plans. Museum News. August/September 1986: 64(6), 25-31.

SAVARD, Réjean. L'enseignement du marketing aux spécialistes de l'information documentaire. Arbido-R. 1987: 2(2), 26-31.

SCHETELICH, Eberhard. 23. CITRA in Austin/Texas (USA). [The 23rd CITRA in Austin, Texas (USA)]. Archiv Mitteilungen. 1986: 36(4), 128-129.

SHEPPARD, John. Creating a public image. *Museum News.* August/September 1986: 64(6), 5-13.

STANSFIELD, Geoff. Nature on display: trends in natural history museum exhibitions. *Museums Journal.* September 1986: 86(2), 97-103.

STOCKFORD, Bridget. Company archives in print: producing a company brochure. *Business Archives.* May 1987: (53), 31-38.

Surveying your arts audience. Washington, D.C.: National Endowment for the Arts, 1985. 77 p.

THORSON, Sandra J. The changing art of museum communication. *Museum News.* June 1986: 64(5), 61-65.

VSA-GILDUNGSAUSSCHUSS. Die Ausleihe von Archivalen für Ausstellungen, das Photokopieren und die Gebührenerhebung in den Archiven der Schweiz und des Fürstentums Liechtenstein. *Arbido-R.* 1987: 2(3), 74-79.

VERNON, John Ed. Teaching with documents. It's in the cards: archives and baseball. *Social Education.* February 1988: 52(2), 124-126.

3.0.4.3   Copyright / Droit d'auteur

BUCHER, Peter. *Les questions de droit dans la communication et la reproduction des archives audiovisuelles.* Congrès international des archives (11ᵉ: 1988: Paris). Paris, 1988. 12 p.

Copyright Act Amendments. *ACA Bulletin.* July 1987: 11(6), 10.

GIFFARD, Alain et Francine FONTANEL. Droit sans frontières: le droit d'auteur en Europe. *Bulletin des bibliothèques de France.* 1988: 33(1/2), 82-87.

HOPKINS, Richard. Complexities and concerns: copyright. *Canadian Library Journal.* October 1987: 44(5), 273-278.

LARIVIÈRE, Jules. Problèmes de droit d'auteur dans les bibliothèques. *Documentation et bibliothèques.* Juillet/septembre 1987: 33(3), 79-85.

Législation proposée sur les droits d'auteur: un point de vue sur la question de « l'utilisation équitable ». *Muse.* Hiver/janvier 1987: 4(4), 59-61.

Proposed copyright legislation: a look at the issue of "fair dealing". *Muse.* Winter/January 1987: 4(4), 57-58.

SARNIA, Lazar. *Authors and publishers: agreements and legal aspects of publishing.* 2nd ed. Toronto: Butterworths, 1987. xiv, 216 p.

3.0.4.4   Security and access / Sécurité et accès

ANDERSON, Hazel and John E. MCINTYRE. *Planning manual for disaster control in Scottish libraries and records offices.* Edinburgh: National Library of Scotland, 1985. 75 p.

BAUMANN, Roland M. The administration of access to confidential records in State archives: common practices and the need for a model law. *The American Archivist.* Fall 1986: 49(4), 349-369.

BEARMAN, T.C. Library and archives policy [questions of access]. *Bulletin of the American Society for Information Science.* June/July 1986: 12, 22-23.

BRADSHER, James Gregory. Researchers, archivists, and the access challenge of the FBI Records in the National Archives. *The Midwestern Archivist.* 1986: 11(2), 95-110.

Britain's National Preservation Office steps up library and archive security. *Library Hi Tech News.* November 1988: (54), 13.

BUCHANAN, Sally. *Disaster planning: preparedness and recovery for libraries and archives.* Paris: Unesco, 1988. vi, 187 p. (PGI-88/WS/6)

Court holds that Privacy Act requires federal agencies to maintain accurate records. *Information Hotline.* May 1986: 18(5), 1, 13-14.

DIAMOND, Sigmund. Archival adventure along the Freedom of Information Trail: what archival records reveal about the FBI and the universities in the McCarthy period. *The Midwestern Archivist.* 1987: 12(1), 29-42.

DOWLER, Lawrence. The role of use in defining archival practice and principles: a research agenda for the availability and use of records. *The American Archivist.* Winter/Spring 1988: 51(1/2), 74-95.

DUNN, F. Ian. The security marking of documentary materials. *Journal of the Society of Archivists.* April 1987: 8(3), 189-191.

ENGLAND, Claire and Karen EVANS. *Disaster management for libraries planning and process.* [Ottawa]: Canadian Library Association, 1988. xi, 207 p.

The FBI and the farm equipment workers: FBI surveillance records as a source for C10 Union history. *Labour History.* Fall 1986: 27(4), 485-505.

FRANZ, Eckhart G. 23 Internationale Konferenz der "Table Ronde des Archives" in Austin (Texas) [23rd International Conference of the "Table Ronde des Archives" in Austin (Texas)]. *Archivar.* May 1986: 39(2), 195-198.

La gestion de l'information gouvernementale. IN Traité de droit administratif, tome II, par René Dussault et Louis Borgeat. 2ᵉ éd. Québec: Presses de l'Université Laval, 1986: 769-1160.

GILLIS, Peter. "Revamping information policies: a Federal approach". IN Proceedings: Conference of the Association of Canadian Archivists (1987: McMaster University). Hamilton, Ont., 1987. 7 p.

GILMORE, Matthew B. Increasing access to archival records in library online public access catalogs. *Library Trends.* Winter 1988: 36(3), 609-623.

GRANSTROM, Claes. *Problèmes juridiques d'accès aux archives informatiques.* Congrès international des archives (11ᵉ: 1988: Paris). Paris, 1988. 10 p.

GRAY, V. Information as a social need. The archivist's view. IN Information '85.

Knowledge to Shape the Future. London: Aslib, 1986: 57-60.

GREENE, Mark A. Developing a research access policy for student records: a case study at Carleton College. *The American Archivist.* Fall 1987: 50(4), 570-579.

HICKERSON, H. Thomas and Anne R. KENNEY. Expanding access: loan of original materials in special collections. *Rare Books & Manuscripts Librarianship.* Fall 1988: 3(2), 113-119.

HYAM, Grace Maurice. Accès aux documents. *L'Archiviste.* Mars/avril 1986: 13(2), 1, 4.

HYAM, Grace Maurice. Access to records and manuscripts. *The Archivist.* March/April 1986: 13(2), 1, 3-4.

JOHNSON, Jeffery O. The documents diggers and their discoveries: a panel: the damage done: an archivist's view. *Dialogue.* Winter 1986: 19, 52-60.

JOHNSTON, R.E. (Bob). Standard threats. *Infosystems.* July 1987: 34(7), 35.

KIRBY, M.D. Access to information and privacy: the ten information commandments. *Archivaria.* Winter 1986-87: (23), 4-15.

La loi sur l'accès aux documents des organismes publics et sur la protection des renseignements. *Le Bureau.* Juillet/août 1986: 23.

MADDEN, Dennis D. *Offsite storage at the Nebraska State Archives: learning by strategy, trial, and error.* [Vancouver]: Association of British Columbia Archivists, [1988]. [7] p. (A.B.C.A. Publications; no. 6)

MOTLEY, Archie. Opinion [Researcher access to unprocessed collections]. *ABCA Newsletter.* Spring 1986: 12(2), 2.

PADFIELD, Tim. Disaster planning. *Business Archives.* May 1988: (55), 39-47.

PADFIELD, Tim. Further readings [disaster planning]. *Business Archives.* May 1988: (55), 45-47.

PETERSON, Trudy Huskamp. Archives fédérales, vie privée et personnages publics aux États-Unis. *Janus*. 1987: (2), 3-19.

PETERSON, Trudy Huskamp. Federal records, privacy and public officials in the United States. *Janus*. 1987: (2), 3-17.

Resolution on declassification policy adopted on April 3, 1987 by the National Coordinating Committee for the promotion of history. *Perspectives*. May/June 1987: 25(5), 9.

ROBBINS, Renee M. Disaster recovery: no longer the "loneliest people in the world". *Infosystems*. June 1987: 34(6), 38-40.

ROESSLER, Monika. Erste Erfahrungen mit dem Archivpass im Staatsarchiv Schwerin [Initial experiences from using the archives control pass in Schwerin State Archives]. *Archiv Mitteilungen*. 1986: 36(4), 118-119.

The Strange and convoluted history of the Nixon material: a retrospective, part I. *SAA Newsletter*. January 1987: 11-14.

The Tale of a frog prince [theft of national historical treasures]. *Newsweek*. 31 August 1987: 110(9), 22.

TAPSCOTT, Bob. "Access and archives: the Manitoba experience". IN Proceedings: Conference of the Association of Canadian Archivists (1987: McMaster University). Hamilton, Ont., 1987. 21 p.

THOMAS, D.L. *Study on control of security and storage of holdings: a RAMP study with guidelines*. Paris: United Nations Educational, Scientific and Cultural Organization, 1987. 62 p.

UHL, Bodo, [et al.]. Berichte der Fachgruppen ueber ihre Arbeitssitzungen auf dem 57. Deutschen Archivtag [Reports from the specialist groups on their working sessions during the 57th German Archive Conference]. *Archivar*. February 1986: 39(1), 59-70.

ULATE-SEGURA, Bodil. *Access to the archives of United Nations agencies: a*

RAMP study with guidelines. Paris: United Nations Educational, Scientific and Cultural Organization, 1987. 123 p.

Walking papers: the FBI nabs a historian. *Time*. 31 August 1987: 130(9), 18.

WALSH, Betty. Salvage of water-damaged archival collections. *ACA Bulletin*. March 1988: 12(4), [17-18].

WURZBURGER, Marilyn. Current security practices in college and university special collections. *Rare Books & Manuscripts Librarianship*. Spring 1988: 3(1), 43-57.

ZEIDBERG, David S. We have met the enemy... collection security in libraries. *Rare Books & Manuscripts Librarianship*. Spring 1987: 2(1), 19-26.

3.0.5 Information processing / Techniques d'information

ACTON, Patricia. Indexing is not classifying — and vice versa. *Records Management Quarterly*. July 1986: 20(3), 10-15.

ALLEN, Marie. Optical character recognition: technology with new relevance for archival automation projects. *ADPA*. 1986: 5(2), 9-24.

ALLEN, Marie. Optical character recognition: technology with new relevance for archival automation projects. *The American Archivist*. Winter 1987: 50(1) 88-99.

ALLEN, Percy and Russell L. MOBLEY. A bank in search of good records management. *The Office*. October 1987: 106(4), 15, 18.

AMBROSIO, Johanna. Micrographics remains a viable medium. *Government Computer News*. March 27, 1987: 6(6), 40.

AMBROSIO, Johanna. Moving the mountain: automating high-density paper storage. *Today's Office*. September 1987: 22(4), 33-37.

ANDORS, Alice. Micrographics service in the information age. *INFORM: the Magazine of Information and Image Management*. June 1987: 1(6), 26-29.

ARAD, A. Indexing from "non-structured" input. *ADPA*. 1987: 5(3), 29-46.

ARMA INTERNATIONAL CONFERENCE (32ND: 1987: ANAHEIM, CA.). *Proceedings of the ARMA International 32nd Annual Conference*. Prairie Village, K.S.: Association of Records Managers and Administrators, 1987. 482 p.

ARONSSON, Patricia and Thomas Elton BROWN. Government archivists and government automation: the odd couple. *Government Publications Review*. September/October 1986: 13, 561-570.

ARONSSON, Patricia and Thomas Elton BROWN. Information automation changes role of archivist. *Government Computer News*. 9 October 1987: 6(20), 40-43.

ART task force: learning objectives. *Archival Informatics Newsletter*. Spring 1987: 1(1), 7.

Automation: the latest good idea at the U.S. Patent Office. *IMC Journal*. 1987: 23(5), 37-40.

BABICKA, Vacslav. Vyuziti pocitace pro zpracovani rejstriku k archivnim pomuckam [Use of computers in the working out of indexes on finding aids]. *Archivni Casopis*. 1986: 36(3), 133-140.

BANNASCH, Hermann. Archiv und Registratur auf dem Weg in die Informationsgesellschaft: die Reform des Registraturwesens und die Einfuehrung der elektronsichen Buerolkommunikation in der Landesverwaltung Baden-Wuerttemberg [The archive and the document registry on the way to an information society: reform of registry practices and the introduction of electronic mailing in Baden Wuerttemburg's State administration]. *Archivar*. July 1986: 39(3), 291-312.

BEARMAN, David. Automated systems. *Archival Informatics Newsletter*. Spring 1987: 1(1), 2-4.

BEARMAN, David. Automated systems for archives and museums: acquisition and implementation issues. *Archival Informatics Technical Report*. Winter 1987/1988: 1(4), 88 p.

BEARMAN, David. Collecting software: a new challenge for archives and museums. *Archival Informatics Technical Report*. Summer 1987: 1(2), 80 p.

BEARMAN, David. MARCON PLUS: text retrieval software: a review. *Archival Informatics Newsletter*. Winter 1987: 1(4), 66-70.

BEARMAN, David. Micro-MARC: amc: a review. *Archival Informatics Newsletter*. Fall 1987: 1(3), 46-48.

BEARMAN, David. Optical media: their implications for archives and museums. *Archival Informatics Technical Report*. Spring 1987: 1(1), 1-73.

BEARMAN, David. Software vendors at the AAM. *Archival Informatics Newsletter*. Summer 1988: 2(2), 26-32.

BENDER, Avi. Full text search and image retrieval. *IMC Journal*. 1987: 23(4), 28-30.

Bibliography on recent automation articles. *SAA Newsletter*. January 1988: 5.

BIDA, Michael C. Scanning, OCR devices complement microfilm in solving data entry bottlenecks. *AIIM Conference Daily*. April 30, 1987: 5, 14, 39.

BIRRELL, A.J. Microcomputers and operational necessity: the experience of the National Photography Collection. IN The Application of micro-computers in information, documentation and libraries. Amsterdam: North-Holland, 1987: 746-751.

BOGGE, Alfonso. Histoire et informatique. *ADPA*. 1986: 5(2), 79-89.

BOLNICK, Franklin I. and Susan LAW. Managing concept: putting system design to work. *INFORM: the Magazine of Information and Image Management*. January 1987: 1(1), 12-15, 44.

BOURKE, Thomas A. Retrospect and prospect: micrographics evolution in research libraries. *INFORM: the Magazine of Information and Image Management.* October 1987: 1(10), 28-30.

BOZEVICH, Ken. Bar code technology: a basic glossary of terms. *IMC Journal.* November/December 1988: 24(6), 16-17.

BROWN, Marlene. Image retrieval keeps PM in touch with public. *Government Computer News.* 9 October 1987: 6(20), 44, 48.

BROWN, Thomas Elton and William A. READER. Archival management of machine-readable records from database management systems: a technical leaflet. *Archival Informatics Newsletter.* Spring 1987: 1(1), 9-12.

BROWN, Thomas Elton. The evolution of an appraisal theory for automated records. *Archival Informatics Newsletter.* Fall 1987: 1(3), 49-51.

BROWN, Thomas Elton and Patricia ARONSSON. Government archivists and government automation: the odd couple. *Government Publications Review.* September/October 1986: 13(5), 561-570.

BROWN, Thomas Elton. Machine-readable: view. *Archival Informatics Newsletter.* Spring 1987: 1(1), 5-7.

BROWN, William E., Jr. and Lofton WILSON. The AMC format: a guide to the implementation process. *Provenance.* Fall 1987: 5(2), 27-36.

BUCKINGHAM, M. The knowledge warehouse: technical issues. *The Electronic Library.* February 1988: 6, 6-9.

Buying a microcomputer. *Records and Retrieval Report.* December 1986: 2(10), 11-12.

CALMES, Alan. *Preservation of permanently valuable information on paper, film, tape and disk.* Washington, D.C.: National Archives and Records Administration, 1987. 8 p.

CAMPBELL, T.M. "Archives and Information Management — Ships passing in the right". IN Proceedings: Conference of the Association of Canadian Archivists (1987: McMaster University). Hamilton, Ont., 1987. 5 p.

CANNING, Bonnie. Backup and redundancy for automated records systems. *Administrative Management.* September 1987: 48(9), 41.

CANNING, Bonnie. Les disques optiques au bureau. *IMC Journal.* 1987: 23(5), 11-12.

CANNING, Bonnie. Optical disk systems: pros and cons. *Administrative Management.* March 1987: 48(3), 51.

CANNING, Bonnie. Optical disks in the office. *IMC Journal.* 1987: 23(5), 9-10.

CANNING, Bonnie. Records automation: careers in records automation. *Administrative Management.* November 1987: 48(11), 39.

CANNING, Bonnie. Technology marches on. *Administrative Management.* January 1987: 48(1), 55.

CARGILL, Jennifer. Paying attention to basics: selecting micro-computer hardware and software, part I. *Technicalities.* October 1987: 8-10.

CASURELLA, Joseph. Document management software. *AIIM Conference Daily.* April 28, 1987: 5, 20.

Le Centre des archives contemporaines des Archives nationales; l'accès au contenu: la base Priam 3. *La Gazette des archives.* 1988: (141), 79-84.

CHARTRAND, Robert Lee. Glossary of selected terms of key information technologies. *Special Libraries.* Spring 1987: 78(2), 86-87.

CINNAMON, Barry. Optical disk applications. *IMC Journal.* July/August 1988: 24(4), 19-22.

CITARELLA, Judith and Lynne LEAHY. Integrated CAR takes charge at Barclay's Bank. *INFORM: the Magazine of Information and Image Management.* July 1987: 1(7), 26-28.

CLITES, Lorraine and William TUTTLE. Industrial document management: an optical system. *INFORM: the Magazine of Information and Image Management.* August 1987: 1(8), 30-33.

CLOUD, Patricia D. Fitting in: the automation of the archives at Northwestern University. *Provenance.* Fall 1987: 5(2), 14-26.

CLOUD, Patricia D. RLIN, AMC, and retrospective conversion: a case study. *The Midwestern Archivist.* 1986: 11(2), 125-134.

COLES, Laura Millar. A.B.C.A. MARC workshop. *ABCA Newsletter.* Summer 1988: 14(1), 1, 5 .

Computer-assisted retrieval (CAR) systems. *Records and Retrieval Report.* December 1986: 1(10), 149-158.

Computer indexing at the National Archives and Records Administration. *Library Hi Tech News.* September 1988: (52), 5.

Computer software for records management. *Records and Retrieval Report.* January 1986: 2(1), 1-14.

Computer software for records management — part II. *Records and Retrieval Report.* February 1986: 2(2), 1-6.

Computerized records management software. *Records and Retrieval Report.* May 1987: 3(6), 5-8.

Converting to an automated system. *Records and Retrieval Report.* May 1987: 3(6), 5-8.

COOK, Michael. *Archives and the computer.* London: Butterworths, 1986. 170 p.

COOK, Michael. International survey of automated applications in archival management. *ADPA.* 1986: 5(2), 53-67.

COOK, Michael. *An introduction to archival automation: a RAMP study with guidelines.* Rev. Paris: Unesco, 1986. 45 p. (PGI-86/WS/15)

COONEY, James P. What is information really worth? *Canadian Library Journal.* October 1987: 44(5), 293-297.

CORTISSOZ, Anne. Telco transition. *INFORM: the Magazine of Information and Image Management.* March 1987: 1(3), 14-18.

CRAVEN, Paul Taylor. Optical records management: application development in action. *INFORM: the Magazine of Information and Image Management.* February 1987: 1(2), 35-39.

CUNNINGHAM, Roger B. Microcomputer-based CAR system increases electronic filing flexibility. *Micro-notes.* Winter 1986: 15(1), 12, 22.

DAVIS, Douglas L. Optical archiving: where are we now and where do we go from here? *Optical Information Systems.* January/February 1987: 7(1), 66-71.

DESMARAIS, Norman. Information management on a compact silver disc. *Optical Information Systems.* May/June 1987: 7(3), 193-204.

DICKEY, Sam. New directions in micrographics. *Today's Office.* August 1987: 22(3), 34-38.

DOLLAR, Charles M. *Electronic records management and archives in international organizations: a RAMP study with guidelines.* Paris: UNESCO, 1986. 159 p. (PGI-86/WS/12)

Don't stuff your backup tapes in a box and stash them in a cave. *Infosystems.* August 1987: 34(8), 18.

DOOLEY, Jackie M. An introduction to authority control for archivists. *Archival Informatics Technical Report.* Summer 1988: 2(2), 5-20.

DUCROT, Marie-Odile. La place de l'informatique aux archives. *La Gazette des archives.* 1988: (141), 97-100.

DUKE, David. Electronic records: access documents instantly. *Administrative Management.* October 1987: 48(10), 28-32.

DURR, Theodore W. At the creation: chaos, control, and automation-commercial software development for archives.

Library Trends. Winter 1988: 36(3), 593-607.

Een kritische doorlichting van de huidige methoden tot ontsluiting van archieven; handelingen van de studiedag ingericht door de Sectie Archief van de VVBAD te Brussel op 18 april 1986 [A critical view on actual finding aids at archives; proceedings of the colloquy of the Archives Section of the VVBAD, Brussels, April 18, 1986]. *Bibliotheek-en Archiefgids.* May 1987: (63), 101-144.

EFIMENKO, R.N. et V.N. KOUZELEN-KOV. Le système automatisé de l'information scientifique et technique pour les documents du Fonds d'Archives d'État: l'organisation de l'exécution des demandes [en russe]. *Sovietskje Arkhivy.* 1987: (2), 82-84.

ENDELMAN, Judith E. Software for the archives. [MARCON, Cactus, Micro MARC: AMC, dBase III Plus]. *MAC Newsletter.* January 1988: 15(3), 9/10.

ENSMAN, Richard G. Paper free, not paperless. *Modern Office Technology.* April 1987: 32(4), 56, 58, 60.

FABREGUETTES, Catherine. L'ABC du CD: où en est le CD-ROM? *Bulletin des bibliothèques de France.* 1987: 32(2), [150]-159.

FELDHAUSEN, Mark. Microfilm retrieval enhanced by CAR. *INFORM: the Magazine of Information and Image Management.* October 1987: 1(10), 40.

Financial markets: Filenet automates the flow. *INFORM: the Magazine of Information and Image Management.* July 1987: 1(7), 22-25.

FINLAY, Douglas. Archives: old records meet new technologies. *Administrative Management.* December 1986: 37-40.

FISHBEIN, Meyer H. Reflections of the impact of automation on archives. *Archives et bibliothèques de Belgique.* 1986: 57(1/2), 159-172.

FLEIG, Clare. "Managing records" has new meaning. *Government Computer News.* 9 October 1987: 6(20), 38.

FLUBACHER, F. Shirley. Old-line bank's approach to new records management. *The Office.* December 1987: 106(6), 15-19.

FLUTY, Steve. Growth management: American Express goes the distance. *INFORM: the Magazine of Information and Image Management.* January 1987: 1(1), 34-36.

FLUTY, Steve. Online reduction innovation at Chemical Bank. *INFORM: the Magazine of Information and Image Management.* July 1987: 1(7), 6-7.

FLUTY, Steve. Streamlining the flow: information management at CBS. *INFORM: the Magazine of Information and Image Management.* January 1987: 1(1), 32-33, 45-46.

FONNES, Ivar. Seminar for edb-medarbeidere i de nordiske riksarkiver [Seminar for computer officers in the Nordic National Archives]. *Nordisk Arkivnyt.* 1986: 31(2), 45-47.

FRANZ, Eckhart G. Zwischen Tradition und Innovation: die Arbeit des Archivars heuteund morgen [Between tradition and innovation: the archivist's work today and tomorrow]. *Archivar.* February 1986: 39(1), 19-26.

FRASE, H. Michael. Videomicrographics: multi-media image management. *INFORM: the Magazine of Information and Image Management.* April 1987: 1(4), 26-29.

FRUSCIONE, James J. A managerial framework for machine-readable data management. *Records Management Quarterly.* July 1986: 20(3), 3-9.

FRUSCIONE, James J. The offline factor: information storage and security. *INFORM: the Magazine of Information and Image Management.* June 1987: 1(6), 20-23.

The Future is in automation. *Records and Retrieval Report*. May 1987: 3(6), 1-4.

GILDEMEISTER, Glen A. Automation, reference, and the small repository, 1967-1997. *The Midwestern Archivist*. 1988: 13(1), 5-15.

GILLILAND, Anne J. Automating intellectual access to archives [special issue]. *Library Trends*. Winter 1988: 36(3), 495-623.

GILLILAND, Anne J. The development of automated archival systems: planning and managing change. *Library Trends*. Winter 1988: 36(3), 519-537.

GILMORE, Matthew B. Increasing access to archival records in library online public access catalogs. *Library Trends*. Winter 1988: 36(3), 609-623.

GONZALEZ, Pedro. *Des salles de lecture sans papier?* Congrès international des archives (11e: 1988: Paris). Paris, 1988. 4 p.

GRECO, Edgar J. Microfilm will help bridge technologies of integrated systems, artificial intelligence. *IMC Journal*. 1987: 23(1), 21-22.

GRIGSBY, Mason. The integration and use of write-once optical information systems automation (DDA) right decision. *IMC Journal*. 1987: 23(4), 9-13.

GRIGSBY, Mason. Write-one optical disk systems in the automated office. *Records Management Quarterly*. July 1986: 20(3), 30-34.

HAMILTON, Angela. Solving a diskette dilemna. *Records Management Quarterly*. April 1986: 20(2), 28-29, 52.

HAWORTH, Kent M. Putting the cart before the horse: automation and descriptive standards for archives. *ABCA Newsletter*. Winter 1987: 13(3), 6-7.

HELGERSON, Linda W. *Introduction to optical technology*. Silver Spring, Md.: Association for Information and Image Management, 1987. iii, 44 p.

HELGERSON, Linda W. Optical storage peripherals: the right format. *INFORM: the Magazine of Information and Image Management*. February 1987: 1(2), 14-16, 18-19.

HEREDIA HERRERA, Antonia. Archivos e informatica: un proyecto de mecnizacion documental en Espana [Archives and information science: a project for automated documentation in Spain]. *Information Development*. April 1988: 4(2), 91-93.

HESSLER, David. Info Station: a low-cost electronic document storage, retrieval and transmission system. *Library Hi-Tech*. Spring 1987: 81-86.

HICKERSON, H. Thomas. Archival information exchange and the role of bibliographic networks. *Library Trends*. Winter 1988: 36(3), 553-571.

HIGGINS, Kevin B. Optical disk and micrographic document management system. *Micro-notes*. September 1986: 14(3), 5-6.

HIRTLE, Peter B. Artificial intelligence, expert systems, and archival automation. *Provenance*. Spring 1987: 5(1), 76-88.

HIVES, Christopher L. and Laurenda DANIELLS. The computer/archives interface: getting started. *ABCA Newsletter*. Winter 1987: 12(5), 6-8.

HOBBS, Brenda. "Automating the life-cycle — a municipal perspective". IN Proceedings: Conference of the Association of Canadian Archivists (1987: McMaster University). Hamilton, Ont., 1987. 7 p.

HONHART, Frederick L. The application of microcomputer-based local systems with the MARC AMC format. *Library Trends*. Winter 1988: 36(3), 585-592.

HOOTEN, Bill. Archiving the archives. *Computerworld*. 24 August 1987: 21(34), 63.

HOPKINS, Mark. Computerizing a government records archives — The FEDDOC Experience. *Records Management Quarterly*. July 1986: 20(3), 36-39.

HUNTER, Gregory S. Microcomputing and micrographic control. *INFORM: the Magazine of Information and Image Management.* October 1987: 1(10), 22-23.

HUSSEY, Harold E. COM for the Pepsi generation. *AIIM Conference Daily.* April 28, 1987: 10, 31.

Image computer enhances records management. *Modern Office Technology.* August 1987: 32(8), 28.

IMPRESSION: document archival and retrieval system. *Library Hi Tech News.* November 1988: (54), 16.

Information management sourcebook. Silver Spring, M.D.: Association for Information and Image Management, 1987. 430 p.

L'informatique au service des fonds clos: réflexions à partir des expériences faites aux Archives nationales. *La Gazette des archives.* 1988: (141), 118-127.

INGEBRETSEN, Dorothy L. Information management software: a selected bibliography. *Database.* December 1987: 27-34.

Is the future of records on cards? *Records and Retrieval Report.* February 1987: 3(2), 12-15.

JANELLI, Harvey. Evolving information management. *INFORM: the Magazine of Information and Image Management.* May 1987: 1(5), 28-31, 33.

JOHNSON, Don S. Creeping towards the paperless office. *Administrative Management.* October 1987: 48(10), 5.

JOHNSTON, R.E. (Bob). Standard threats. *Infosystems.* July 1987: 34(7), 35.

KAEBNICK, Gregory. Microfilm and the Benedictine tradition: Hill Monastic Manuscript Library preserves the past. *INFORM: the Magazine of Information and Image Management.* October 1987: 1(10), 34-35.

KALTHOFF, Robert J. 1987: industry leaders on the outlook for digital document automation (DDA) right decision. *IMC Journal.* 1987: 23(4), 15-19.

KATZ, Richard N. and Victoria A. DAVIS. The impact of automation on our corporate memory. *Records Management Quarterly.* January 1986: 20(1), 10-14.

LACY, John A. The future of document management: the "fourth stage" and beyond. *AIIM Conference Daily.* April 30, 1987: 5, 14, 16.

LANCASTER, Wilfrid. *Vocabulary control for information retrieval.* Arlington, Va.: Information Resources Press, 1986. 270 p.

LANGEMO, Mark. Major trends in the managing of records. *Office.* January 1987: 105(1), 65.

The Leading edge of CALS. *INFORM: the Magazine of Information and Image Management.* September 1987: 1(9), 30.

LEGARE, Jacques and Louise PELLETIER. "Computer use in an Historical demography research". IN Proceedings: Conference of the Association of Canadian Archivists (1987: McMaster University). Hamilton, Ont., 1987. 13 p.

LI-KUEI, Hsueh. Perspectives in archives management automation [in Chinese]. *Journal of Educational Media & Library Sciences.* Winter 1986: 23(2), 187-204.

LINDER, C.E. (Ted). COM services offer records-keeping alternative. *Micro-notes.* Spring 1987: 15(2), 13.

LUNDGREN, Terry D. and Carol A. LUNDGREN. Introduction to computer-based records management systems. *Records Management Quarterly.* July 1987: 21(3), 31-34.

LYNCH, Clifford A. and Edwin B. BROWNRIGG. Conservation, preservation and digitization. *College and Research Libraries News.* July 1986: 47(4), 379-382.

LYNCH, Clifford A. Optical storage media, standards and technology life-cycle management. *Records Management Quarterly.* January 1986: 20(1), 44-54.

MACHOVEC, George S. Automating archives: choices with new information technology. *Library Hi Tech News.* May 1986: 4(5), 1-3.

MACLEOD, A. and A.R. REUBER. The Array model: conceptual modeling approach to document retrieval. *Journal of the American Society for Information Science.* May 1987: 162-170.

A Major utility builds automated records center. *Office.* March 1987: 105(3), 88-94.

MAROTEAUX, Vincent. Informatique et archives contemporaines, une approche nouvelle. *La Gazette des archives.* 1987: (137-138), 144-149.

MARTIN, Craig. Video technology in the computer industry. *International Journal of Micrographics and Video Technology.* 1986: 15(3/4), 185-198.

MATTERS, Marion. Authority files in an archival setting. *Archival Informatics Technical Report.* Summer 1988: 2(2), 29-34.

MENKUS, Belden. Records managers fail to meet MIS challenge. *Journal of Systems Management.* August 1987: 38(8), 36-37.

MENNE-HARITZ, A. Microcomputers in archives: requirements and consequences. IN The application of micro-computers in information, documentation and libraries. Amsterdam: North-Holland, 1987: 684-689.

MICHELS, Fredrick and Terry LOVE-GROVE. PC Corner: MicroMARC: AMC. *Library Hi Tech News.* March 1988: (47), 14-15.

MICHELSON, Avra. Description and reference in the age of automation. *The American Archivist.* Spring 1987: 50(2), 192-208.

Microfilm or optical disc: choose the system. *The Office.* October 1987: 106(4), 130.

Micrographics at the Royal Bank. *Micronotes.* September 1986: 14(3), 10-11.

MicroMARC: AMC — Microcomputer bibliographic control for manuscripts and archives. *Information Intelligence Online Libraries and Microcomputers.* September 1986: 4(8-9), 11.

MORAN, Robert. Courting midrange calamities. *Computer & Communications Decisions.* August 1987: 19(11), 69-72, 74-76.

MOSELEY, Eva. Sharing archives of women's organizations. *SAA Newsletter.* July 1988: 9.

MOTZ, Arlene. Applying records management principles to magnetic media. *Records Management Quarterly.* April 1986: 20(2), 22-26.

New document processing system boosting productivity at NEC American, Inc. *IMC Journal.* 1987: 23(3), 49-50.

NIKOLAISON, Ray. Two directions in the future of micrographics. *The Office.* October 1987: 106(4), 54, 56.

NOBLE, Richard A. The NHPRC Data Base Project: building the "Interstate Highway System". *The American Archivist.* Winter/Spring 1988: 51(1/2), 98-105.

NORBERG, Erik. ADP and archives in the Swedish Armed Forces. *ADPA.* 1986: 5(2), 43-52.

NOVINGER, Walter B. Optical storage: a conversion perspective. *INFORM: the Magazine of Information and Image Management.* September 1987: 1(9), 22-23.

Optical character recognition. *Records and Retrieval Report.* February 1987: 3(2), 1-11.

Optical disk may preserve millions of National Archives documents. *Infosystems.* July 1987: 34(7), 14.

An Optical disk primer. *Records and Retrieval Report.* October 1987: 3(8), 1-16.

Optical disk systems. *Records and Retrieval Report.* January 1987: 3(1), 1-15.

ORBELL, John. The introduction of a computer modern records control system at Barings Merchant Bank. *Business Archives.* May 1988: (55), 29-37.

OSTERLUND, Steve. Optical archiving systems. *DEC Professional.* June 1987: 7(7), 66-69, 72.

OTTEN, Klaus. *Integrated document and image management.* Silver Spring, Md.: Association for Information and Image Management, 1987. 66 p.

PERRON-CROTEAU, Lise. Aide et entraide — Les Archives appuient de façon concrète la collectivité archivistique. *L'Archiviste.* Janvier/février 1988: 15(1), 16-17.

PERRON-CROTEAU, Lise. NA support to the Canadian Archival Community. *The Archivist.* January/February 1988: 15(1), 16-17.

PERRY, Meg Woollen. An inside look at a LAW data archive system. *Byte.* July 1987: 169-170, 172-176.

PFEIFFER, Ken. The paper challenge and progressive records management. *INFORM: the Magazine of Information and Image Management.* April 1987: 1(4), 18-20, 24, 44.

PHILLIPS, Trudy M. Managing choice: single and multivendor options. *INFORM: the Magazine of Information and Image Management.* January 1987: 1(1), 20-23.

PINEAU, Guy. L'Europe des programmes. *Dossiers de l'audiovisuel.* Mai/juin 1987: 13, 13-54.

PLAYOUST, Arlette. L'informatisation des archives contemporaines: bilan d'expériences et propositions. *La Gazette des archives.* 1988: (141), 101-117.

POOR, William E. Docu/Master information retrieval system. *Special Libraries.* Summer 1987: 78(3), 170-176.

The Quiet Revolution: managing New York's local government records in the information age. Albany: N.Y. State Archives and Records Administration, 1988.

RASCH, M. Uberlegungen zu Aufbau und Organisation eines DV-Programmes für das Archiv-dargestellt an, Archibald [Reflections on construction and organization of the computer program, Archibald, designed for archives]. *Nachrichten für Dokumentation.* April 1988: 39, 87-92.

The Real revolution in office automation. *Records and Retrieval Report.* April 1987: 3(4), 1-3.

Records retention schedules. *Records and Retrieval Report.* April 1987: 3(4), 4-14.

Retrieval terminals will be a key component in microfilm access systems of the future. *AIIM Conference Daily.* April 30, 1987: 16.

RICHARDSON, Lee D. Retention of engineering documentation. *IMC Journal.* 1987: 23(3), 46-48.

RODRIGUEZ, Manuel and Jeffrey C. SCHOWEN. System management from start to finish. *INFORM: the Magazine of Information and Image Management.* January 1987: 1(1), 26-31, 45-46.

ROWH, Mark C. Records management systems are better than ever before. *The Office.* October 1987: 106(4), 92-93.

RUMSCHOETTEL, Hermann. Der 57. Deutsche Archivtag 1985 in Hannover: Vortraege Berichte, Referate-Rationalisierung im Archivwesen-Moeglichkeiten und Grenzen [The 57th German Archive Conference 1985 in Hanover: lectures, reports, talks-rationalisation in archives-possibilities and limitations. *Archivar.* February 1986: 39(1), 5-20.

SAERGEL, Dagobert. Organizing information: principles of data base and retrieval systems. *Journal of Academic Librarianship.* May 1987: 105-106.

SAFFADY, William. Optical disks: an overview. *AIIM Conference Daily.* April 29, 1987: 10, 20, 30.

SAFFADY, William. *Optical disks for data and document storage.* Westport, Ct.: Meckler, 1986. 94 p.

SAVIERS, Shannon Smith. Reflections on CD-ROM: bridging the gap between technology and purpose. *Special Libraries.* Fall 1987: 78(4), 288-294.

SBAITI, A.A. Archives automation at the Arab Fund for Economic and Social Development. *ADPA.* 1987: 5(3), 23-27.

SCALA, Bea. Telco conversion: from paper records to online information system. *INFORM: the Magazine of Information and Image Management.* March 1987: 1(3), 20-23.

SCELI, W. Clair. Document management systems today and tomorrow. *AIIM Conference Daily.* April 28, 1987: 5, 20.

SCELI, W. Clair. Micrographics and/or optical disk? Ideas to help you make the right decision. *IMC Journal.* 1987: 23(4), 44-49.

SCHOWEN, Jeffrey C. Information management: a matter of fact. *INFORM: the Magazine of Information and Image Management.* August 1987: 1(8), 18, 46.

SEC and GAO at odds on a "paperless" system. *Office.* January 1987: 105(1), 50.

SEIGLE, David C. Document image processing: breaking the productivity barrier in today's office microfilm images of engineering drawings. *IMC Journal.* 1987: 23(4), 55-57.

SHAW, Abigail. Integrating document storage: an end user's view. *INFORM: the Magazine of Information and Image Management.* May 1987: 1(5), 34-37.

SHERVINGTON, Christine. Automating records management. *Archives and Manuscripts.* November 1986: 14(2), 129-143.

SILBER, Sigmund. A case for electronic document interchange. *Infosystems.* January 1987: 34(1), 58.

SMELTZER, Dennis K. Producing a computerized media catalog. *Small Computers in Libraries.* September 1987: 7(8), 19-25.

SOAPES, Thomas F. Progress continues on PRESNET: the Presidential Library Information System. *SAA Newsletter.* March 1987: 12.

Solving the paper problem: an introduction to document processing. Sunnyvale, Calif.: Interfile, [1987?]. 8 p.

SPAULDING, George. An HMO chooses CAR. *IMC Journal.* 1987: 23(1), 31-33.

SPENCER, DON. "Information systems planning: the role of strategic data design". IN Proceedings: Conference of the Association of Canadian Archivists (1987: McMaster University). Hamilton, Ont., 1987. 6 p.

SPILKER, Chris. Medical imaging: merging picture archives and communications. *INFORM: the Magazine of Information and Image Management.* February 1987: 1(2), 24-27.

STILLGER, Josef. The German Patent Office and microfilm integrated retrieval. *INFORM: the Magazine of Information and Image Management.* November 1987: 1(11), 28-30, 43.

STOCKSLAGER, Todd. Office automation: cost justification or management? *Records Management Quarterly.* October 1987: 21(4), 15-19.

SZARY, Richard V. Technical requirements and prospects for authority control in the SIBIS-Archives databases. *Archival Informatics Technical Report.* Summer 1988: 2(2), 41-46.

TATEM, Jill M. and Jeffrey ROLLISON. *Thesaurus of university terms developed at Case Western Reserve University Archives.* Chicago: Society of American Archivists, 1986. 46 p.

TENER, Jean. "Automation and small archives". IN Proceedings: Conference of the Association of Canadian Archivists (1987: McMaster University). Hamilton, Ont., 1987. 5 p.

THIEME, B. and H. SMITH. Automating search and retrieval of patents in the U.S. Patent and Trademark Office. *Government Publications Review.* July/August 1986: 13, 431-449.

THOMA, G., [et al.]. Design consideration affecting throughput in an optical disk-based document storage system. IN ASIS' 87: Proceedings of the 50th ASIS annual meeting, Boston, Mass., Oct. 4-8, 1987. Medford, N.J.: Learned Information, 1987: 225-233.

TIMBERS, Michael J. Microfilm: information management mainstay at IHS. *INFORM: the Magazine of Information and Image Management*. June 1987: 1(6), 30-31.

TIMBERS, Michael J. We are working to solve the problems of paper. *Office*. January 1987: 105(1), 122.

TYNDALL, R.M., J.A. CLARKE and J. SHIMMINS. An automated procedure for determining patient numbers from episode of care records. *Medical Informatics*. April/June 1987: 12(2), 137-146.

U.S. Postal Service stores constituent letter files on optical disk. *IMC Journal*. July/August 1988: 24(4), 43-44.

USDIN, Steve. Like it or not, plan for a disaster recovery. *Office*. March 1987: 105(3), 90-92.

VAN DER SAAG, Bert J. Automatic data processing in a municipal record office: managing information by micro-computers using Ask Sam (the text based management system). *ADPA*. 1987: 5(3), 47-59.

Vendors of CAR systems. *Records and Retrieval Report*. December 1986: 1(10), 159-165.

Vendors of computer software for records management. *Records and Retrieval Report*. February 1986: 2(2), 7-15.

WALFORD, John, Henry GILLETT and J.B. POST. Introducing computers to the record office: theory and practice. *Journal of the Society of Archivists*. January 1988: 9(1), 21-29.

WALKER, Cathy. "Automating the life cycle at Ontario Hydro". IN Proceedings: Conference of the Association of Canadian Archivists (1987: McMaster University). Hamilton, Ont., 1987. 5 p.

WALTER, Gerry. An overview: technology and application status of optical disk systems. *IMC Journal*. July/August 1988: 24(4), 10-13.

WEBER, Lisa B. Archival automation: the MARC AMC format. *SAA Newsletter*. May 1987: 13.

WEBER, Lisa B. Automation survey results. *SAA Newsletter*. November 1987: 4-5.

WEBER, Lisa B. Status report on SAA's automated archival information program. *SAA Newsletter*. March 1987: 7.

WILKINSON, David G. Where is hardware taking information management? *IMC Journal*. 1987: 23(4), 35-38.

Will optical disks ever forget? *The Economist*. 28 September 1987: 9(39), 90-91.

WILLIAMS, Bernard. Optical disks at the Public Records Office. *Information Media & Technology*. September 1987: 20(5), 204-205.

WILLIAMSON, R. The knowledge warehouse: legal and commercial issues. *The Electronic Library*. February 1988: 6, 10-16.

WOLCHAK, William H. Conducting a systems analysis. *Records Management Quarterly*. July 1986: 20(3), 16-19.

WOOD, Lamont. Computer-assisted retrieval accesses microfilm. *Government Computer News*. 9 October 1987: 6(20), 56-57.

WOOLGAR, C.M. The Wellington papers database: an interim report. *Journal of the Society of Archivists*. January 1988: 9(1), 1-20.

YERBURGH, Mark. Studying all those "tiny little tea leaves": the future of microforms in a complex technological environment. *Microform Review*. Winter 1987: 16(1), 14-20.

ZAGAMI, Robert W. Record conversion to microfilm safe, stabilized procedure.

Administrative Management. July 1987: 48(7), 48.

ZAGAMI, Robert W. State-of-the-art report on micrographics and optical disks. *Administrative Management.* April 1987: 48(4), 24-29.

ZBORAY, Ronald J. dBASE III Plus and the MARC AMC format: problems and possibilities. *The American Archivist.* Spring 1987: 50(2), 210-225.

3.1 Cartographical archives / Archives cartographiques

Les archives d'architecture et d'urbanisme. *La Gazette des archives.* 1988: (141), 181-197.

BEECH, Geraldine. Cartography and the State: the British Land Registry Experience. *Journal of the Society of Archivists.* October 1988: 9(4), 190-196.

BERGEN, Kathleen. Hidden cartographic archives. *SLA. Geography & Map Division. Bulletin.* March 1986: 143, 15-28.

BOSSE, David. Cartographia Americana: the collections of the William L. Clements Library. *The Map Collector.* December 1986: 37, 10-18.

CHRISTIAN, Helen. A map collection to be sneezed at. *The Map Collector.* December 1986: 37, 28-29.

CRUSE, Larry. MIMI, the map and graphic information index to major microform sets. *Microform Review.* Fall 1986: 15(4), 224-227.

The Cumberland map collection from the Royal Library, Windsor Castle. *SLA. Geography & Map Division. Bulletin.* 1988: 153, 66-68.

HAGEN, Carlos B. Disaster planning analysis study: seismic dangers at the UCLA Map Library. *Western Association of Map Libraries. Information Bulletin.* March 1987: 18(2), 102-120.

HARTWIG, Robert. Archivorganisation von historischen Plaenen und Karten [Archive organisation of historical plans and maps]. *Scrinium.* 1986: (34), 168-174.

HILDESHEMEIR, Françoise. *The Processing of Architects' records a case study: France.* Paris: Unesco, 1987. 74 p. (PGI-86/WS/13)

HILDESHEIMER, Françoise. *Le traitement des archives des architectes: étude de cas: la France.* Paris: UNESCO, 1986. 85 p. (PGI-86/WS/13)

HODSON, Yolande. Prince William, royal map collector. *The Map Collector.* 1988: 44, 2-12.

HOOD, Annie. The map collection of William Wyndham Grenville. *The Map Collector.* March 1987: 38, 2-8.

HOSTE, Frans E. Ch. Maps and technical drawings in archives — special problems and special solutions. *LIBER Bulletin.* 1986: (28), 47-49.

HUDSON, Alice C. and Maude D. COLE. The cartographic treasures in the New York Public Library, Astor, Lennox and Tilden Foundations. *The Map Collector.* Summer 1988: 43, 2-10.

ISDALE, Les. Summap historical map collection. *The Globe.* 1988: 29, 34-37.

KIDD, Betty. Les collections de cartes au Canada: développement et coopération. *L'Archiviste.* Mai/juin 1987: 14(3), 16-18.

KIDD, Betty. Map collections in Canada: growth and co-operation. *The Archivist.* May/June 1987: 14(3), 16-18.

LAING, Josie. Maps or misfits. *Archifacts.* 1988: (2), 28-31.

LOVELL-SMITH, Brian. Notes on the Canterbury Museum Map Collection. *Archifacts.* 1988: (2), 31.

MACIEROWSKI, E.M. British naval geography in World War I: holdings in the Library of Congress. *SLA. Geography & Map Division. Bulletin.* March 1987: 147, 9-17.

MARLEY, Carol. The role of NCIP (National Collections Inventory Project). *Association of Canadian Map Libraries. Bulletin.* September 1986: 60, 1-7.

MARTIN-MERAS, Luisa. Cartographic materials in microform at the Museo Naval, Madrid. *Microform Review*. February 1988: 17(1), 14-16.

MATKOVIC, Ivan. The Zagreb national and university library map collection. *The Map Collector*. 1988: 44, 40-41.

MILLER, Rosana. The map collection, Arizona State University Library. *Western Association of Map Libraries. Information Bulletin*. March 1987: 18(2), 149-156.

MORRISON, Walter K. Manuscript maps from the Earl of Dalhousie's Library located at Dalhousie and Acadia Universities, in the Nova Scotia Museum, and in the National Archives of Canada. *Association of Canadian Map Libraries. Bulletin*. June 1987: 63, 1-11.

MURRAY, Jeffrey S. British-Canadian military cartography on the Western Front, 1914-1918. *Archivaria*. Summer 1988: (26), 52-65.

NAGY, Tom. New microfilm camera for maps. *The Archivist*. May/June 1988: 15(3), 21-22.

NAGY, Tom. Un nouvel appareil pour microphotographie. *L'Archiviste*. Mai/juin 1988: 15(3), 21-22.

NICHOLSON, Tim. The Ordnance Survey and Smaller Scale Military Maps of Britain 1854-1914. *The Cartographic Journal*. December 1988: 25(2), 109-127.

PASTOUREAU, Mireille. Maps at the Bibliothèque nationale: a collection of collections. *The Map Collector*. Autumn 1987: 40, 8-16.

PELLETIER, Monique. Geography for all: the founding of the department of maps and plans at the Bibliothèque nationale. *The Map Collector*. Autumn 1987: 40, 2-6.

PELLETIER, Monique and Jean-Marie ARNOULT. Reproduction on microfiche of the ancient cartographic holdings of the Bibliothèque nationale, Paris sets. *Microform Review*. Fall 1986: 15(4), 221-227.

PERKINS, C.R. Map libraries [bibliographical essay]. IN British librarianship and information work, 1981-1985. London: Library Association, 1988: 116-131.

PRESCOTT, Dorothy F. Education for map curatorship in Australia: a discussion paper. *The Globe*. 1988: 30, 14-22.

SHERWOOD, Arlyn. "Heinz 57 Varieties": a taste of Illinois State Document Maps. *Illinois Libraries*. September 1987: 69(7), 505.

SORRELL, Patrick. Optimal mapping and the determination of cartographic design principles. *The Cartographic Journal*. December 1988: 25(2), 128-138.

STONE, Jeffrey. The cartographic treasures of Aberdeen University Library. *The Map Collector*. September 1986: 36, 30-34.

SUTHERLAND, Johnnie D. Collection policies. *SLA. Geography & Map Division. Bulletin*. December 1985: 142, 2-11.

TURNER, James. Unrolling maps for flat storage. *Archivaria*. Winter 1987-1988: (25), 171-176.

3.1.1 Acquisition, selection, appraisal and evaluation / Acquisition, sélection et évaluation historique et monétaire

DAHL, Edward H. Earliest printed map bearing the name "Canada" now at Archives. *The Archivist*. September/October 1988: 15(5), 13.

DAHL, Edward H. Un trésor national aux Archives. *L'Archiviste*. Septembre/octobre 1988: 15(5), 13.

ISAAC, Glen. *The arrangement, description, and appraisal of archival map series*. [Vancouver]: Association of British Columbia Archivists, c1988. 7 p. (A.B.C.A. publications; no. 2)

KISTNER, Hans-Juergen and Ruediger OSTERMANN. Zur Aufbereitung historischer Archivdaten mit statistischen Methoden am Beispiel der Stadt Kamen [Handling and analysing of historical archive data by means of statistical methods — some examples of the city of Kamen]. *Archivar*. February 1987: 40(1), 87-94.

LARSGAARD, Mary Lynette. *Map librarianship: an introduction*. 2nd ed. Littleton, Colo.: Libraries Unlimited, 1987. xxvii, 382 p.

MCGING, Angela and Anne PICOT. The conservation of building plans project. *Archives and Manuscripts*. November 1988: 16(2), 97-118.

SCADDEN, Ken. Maps-mainstream or misfits. *Archifacts*. 1988: (2), 32-34.

SCHROCK, Nancy Carlson. Images of New England: documenting the built environment. *The American Archivist*. Fall 1987: 50(4), 474-498.

VAN DEN BROECKE, Marcel P.R. How rare is a map and the atlas it comes from? Facts and speculations on production and survival of Ortelius Theatrum Orbis Terrarum and its maps. *The Map Collector*. September 1986: 36, 2-12.

3.1.2 Arrangement / Classement

DODGE, Bernadine. The Application of INMAGIC in a University Archive. *Association of Canadian Map Libraries and Archives. Bulletin*. September 1988: 68, 1-5.

GERENCHER, Joseph J. An inexpensive horizontal map storage facility. *SLA. Geography & Map Division. Bulletin*. September 1985: 141, 2-6.

HILDESHEMEIR, Françoise. *The Processing of Architects' records a case study: France*. Paris: Unesco, 1987. 74 p. (PGI-86/WS/13)

ISAAC, Glen. *The arrangement, description, and appraisal of archival map series*. [Vancouver]: Association of British Columbia Archivists, c1988. 7 p. (A.B.C.A. publications; no. 2)

LARSGAARD, Mary Lynette. *Map librarianship: an introduction*. 2nd ed. Littleton, Colo.: Libraries Unlimited, 1987. xxvii, 382 p.

MACDONALD, Kirk and Lori COLLINS. All adrift about Oceanic mapping: the problems of using the Library of Congress classification with Oceanic and Coastal zone mapping. *Association of Canadian Map Libraries and Archives. Bulletin*. December 1987: 65, 5-12.

MORRIS, Barbara. CARTO-NET: graphic retrieval and management in an automated map library. *SLA. Geography & Map Division. Bulletin*. June 1988: (152), 19-35.

S.L.A. GEOGRAPHY AND MAP DIVISION. COMMITTEE ON STANDARDS. Draft standards for university map collections. *SLA. Geography & Map Division. Bulletin*. March 1986: 143, 7-14.

SCADDEN, Ken. Maps — mainstream or misfits. *Archifacts*. 1988: (2), 32-34.

SUTHERLAND, Johnnie D. Map librarianship the old fashion way-book format. *SLA. Geography & Map Division. Bulletin*. September 1985: 141, 7-11.

TURNER, James. Unrolling maps for flat storage. *Archivaria*. Winter 1987-1988: (25), 171-176.

3.1.3 Description and finding aids / Description et instruments de recherche

HEALEY, Richard and Barbara MORRIS. CARTO-NET: a relational database approach to automated map cataloguing. *The Cartographic Journal*. June 1987: 24(1), 15-18.

ISAAC, Glen. *The arrangement, description, and appraisal of archival map series*. [Vancouver]: Association of British Columbia Archivists, c1988. 7 p. (A.B.C.A. publications; no. 2)

LARSGAARD, Mary Lynette. Map cataloging from an American perspective. *Association of Canadian Map Libraries. Bulletin*. December 1986: 61, 9-18.

LARSGAARD, Mary Lynette. *Map librarianship: an introduction*. 2nd ed. Littleton, Colo.: Libraries Unlimited, 1987. xxvii, 382 p.

S.L.A. GEOGRAPHY AND MAP DIVISION. COMMITTEE ON STANDARDS. Draft standards for university map collections. *SLA. Geography & Map Division. Bulletin.* March 1986: 143, 7-14.

SCADDEN, Ken. Maps — mainstream or misfits. *Archifacts.* 1988: (2), 32-34.

SCHREIBER, Robert E. Defining map areas in cartographic cataloging. *Western Association of Map Libraries. Information Bulletin.* November 1986: 18(1), 29-34.

STUDWELL, William E. Inconsistency in LC policy for some place names as subjects, a problem for map catalogers. *Western Association of Map Libraries. Information Bulletin.* June 1986: 17(3), 233-234.

STUDWELL, William E. Map libraries and a subject heading code. *Western Association of Map Libraries. Information Bulletin.* March 1987: 18(2), 157-159.

WATT, I. and Thomas Elton BROWN. Using computers to catalogue map collections (Part 2). *The Cartographic Journal.* June 1987: 24(1), 50-52.

3.1.4 Public service / Service au public

CLARKE, Keith C. Geographica information systems. *SLA. Geography & Map Division. Bulletin.* December 1985: 142, 12-17.

WALSH, Jim. The four editions of Map Collections in the United States and Canada: a comparison. *SLA. Geography & Map Division. Bulletin.* June 1986: 144, 16-27.

WILSON, Pam. Archives and architectural history. *Archifacts.* 1988: (2), 47-52.

3.1.4.1 Reference and research / Référence et recherche

ARCHIVES NATIONALES DU CANADA. *Au-delà de l'écrit: actualités filmées et reportages radio et télé diffusés au Canada.* Ottawa: Les Archives, 1988. 348 p.

BAIRD, Dennis. Life after Michelin. *SLA. Geography & Map Division. Bulletin.* March 1987: 147, 3-8.

BALOGUN, Olayinka Y. The directorate of overseas surveys and mapping in Nigeria. *The Cartographic Journal.* June 1987: 24(1), 3-14.

BARTZ PETCHENIK, Barbara. Fundamental considerations about atlases for children. *Cartographica.* Spring 1987: 24(1), 16-23.

BOSSE, David. Who was Hurricane Tom? *The Map Collector.* 1988: 44, 26-28.

BOUD, R.C. Institutional and individual influence on Scottish geological maps. *The Cartographic Journal.* June 1988: 25(1), 5-19.

BRANNON, Garry. Some observations on map and book publishing in early America. *The Cartographic Journal.* December 1987: 24(2), 159-162.

BROOKE-SMITH, Peter. Geographic information systems — is this the end of the map? *The Globe.* 1987: 27, 48-70.

BROWN, Thomas Elton. Machine readable views. *Archival Informatics Newsletter.* Spring 1988: 2(1), 5-6.

CARSWELL, R.J.B. and G.J.A. LEEUW. Curriculum relationships and children's atlases. *Cartographica.* Spring 1987: 24(1), 135-145.

CASTNER, Henry W. Education through mapping / a new role for the school atlas? *Cartographica.* Spring 1987: 24(1), 82-100.

COOPER, B.J. Early geological mapping in South Australia. *The Globe.* 1987: 27, 11-33.

COOPER, Graham H. The impact of LIS on the production and use of urban mapping. *The Globe.* 1988: 30, 42-49.

CROTTS, Joe. An index to the Defense Mapping Agency — Army Map Service depository catalogs. Supplement, 1977-1987. *Western Association of Map*

Libraries. Information Bulletin. November 1987: 19(1), 51-52.

DAHL, Edward H. "The Veriest Rubbish": an example of cartographic records management at the Royal Engineers Office, Kingston, 1862. *Association of Canadian Map Libraries and Archives. Bulletin.* March 1988: 66, 9-10.

DAVID, Andrew C.F. James Cook's sailing directions for Nova Scotia (Including present-day New Brunswick), Newfoundland and the St. Lawrence River: a preliminary study. *Association of Canadian Map Libraries and Archives. Bulletin.* March 1988: 66, 1-7.

DEMPSEY, Patrick E. Irish maps: a catalog of maps, atlases and charts. *SLA. Geography & Map Division. Bulletin.* December 1985: 142, 36-41.

DOLL, John G. Cloth maps of World War II. *Western Association of Map Libraries. Information Bulletin.* 1988: 20(1), 23-35.

ERLING, Paul A. The first printed map of the Swedish Colony on the Delaware. *The Map Collector.* Spring 1988: 42, 39.

FINLAYSON, Brian. The impact of an explorer's map. *The Globe.* 1987: 27, 1-10.

FRY, Caroline M. Maps for the physically disabled. *The Cartographic Journal.* June 1988: 25(1), 20-28.

GALE, Fay. Art as a cartographic form. *The Globe.* 1986: 26, 32-41.

GERBER, Rodney. A form-function analysis of school atlases. *Cartographica.* Spring 1987: 24(1), 146-159.

GODLEWSKA, Anne. The Napoleonic Survey of Egypt: a masterpiece of cartographic compilation and early-nineteenth century fieldwork. *Cartographica.* 1988: 25(1,2), 1-171.

GOLE, Susan. An early atlas of Asia. *The Map Collector.* 1988: 45, 20-26.

HAILS, John R. Beneath the surface — pitfalls in hydrographic mapping. *The Globe.* 1988: 30, 50-60.

HARDING, Kathy. The national atlas of Canada fifth edition: format, scale and distribution. *Association of Canadian Map Libraries and Archives. Bulletin.* December 1987: 65, 13-14.

HECKROTTE, Warren. Aaron Arrowsmith's map of North American and the Lewis and Clark Expedition. *The Map Collector.* Summer 1987: 39, 16-20.

HEIDENREICH, Conrad E. An analysis of the 17th century map Novvelle France. *Cartographica.* 1988: 25(3), 67-111.

HERBERT, Francis. A cartobibliography (with locations of copies) of the Arrowsmith/Stanford North Pole Map, 1818-1937. *Association of Canadian Map Libraries. Bulletin.* March 1987: 62, 1-16.

HOOKER, Brian. The French contribution to early printed charts of New Zealand — Part 2. *The Map Collector.* 1988: 44, 30-38.

KAY, Terry. Helen M. Wallis: a bibliography of published works. *The Map Collector.* Autumn 1987: 40, 30-38.

LAMPRECHT, Sandra J. The geography librarian and online information retrieval. *SLA. Geography & Map Division. Bulletin.* March 1986: 143, 2-6.

LAMPRECHT, Sandra J. The Vinland map: a selected bibliography. *SLA. Geography & Map Division. Bulletin.* June 1988: (152), 2-9.

LARSGAARD, Mary Lynette and Alice CARLBERGER. Alphabetical index to geological maps of Colorado. *Western Association of Map Libraries. Information Bulletin.* November 1987: 19(1), 8-29.

LARSGAARD, Mary Lynette. *Map librarianship: an introduction.* 2nd ed. Littleton, Colo.: Libraries Unlimited, 1987. xxvii, 382 p.

LEUNG, C.K. The Population Atlas of China: a preview. *Cartographica.* 1987: 24(3), 23-32.

LLOYD, Robert and Patricia GILMARTIN. The South Caroline coastline on historical maps: a cartometric analysis. *The*

Cartographic Journal. June 1987: 24(1), 19-26.

LUCEY, C.J. Maps and mining. *The Globe.* 1987: 28, 32-36.

MACEACHREN, Alan M. and Gregory JOHNSON. The evolution, application and implications of strip format travel maps. *The Cartographic Journal.* December 1987: 24(2), 147-158.

MCMINN, Stuart. Mapping of Arabia: real or imagined. *The Map Collector.* December 1986: 37, 36-40.

MALING, Derek. Maps for mountaineers. *The Cartographic Journal.* June 1988: 25(1), 29-36.

MARCOTTE, Louise and Yves TESSIER. Applied research and instructional atlas design/the "Ten Commandments" of L'Interatlas. *Cartographica.* Spring 1987: 24(1), 101-117.

MARLEY, Carol. McGill University's 'Nova Francia'. *Association of Canadian Map Libraries and Archives. Bulletin.* June 1988: 67.

MODELSKI, Andrew M. Preliminary chronology of the naming of America on maps. *SLA. Geography & Map Division. Bulletin.* June 1986: 144, 40-42.

MORRISON, Walter K. The Porcupine map. *Association of Canadian Map Libraries. Bulletin.* March 1987: 62, 18.

MURRAY, Jeffrey S. British-Canadian military cartography on the Western Front, 1914-1918. *Archivaria.* Summer 1988: (26), 52-65.

MURRAY, Jeffrey S. The map is the message. *The Geographical Magazine.* May 1987: 59(5), 237-241.

NATIONAL ARCHIVES OF CANADA. *Beyond the printed word: newsreel and broadcast reporting in Canada.* Ottawa: The Archives, 1988. 348 p.

NOGA, Michael Mark. Index to geologic maps of Hawaii, by USGS Topographic Quadrangle Name, 1883-1986. *Western*

Association of Map Libraries. Information Bulletin. 1988: 19(2), 64.

PICKLES, John. Bibliography on propaganda maps. *SLA. Geography & Map Division. Bulletin.* December 1986: 146, 2-7.

POST, J.B. Maps for genealogists. *SLA. Geography & Map Division. Bulletin.* March 1986: 143, 29-32.

POTTER-MEDWELL, M.R.R. The early pastoral plans of South Australia. *The Globe.* 1987: 27, 34-37.

RANDHAWA, Bikkar S. Atlases for children/a legacy of perceptual and cognitive processes. *Cartographica.* Spring 1987: 24(1), 47-60.

ROSTECKI, Randy R. The Canadian Chicago. *SLA. Geography & Map Division. Bulletin.* December 1985: 142, 30-35.

ROWLAND, John and Trevor EGAN. Geological mapping — historical aspects. *The Globe.* 1987: 28, 51-58.

SABLE, Martin H. The Northwest ordinance of 1787: an interdisciplinary bibliography. *SLA. Geography & Map Division. Bulletin.* September 1987: 149, 16-43.

SANDFORD, Herbert A. The state of canadian children's atlases from a European perspective. *Cartographica.* Spring 1987: 24(1), 1-15.

SCHILDER, Günter. Rare seventeenth century wall map of the British Isles found. *The Map Collector.* Summer 1988: 43, 12-15.

SCURFIELD, J.M. and G. SCURFIELD. The cartographic record of urban development in Victoria. *The Globe.* 1988: 30, 1-13.

SEBERT, L.M. Canada's first aeronautical charts and the eight-mile map series. *Cartographica.* 1986: 23(4), 79-118.

SHIRLEY, Rodney W. The decorative cartographic title-page. *The Map Collector.* 1987: 41, 2-6.

SHIRLEY, Rodney W. The decorative cartographic title-page. Part 2. *The Map Collector*. Spring 1988: 42, 10-17.

SIDER, Sandra. Sebastian Munster. *The Map Collector*. December 1986: 37, 32-34.

SMITH, Catherine Delano. Maps in bibles in the sixteenth century. *The Map Collector*. Summer 1987: 39, 2-14.

SMITH, David. The Cary Family. *The Map Collector*. Summer 1988: 43, 40-47.

SMITH, David and David WEBB. James Baker's picturesque plan of England and Wales. *The Map Collector*. Spring 1988: 42, 20-26.

SMITH, David. Jansson versus Blaeu. *The Cartographic Journal*. December 1986: 23(2), 106-114.

SMITH, David. Map publishers of Victorian Britain: the Philip Family Firm 1834-1902. *The Map Collector*. March 1987: 38, 28-34.

STARK, Peter L. and Susan TREVITT-CLARK. Index to geologic maps of Oregon, by USGS Topographic Quadrangle Name, 1883-1987. Part I: A-Elgin. *Western Association of Map Libraries. Information Bulletin*. 1988: 20(1), 2-17.

STERETT, Jill Norton. Identification of print media. *The Globe*. 1988: 29, 38-55.

STUART, Elizabeth A. Armada maps of Plymouth. *The Map Collector*. Spring 1988: 42, 2-8.

THORNDALE, William. Reconstructing historical U.S. county boundaries. *Western Association of Map Libraries. Information Bulletin*. March 1987: 18(2), 159-164.

TOMPKINS, Edward. French Mapping of Newfoundland. *Association of Canadian Map Libraries. Bulletin*. September 1987: 64, 10-12.

VALERIO, Vladimiro. Italian atlases and their makers 1770-1830. *The Map Collector*. 1988: 45, 10-18.

WARD, Bob. Lost harbour found! The truth about Drake and the Pacific. *The Map Collector*. 1988: 45, 3-8.

WATERS, N.M. and G.J.A. DE LEEUW. Computer atlases to complement printed atlases. *Cartographica*. Spring 1987: 24(1), 118-134.

WEIR, Thomas R. Problems associated with the production of atlases. *SLA. Geography & Map Division. Bulletin*. December 1985: 142, 26-29.

WHISTANCE-SMITH, Ron. Hunting maps in Vienna. *Association of Canadian Map Libraries. Bulletin*. September 1987: 64, 1-10.

WINN, William. Communication, cognition and children's atlases. *Cartographica*. Spring 1987: 24(1), 61-81.

WISE, Donald A. Eddie Hastain, map publisher. *SLA. Geography & Map Division. Bulletin*. 1988: 153, 14-18.

WOLF, Eric W. Cartobibliography: whither and why. *SLA. Geography & Map Division. Bulletin*. June 1986: 144, 28-36.

WOLF, Eric W. Toward a bibliography of cartobibliographies. *SLA. Geography & Map Division. Bulletin*. September 1987: 149, 12-15.

WOOD, Denis. Pleasure in the idea/the atlas as narrative form. *Cartographica*. Spring 1987: 24(1), 24-46.

WOODWARD, David. The analysis of paper and ink in early maps. *Library Trends*. Summer 1987: 36(1), 85-107.

WORAM, John M. On the cartography of the Galapagos Islands. *The Map Collector*. 1988: 44, 16-24.

3.1.4.2 Conferences, displays, diffusion and publications / Conférences, expositions, diffusion et publications

DELLER, Howard. Reaching the public: the AGS collection's annual Chrismas/Hanukkah map exhibit. *SLA. Geography & Map Division. Bulletin*. September 1986: 145, 3-7.

HOLTON, Mark. Maps and the Art Gallery. *Association of Canadian Map Libraries and Archives. Bulletin.* December 1987: 65, 1-4.

KIDD, Betty. Les collections de cartes au Canada: développement et coopération. *L'Archiviste.* Mai/juin 1987: 14(3), 16-18.

KIDD, Betty. Map collections in Canada: growth and co-operation. *The Archivist.* May/June 1987: 14(3), 16-18.

STRICKLAND, Muriel. Map displays: a means of promoting map use. *Western Association of Map Libraries. Information Bulletin.* June 1986: 17(3), 257-260.

WILSON, Bruce. Identités coloniales — Le Canada de 1760 à 1815. *L'Archiviste.* Novembre/décembre 1988: 15(6), 9.

WILSON, Bruce. New book illustrates richness of National Archives holdings, 1760 to 1815. *The Archivist.* November/December 1988: 15(6), 15.

3.1.4.3   Copyright / Droit d'auteur

LATHROP, Alan K. Copyright of architectural records: a legal perspective. *The American Archivist.* Fall 1986: 49(4), 409-423.

3.1.5   Information processing/ Techniques d'information

AZEVEDO, Carmen Lucia de, Luciano FIGUEIREDO and Maria Regina HIPPOLITO. MAPA data base — Brazilian public administration memory. *ADPA.* 1986: 5(2), 69-77.

COOKE, Donald F. Map storage on CD-ROM. *Byte.* July 1987: 129-130, 132, 134-136, 138.

SHAFFER, Norman J. Maps on microfiche: a success story at the Library of Congress. *INFORM: the Magazine of Information and Image Management.* November/December 1988: 2(10), 21-22.

3.2   Documentary art archives / Archives de l'art documentaire

Les archives et les techniques audiovisuelles. Rapports et débats sur les films projetés l'après-midi. *La Gazette des archives.* 1988: (140), 38-50.

Audio-visual archives in the United Kingdom. *ACA Bulletin.* September 1988: 13(1), [2-4].

BOUVIER, Jean-Claude. *Collecte des documents audiovisuels: la production des associations et des chercheurs.* Congrès national des archivistes français (28e: 1986: Paris, France). Paris, 1987: 114-117.

BURANT, Jim. The military artist and the documentary art record. *Archivaria.* Summer 1988: (26), 33-51.

CLAUZADE, Sophie de. Pour une archivistique audiovisuelle internationale. Analyse d'un ouvrage récent. *La Gazette des archives.* 1988: (140), 54-64.

CORNISH, Graham P. Audiovisual archives in the United Kingdom. *College and Research Libraries News.* February 1988: 14(1), 17-23.

COUEDELO, Rose-Anne, Jean-Pierre DEFRANCE et Perrine CANAVAGGIO. *Bilan de l'enquête effectuée par la section des missions sur les archives audiovisuelles des administrations centrales.* Congrès national des archivistes français (27e: 1985: Limoges, France). Paris, 1986: 79-82.

DEFRANCE, Jean-Pierre. Les archives audiovisuelles des services centraux de l'État. *La Gazette des archives.* 1987: (137-138), 150-161.

JIRAT-WASIUTYNSKI, Thea. Caring for works on paper. Part IV: care of watercolours. *Canadian Collector.* January/February 1987: 22(1), 30-33.

KLAUE, Wolfgang. *Les documents audiovisuels en tant qu'archives.* Congrès international des archives (11e: 1988: Paris). Paris, 1988. 5 p.

Panorama des archives audiovisuelles: contribution à la mise en œuvre d'une archivistique internationale. Paris: La documentation française, 1986. 298 p.

PETIT, Roger. Les affiches aux archives de l'État. *Archives et bibliothèques de Belgique*. 1988: 59(3/4), 111-125.

ROOS, Arnold E. A case study in frustration: archives, the history of technology and the restoration of Yukon Riverboats. *Archivaria*. Winter 1987-1988: (25), 51-72.

3.2.1 Acquisition, selection, appraisal and evaluation / Acquisition, sélection et évaluation historique et monétaire

KALNY, Adolf. Zpracovani obrazovych dokumentu v trebonskem archivie [Processing of iconographic documents in the Archives of Trebon]. *Archivni Casopis*. 1986: 36(3), 141-149.

NORTH, Susan. New faces at the Canadian Centre for Caricature. *The Archivist*. January/February 1988: 15(1), 9.

NORTH, Susan. Sourires tous azimuts. *L'Archiviste*. Janvier/février 1988: 15(1), 9.

SCHROCK, Nancy Carlson. Images of New England: documenting the built environment. *The American Archivist*. Fall 1987: 50(4), 474-498.

3.2.2. Arrangement / Classement

KALNY, Adolf. Zpracovani obrazovych dokumentu v trebonskem archivie [Processing of iconographic documents in the Archives of Trebon]. *Archivni Casopis*. 1986: 36(3), 141-149.

3.2.4 Public service / Service au public

GIGNAC, Gilbert. L'histoire en miniature... *L'Archiviste*. Septembre/octobre 1986: 13(5), 8-9.

GIGNAC, Gilbert. Look here upon this picture... *The Archivist*. September/October 1986: 13(5), 8-9.

HARRIS, Kevin. Indexing a special visual image collection. *Catalogue & Index*. Winter 1986: (83), 6-8.

3.2.4.1 Reference and research / Référence et recherche

COLLINS, Roger. Pictures as archives: musings and anecdotes and cautionary tales. *Archifacts*. 1988: (2), 53-56.

GIGNAC, Gilbert. L'histoire en miniature... *L'Archiviste*. Septembre/octobre 1986: 13(5), 8-9.

GIGNAC, Gilbert. Look here upon this picture... *The Archivist*. September/October 1986: 13(5), 8-9.

ROOS, Arnold E. A case study in frustration: archives, the history of technology and the restoration of Yukon Riverboats. *Archivaria*. Winter 1987-1988: (25), 51-72.

3.2.4.2 Conferences, displays, diffusion and publications / Conférences, expositions, diffusion et publications

GIGNAC, Gilbert. L'histoire en miniature... *L'Archiviste*. Septembre/octobre 1986: 13(5), 8-9.

GIGNAC, Gilbert. Look here upon this picture... *The Archivist*. September/October 1986: 13(5), 8-9.

VERNON, John Ed. Teaching with documents. It's in the cards: archives and baseball. *Social Education*. February 1988: 52(2), 124-126.

WILSON, Bruce. Identités coloniales — Le Canada de 1760 à 1815. *L'Archiviste*. Novembre/décembre 1988: 15(6), 9.

WILSON, Bruce. New book illustrates richness of National Archives holdings, 1760 to 1815. *The Archivist*. November/December 1988: 15(6), 15.

3.2.4.4 Security and access / Sécurité et accès

MILLER, J. Wesley. Archival security and the Madison People's Poster and Propaganda Collection. *Manuscripts*. Spring 1988: 40(2), 119-125.

3.2.5 Information processing / Techniques d'information

REMINGTON, R.R. The Electronic Museum of Graphic Design History at Rochester Institute of Technology. *Art Libraries Journal.* 1988: 13(2), 21-23.

3.3 Film archives / Archives cinématographiques

Les archives et les techniques audiovisuelles. Rapports et débats sur les films projetés l'après-midi. *La Gazette des archives.* 1988: (140), 38-50.

Audio-visual archives in the United Kingdom. *ACA Bulletin.* September 1988: 13(1), [2-4].

BOUVET, Mireille-Bénédicte. *Les archives des stations locales de télévision FR3 dans les archives départementales.* Congrès national des archivistes français (28e: 1986: Paris, France). Paris, 1987: 89-96.

BOUVIER, Jean-Claude. *Collecte des documents audiovisuels: la production des associations et des chercheurs.* Congrès national des archivistes français (28e: 1986: Paris, France). Paris, 1987: 114-117.

CLAUZADE, Sophie de. Pour une archivistique audiovisuelle internationale. Analyse d'un ouvrage récent. *La Gazette des archives.* 1988: (140), 54-64.

CLAYSSEN, Dominique, Dominique LOBSTEIN et Jean ZEITOUN. *Les nouvelles images: introduction à l'image informatique.* Paris: Dunod, 1987. 164 p.

COCHRANE, C. Regional film archives in Great Britain: the report of a study tour. *Leabharlann.* 1987: 2ND, SER. 4 NO. 2, 35-44.

CORNISH, Graham P. Archival collections of audiovisual materials. *Journal of the Society of Archivists.* October 1987: 8(4), 258-260.

CORNISH, Graham P. Audiovisual archives in the United Kingdom. *College and Research Libraries News.* February 1988: 14(1), 17-23.

CORNISH, Graham P. Audiovisual archives in the United Kingdom [first report from the National Archival Collections of Audiovisual Materials Forum]. *Audiovisual Librarian.* May 1988: 14, 17-23.

COUEDELO, Rose-Anne, Jean-Pierre DEFRANCE et Perrine CANAVAGGIO. *Bilan de l'enquête effectuée par la section des missions sur les archives audiovisuelles des administrations centrales.* Congrès national des archivistes français (27e: 1985: Limoges, France). Paris, 1986: 79-82.

DEFRANCE, Jean-Pierre. Les archives audiovisuelles des services centraux de l'État. *La Gazette des archives.* 1987: (137-138), 150-161.

DJILAS, Hélène. Producteur, une nouvelle génération. *Dossiers de l'audiovisuel.* Juillet/août 1987: 14, 15-40.

L'établissement cinématographique et photographique des armées. Congrès national des archivistes français (28e: 1986: Paris, France). Paris, 1987: 77-82.

FRITZ, Walter. Das oesterreichische Filmarchiv [The Austrian Film Archive]. *Scrinium.* 1986: (34), 162-167.

HARRISON, Helen P. Audiovisual archives. *Audiovisual Librarian.* August 1986: 112(3), 133-141.

KLAUE, Wolfgang. *Les documents audiovisuels en tant qu'archives.* Congrès international des archives (11e: 1988: Paris). Paris, 1988. 5 p.

MCBAIN, J. The Scottish Film Archive. *Audiovisual Librarian.* May 1987: 13, 88-90.

MADELIN, Patrick. L'Europe des télévisions privées. *Dossiers de l'audiovisuel.* Septembre/octobre 1988: 21, 10-51.

MBAYE, Saliou. *Les archives orales.* Congrès international des archives (11e: 1988: Paris). Paris, 1988. 14 p.

O'FARRELL, William S. Cold storage for colour film. *The Archivist.* March/April 1988: 15(2), 18.

O'FARRELL, William S. Entreposage au froid. *L'Archiviste*. Mars/avril 1988: 15(2), 18.

Panorama des archives audiovisuelles: contribution à la mise en œuvre d'une archivistique internationale. Paris: La documentation française, 1986. 298 p.

PEYRON, Jean-Marc. Images de synthèse, un art? *Dossiers de l'audiovisuel*. Septembre/octobre 1987: 15, 13-54.

PONCIN, Philippe. *Archives de l'image: les implications techniques*. Congrès national des archivistes français (27e: 1985: Limoges, France). Paris, 1986: 68-73.

Pourquoi conserver les archives des médias? Rapports et débats de la table ronde tenue en matinée. *La Gazette des archives*. 1988: (140), 9-37.

ROADS, Christopher H. *Les enregistrements de radio et de télévision en tant qu'archives*. Congrès international des archives (11e: 1988: Paris). Paris, 1988. 8 p.

SCHMITT, Frantz. *Le service des archives du film*. Congrès national des archivistes français (28e: 1986: Paris, France). Paris, 1987: 74-76.

TOUCHARD, Jean-Baptiste. *Images numériques*. Paris: Cedic/Nathan, 1987.

TURNER, D. John and Micheline MORISSET. *Canadian feature film index, 1913-1985*. Ottawa: Public Archives Canada, National Film, Television and Sound Archives, 1987. xx, 816 p.

TURNER, D. John et Micheline MORISSET. *Index des films canadiens de long métrage, 1913-1985*. Ottawa: Archives publiques Canada, Archives nationales du film, de la télévision et de l'enregistrement sonore, 1987. xx, 816 p.

VIGNES-DUMAS, Claire. Le Centre des archives contemporaines des Archives nationales: les archives audiovisuelles. *La Gazette des archives*. 1988: (141), 67-72.

3.3.1 Acquisition, selection, appraisal and evaluation / Acquisition, sélection et évaluation historique et monétaire

BERGERON, Rosemary. The selection of television production for archival preservation. *Archivaria*. Winter 1986-87: (23), 41-53.

NATHAN-TILLOY, Michèle. *La collecte des documents audiovisuels dans les archives départementales*. Congrès national des archivistes français (28e: 1986: Paris, France). Paris, 1987: 83-88.

SOWRY, Clive. Film identification by examination of physical characteristics. *Archifacts*. 1988: (2), 1-12.

3.3.2 Arrangement / Classement

ANDROSSOVA, M.E. Le classement des documents cinématographiques et photographiques des Archives d'État. *Sovietskje Arkhivy*. 1988: (6), 33-37.

BERCHE, Claire. *Cotation et catalogage de l'image animée et sonorisée*. Congrès national des archivistes français (27e: 1985: Limoges, France). Paris, 1986: 19-20.

EVANS, A. TELCLASS: a structural approach to TV classification [condensed version of a presentation given at the 1987 conference of the Educational Television Association at the University of York]. *Audiovisual Librarian*. November 1987: 13, 215-216.

3.3.3 Description and finding aids / Description et instruments de recherche

BERCHE, Claire. *Cotation et catalogage de l'image animée et sonorisée*. Congrès national des archivistes français (27e: 1985: Limoges, France). Paris, 1986: 19-20.

SMITH, D.R.A. Mickey Mouse index: indexing and cataloguing the Walt Disney Archives. *Indexer*. April 1987: 15, 154-156.

SMITHER, Roger. Formats and standards: a film archive perspective on exchanging computerized data. *The American Archivist.* Summer 1987: 50(3), 324-337.

WALSH, Steven, David A. HALES and Judith DIAMONDSTONE. Indexing archival films: Alaska Archival Motion Picture Program. *Provenance.* Spring 1987: 5(1), 39-54.

3.3.4 Public service / Service au public

CALAS, Marie-France. *Consultation et conservation d'images animées dans un service d'archives.* Congrès national des archivistes français (28e: 1986: Paris, France). Paris, 1987: 107-113.

ERMISSE, Gérard. Les Archives nationales de France et leur public. *Janus.* 1988: (1), 26-28.

ERMISSE, Gérard. The National Archives of France and its public. *Janus.* 1988: (1), 13-14.

3.3.4.1 Reference and research / Référence et recherche

ARCHIVES NATIONALES DU CANADA. *Au-delà de l'écrit: actualités filmées et reportages radio et télé diffusés au Canada.* Ottawa: Les Archives, 1988. 348 p.

BOURDON, Jérôme. L'esprit des lois ou comment reformer l'audiovisuel (1917-1988). *Dossiers de l'audiovisuel.* Juillet/août 1988: 20, 9-52.

MADELIN, Patrick. L'Europe des télévisions privées. *Dossiers de l'audiovisuel.* Septembre/octobre 1988: 21, 10-51.

NATIONAL ARCHIVES OF CANADA. *Beyond the printed word: newsreel and broadcast reporting in Canada.* Ottawa: The Archives, 1988. 348 p.

PUPPINEK, Bénédicte. La télévision des jeunes. *Dossiers de l'audiovisuel.* Mai/juin 1988: 19, 14-51.

3.3.4.2 Conferences, displays, diffusion and publications / Conférences, expositions, diffusion et publications

Les archives et les techniques audiovisuelles. Rapports et débats sur les films projetés l'après-midi. *La Gazette des archives.* 1988: (140), 38-50.

DJILAS, Hélène. Producteur, une nouvelle génération. *Dossiers de l'audiovisuel.* Juillet/août 1987: 14, 15-40.

3.3.4.3 Copyright / Droit d'auteur

CHESTERMAN, John and Andy LIPMAN. *The electronic pirates: DIY crime of the century.* London: Routledge, 1988. x, 224 p. (A Comedia book)

3.3.4.4 Security and access / Sécurité et accès

BOURDON, Jérôme. L'esprit des lois ou comment reformer l'audiovisuel (1917-1988). *Dossiers de l'audiovisuel.* Juillet/août 1988: 20, 9-52.

CALAS, Marie-France. *Consultation et conservation d'images animées dans un service d'archives.* Congrès national des archivistes français (28e: 1986: Paris, France). Paris, 1987: 107-113.

3.3.5 Information processing / Techniques d'information

PEYRON, Jean-Marc. Images de synthèse, un art? *Dossiers de l'audiovisuel.* Septembre/octobre 1987: 15, 13-54.

SMITHER, Roger. Formats and standards: a film archive perspective on exchanging computerized data. *The American Archivist.* Summer 1987: 50(3), 324-337.

3.4 Machine readable archives / Archives ordinolingues

BAILEY, Catherine Aileen. *Archival theory and machine readable records: some problems and issues.* M.A. thesis, University of British Columbia, August 1988.

BALON, Brett J. and H. Wayne GARDNER. Disaster planning for electronic records. *Records Management Quarterly.* July 1988: 22(3), 20-25, 30.

BONNIN, Hélène. *Les archives informatiques dans les archives communales.* Congrès national des archivistes français (28ᵉ: 1986: Paris, France). Paris, 1987: 160-161.

BROWN, Thomas Elton. Archives law and machine-readable data files: a look at the United States. *ADPA.* 1986: 5(2), 37-42.

CLAYSSEN, Dominique, Dominique LOBSTEIN et Jean ZEITOUN. *Les nouvelles images: introduction à l'image informatique.* Paris: Dunod, 1987. 164 p.

CLERC, Jean-Pierre. *L'évolution des technologies de support et des méthodes de gestion associées à ces supports dans le domaine des archives informatiques.* Congrès national des archivistes français (28ᵉ: 1986: Paris, France). Paris, 1987: 162-164.

CONCHON, Michèle. L'archivage des fichiers informatiques: bilan de la mise en œuvre de Constance (1982-1988). *La Gazette des archives.* 1988: (141), 61-66.

DAVENPORT, L. Archiving electronic files. *Scottish Libraries.* September/October 1987: (5), 7-8.

DAVIS, Douglas L. Optical archiving: where are we now and where do we go from here? *Optical Information Systems.* January/February 1987: 66-71.

DURANTI, Luciana. "Towards automated records paleography". IN Proceedings: Conference of the Association of Canadian Archivists (1987: McMaster University). Hamilton, Ont., 1987. 5 p.

GAVREL, Katharine. National Archives of Canada: Machine Readable Records Program. *Reference Services Review.* 1988: 16(1), 25-29.

GERKEN, Ann. What is a data archive and what should the information specialist know about managing locally maintained numeric data files. *Database.* August 1988: 11(4), 60-65.

HARRISON, Donald Fisher. Computers, electronic data and the Vietnam War. *Archivaria.* Summer 1988: (26), 18-32.

HEDLIN, Edie and D.F. HARRISON. The National Archives and electronic. *Reference Services Review.* 1988: 16(1/2), 13-16.

HEDSTROM, Margaret and Alan KOWLOWITZ. Meeting the challenge of machine-readable records: a state archives perspective. *Reference Services Review.* 1988: 16(1/2), 31-40.

HERSTAD, John. *Le coût et le financement de la recherche.* Congrès international des archives (11ᵉ: 1988: Paris). Paris, 1988. 6 p.

MALLINSON, John C. On the preservation of human and machine-readable records. *Information Technology and Libraries.* March 1988: 7(1), 19-23.

MALLINSON, John C. Preserving machine-readable archival records for the millenia. *Archivaria.* Summer 1986: (22), 147-155.

MAROTEAUX, Vincent. Informatique et archives contemporaines, une approche nouvelle. *La Gazette des archives.* 1987: (137-138), 144-149.

PETERSON, Trudy Huskamp. *Les archives informatiques: principes et pratiques.* Congrès international des archives (11ᵉ: 1988: Paris). Paris, 1988. 10 p.

PEYRON, Jean-Marc. Images de synthèse, un art? *Dossiers de l'audiovisuel.* Septembre/octobre 1987: 15, 13-54.

PIEYNS, Jean. Technologies nouvelles et archivistique: la lecture optique et les disques optiques digitaux. *Archives et bibliothèques de Belgique.* 1988: 59(3/4), 127-132.

PRAX, Hélène. *Synthèse des travaux de l'atelier « archives informatiques ».* Congrès national des archivistes français (28ᵉ: 1986: Paris, France). Paris, 1987: 168-170.

SERGEEV, You V. et N. You GOUREEVA. La production automatisée des documents dans l'institution administrative. *Sovietskje Arkhivy*. 1988: (4), 85-86.

SKUPSKY, Donald S. Legal requirements for computer records containing federal tax information: an update. *Records Management Quarterly*. July 1988: 22(3), 32-35.

STURGES, P. Archival problems of electronic publications. IN New horizons for the information profession. London: Taylor Graham, 1988: 158-168.

TOUCHARD, Jean-Baptiste. *Images numériques*. Paris: Cedic/Nathan, 1987.

3.4.1 Acquisition, selection, appraisal and evaluation / Acquisition, sélection et évaluation historique et monétaire

FISHBEIN, Meyer H. Reflections on appraising statistical records. *The American Archivist*. May 1987: 50(2), 226-234.

GAVREL, Katharine. Scheduling and archival appraisal: an integrated approach for EDP records. *The Archivist*. July/August 1986: 13(4), 6-7.

GAVREL, Katharine. Sélectionner les documents grâce aux calendriers de conservation: une méthode intégrée d'archivage des documents informatisés. *L'Archiviste*. Juillet/août 1986: 13(4), 6-7.

GAVREL, Sue. Preserving machine-readable archival records: a reply to John Mallinson. *Archivaria*. Summer 1986: (22), 153-155.

NAUGLER, Harold. *Évaluation et tri des documents informatiques en archivistique: une étude RAMP, accompagnée de principes directeurs*. Paris: UNESCO, 1986. 155 p. (PGI-84/WS/27)

3.4.3 Description and finding aids / Description et instruments de recherche

AAP announces provisional standard for electronic manuscripts. *Electronic Publishing Review*. June 1986: 6(2), 67-68.

BROWN, Thomas Elton. An experiment with research data. *Archival Informatics Newsletter*. Summer 1988: 2(2), 33-34.

DODD, Sue A. and Ann M. SANDBERG-FOX. *Cataloging microcomputer files: a manual of interpretation for AACR2*. Chicago: American Library Association, 1985. 272 p.

LYNCH, Clifford A. Implications of the Electronic Manuscript Project for libraries, scholarly publications, and universities. *Electronic Publishing Business*. September 1986: 4(8), 22-23, 26.

MARTIN, J. Sperling. The AAP Electronic Manuscript Project — The contractor's final report. *Electronic Publishing Business*. September 1986: 4(8), 14-15, 21.

PAUL, Sandra K. The electronic manuscript project: an AAP perspective. *Electronic Publishing Business*. September 1986: 4(8), 10-11.

3.4.4 Public service / Service au public

3.4.4.1 Reference and research / Référence et recherche

BROWN, Thomas Elton. An experiment with research data. *Archival Informatics Newsletter*. Summer 1988: 2(2), 33-34.

BROWN, Thomas Elton. Machine readable views. *Archival Informatics Newsletter*. Spring 1988: 2(1), 5-6.

BROWN, Thomas Elton. Standards for MRR Reference Service. *Archival Informatics Newsletter*. Summer 1988: 2(2), 34-35.

HARRISON, Donald Fisher. Computers, electronic data and the Vietnam War. *Archivaria*. Summer 1988: (26), 18-32.

KAHIN, Brian. Fair use of electronic archives. *ACA Bulletin*. September 1988: 13(1), [11-12].

3.4.4.3 Copyright / Droit d'auteur

CHESTERMAN, John and Andy LIPMAN. *The electronic pirates: DIY crime of the century*. London: Routledge, 1988. x, 224 p. (A Comedia book)

KAHIN, Brian. Fair use of electronic archives. *Archival Informatics Newsletter*. Summer 1988: 2(2), 35.

3.4.4.4 Security and access / Sécurité et accès

EDDISON, Betty. Protecting valuables: databases and software. *Database*. December 1987: 88-90.

HARRISON, Donald Fisher. Computers, electronic data and the Vietnam War. *Archivaria*. Summer 1988: (26), 18-32.

KAHIN, Brian. Fair use of electronic archives. *ACA Bulletin*. September 1988: 13(1), [11-12].

MCDONALD, John. *Lignes directrices régissant la conservation et l'élimination des données des systèmes automatisés*. Ottawa: Programme des systèmes d'information automatisés, Archives publiques du Canada, 1986. [24] p.

PIEYNS-RIGO, Paulette. *Les conséquences juridiques de la production des documents informatiques par les administrations publiques: une étude RAMP*. Paris: Unesco, 1988. 78 p.

ROBBINS, Renee M. Disaster recovery: trial by flood. *Infosystems*. January 1988: 35(1), 40-46.

3.4.5 Information processing / Techniques d'information

BANKS, Richard L. COM and optical recording — change and challenge. *IMC Journal*. May/June 1988: 24(3), 18-20.

BROWN, Thomas Elton. Machine readable views. *Archival Informatics Newsletter*. Winter 1987: 1(4), 70-71.

CONCHON, Michèle. *L'archivage des fichiers magnétiques des administrations centrales, bilan et perspectives de « Constance »*. Congrès national des archivistes français (28ᵉ: 1986: Paris, France). Paris, 1987: 130-148.

GAVREL, Sue. Preserving machine-readable archival records: a reply to John Mallinson. *Archivaria*. Summer 1986: (22), 153-155.

GRAHAM, Gord. SGML spells relief when handling manuscripts on-line. *Quill & Quire*. January 1987: 53(1), 10.

IMPRESSION: document archival and retrieval system. *Library Hi Tech News*. November 1988: (54), 16.

NOLTE, William. High-speed text search systems and their archival implication. *The American Archivist*. Fall 1987: 50(4), 580-584.

SEIGLE, David C. Office economics and document image processing. *INFORM: the Magazine of Information and Image Management*. January 1988: 2(1), 35-36.

3.5 Photographic archives / Archives photographiques

Les archives et les techniques audiovisuelles. Rapports et débats sur les films projetés l'après-midi. *La Gazette des archives*. 1988: (140), 38-50.

Audio-visual archives in the United Kingdom. *ACA Bulletin*. September 1988: 13(1), [2-4].

BARR, Debra. Photographs as archival documents. *ABCA Newsletter*. Winter 1986: 12(1), 8.

BERCHE, Claire. *Les images fixes dans un nouveau département de la couronne parisienne*. Congrès national des archivistes français (28ᵉ: 1986: Paris, France). Paris, 1987: 32-35.

BOUVIER, Jean-Claude. *Collecte des documents audiovisuels: la production des associations et des chercheurs*. Congrès national des archivistes français (28ᵉ: 1986: Paris, France). Paris, 1987: 114-117.

CAREY, Brian. Archives acquires Karsh photos. *The Archivist*. September/October 1987: 14(5), 13.

CAREY, Brian. La collection Karsh aux Archives. *L'Archiviste*. Septembre/ octobre 1987: 14(5), 13.

CLAUZADE, Sophie de. Pour une archivistique audiovisuelle internationale. Analyse d'un ouvrage récent. *La Gazette des archives*. 1988: (140), 54-64.

CORNISH, Graham P. Archival collections of audiovisual materials. *Journal of the Society of Archivists*. October 1987: 8(4), 258-260.

COUEDELO, Rose-Anne, Jean-Pierre DEFRANCE et Perrine CANAVAGGIO. *Bilan de l'enquête effectuée par la section des missions sur les archives audiovisuelles des administrations centrales*. Congrès national des archivistes français (27e: 1985: Limoges, France). Paris, 1986: 79-82.

CRIBBS, Margaret A. Photographic conservation: an update. *Records Management Quarterly*. July 1988: 22(3), 17-19.

DEFRANCE, Jean-Pierre. Les archives audiovisuelles des services centraux de l'État. *La Gazette des archives*. 1987: (137-138), 150-161.

DU BOISROUVRAY, Xavier. *Les images fixes dans les archives départementales: l'exemple de la Loire-Atlantique*. Congrès national des archivistes français (28e: 1986: Paris, France). Paris, 1987: 26-31.

L'établissement cinématographique et photographique des armées. Congrès national des archivistes français (28e: 1986: Paris, France). Paris, 1987: 77-82.

KLAUE, Wolfgang. *Les documents audiovisuels en tant qu'archives*. Congrès international des archives (11e: 1988: Paris). Paris, 1988. 5 p.

KORCHIA, Robert. *Les collections des archives photographiques*. Congrès national des archivistes français (28e: 1986: Paris, France). Paris, 1987: 44-48.

LEONHIRTH, Janene. Administration of photographic collections: a bibliographic

essay. *Provenance*. Spring 1988: 6(1), 60-66.

Panorama des archives audiovisuelles: contribution à la mise en œuvre d'une archivistique internationale. Paris: La documentation française, 1986. 298 p.

ROSS, David. Military dress and the cataloguing of photographs. *Archivaria*. Summer 1988: (26), 173-175.

VIGNES-DUMAS, Claire. Le Centre des archives contemporaines des Archives nationales: les archives audiovisuelles. *La Gazette des archives*. 1988: (141), 67-72.

WOHLFEIL, Rainer, [et al.]. Archivische Bildbestaende ihre Nutzung [Archival picture collections and their use]. *Archivar*. February 1986: 39(1), 45-60.

3.5.1 Acquisition, selection, appraisal and evaluation / Acquisition, sélection et évaluation historique et monétaire

CAREY, Brian. Archives acquires Karsh photos. *The Archivist*. September/October 1987: 14(5), 13.

CAREY, Brian. La collection Karsh aux Archives. *L'Archiviste*. Septembre/ octobre 1987: 14(5), 13.

CROSS, James Edward. The science of deduction: dating and identifying photographs in twentieth century political collection's. *Provenance*. Spring 1988: 6(1), 45-59.

DIEUZEDE, Geneviève. *Repérage des collections photographiques à l'échelon national et problèmes juridiques posés lors de la collecte*. Congrès national des archivistes français (28e: 1986: Paris, France). Paris, 1987: 49-53.

DINWIDDIE, Robert C. The Lane Brothers Photographic Archive: its provenance, scope and arrangement. *Provenance*. Fall 1988: 6(2), 20-34.

JOUKOVA, M.P. et Z.P. KHODAKOVA. Les listes des sources des accroissements des Archives d'État sont les bases de l'amélioration de la composition du Fonds d'archives photographiques d'État de l'URSS. *Sovietskje Arkhivy.* 1988: (6), 28-32.

NATHAN-TILLOY, Michèle. *La collecte des documents audiovisuels dans les archives départementales.* Congrès national des archivistes français (28ᵉ: 1986: Paris, France). Paris, 1987: 83-88.

SCHROCK, Nancy Carlson. Images of New England: documenting the built environment. *The American Archivist.* Fall 1987: 50(4), 474-498.

3.5.2 Arrangement / Classement

ANDROSSOVA, M.E. Le classement des documents cinématographiques et photographiques des Archives d'État. *Sovietskje Arkhivy.* 1988: (6), 33-37.

DINWIDDIE, Robert C. The Lane Brothers Photographic Archive: its provenance, scope and arrangement. *Provenance.* Fall 1988: 6(2), 20-34.

VOISIN, Jean-Claude. *Comment traiter un patrimoine photographique: l'exemple des archives communales de Montbéliard.* Congrès national des archivistes français (28ᵉ: 1986: Paris, France). Paris, 1987: 36-43.

3.5.3 Description and finding aids / Description et instruments de recherche

DIEUZEDE, Geneviève. *Repérage des collections photographiques à l'échelon national et problèmes juridiques posés lors de la collecte.* Congrès national des archivistes français (28ᵉ: 1986: Paris, France). Paris, 1987: 49-53.

ROSS, David. Military dress and the cataloguing of photographs. *Archivaria.* Summer 1988: (26), 173-175.

3.5.5 Information processing / Techniques d'information

PROKUPETS, Elena A. Electronic photoimaging: the management of color images. *IMC Journal.* September/October 1988: 24(5), 44-46.

3.6 Printed archives / Archives imprimées

COX, Richard J. and Anne S.K. TURKOS. Establishing public library archives. *Journal of Library History.* Summer 1986: 21, 574-584.

GARAY, K.E. The Saturday Night Archive. *Library Research News.* Spring 1988: 12(1), 1-133.

GARAY, K.E. The Saturday Night Archive. *Library Research News.* Fall 1988: 12(2), 1-155.

KOWALEWSKI, Anne-Françoise. Le Centre des archives contemporaines des Archives nationales: nouveaux aspects des bibliothèques. *La Gazette des archives.* 1988: (141), 85-86.

VERSCHAFFEL, A. Een overzicht van het Limburgsch Jaarboek (1892-1896). *Archives et bibliothèques de Belgique.* 1986: 57(3/4), 455-461.

3.6.1 Acquisition, selection, appraisal and evaluation / Acquisition, sélection et évaluation historique et monétaire

ORGAN, Michael. Ephemera in archives: what to do? (A possible solution from the University of New South Wales Archives). *Archives and Manuscripts.* November 1987: 15(2), 105-118.

3.6.2 Arrangement / Classement

ORGAN, Michael. Ephemera in archives: what to do? (A possible solution from the University of New South Wales Archives). *Archives and Manuscripts.* November 1987: 15(2), 105-118.

3.6.3 Description and finding aids / Description et instruments de recherche

ORGAN, Michael. Ephemera in archives: what to do? (A possible solution from the University of New South Wales Archives). *Archives and Manuscripts.* November 1987: 15(2), 105-118.

3.6.5 Information processing / Techniques d'information

FOSSIER, Lucie and Marie-Josèphe BEAUD. Introducing the Institut de Recherche et d'Histoire des Textes (C.N.R.S.): medieval book and computer. *Computers and the Humanities*. October/December 1986: 20(4), 267-268.

GUILLAUMONT, Agnès and Jean-Luc MINEL. MEDIUM: realities and projects. *Computers and the Humanities*. October/December 1986: 20(4), 269-271.

3.7 Sound archives / Archives sonores

ALLERSTRAND, Sven. Arkivet foer Ljud och Bild (ALB) — The National Archives of Recorded Sound and Moving Images. *Phonographic Bulletin*. June 1986: (45), 7-11.

ARCHIVES PUBLIQUES CANADA. *Catalogues des fonds sur la société Radio-Canada déposés aux Archives publiques.* Préparé sous la direction de Ernest J. Dick. Ottawa: Archives publiques Canada, 1987. viii, 141, 125, viii p.

ARNAULD, Marie-Paule. *Enquête sur les documents sonores et audiovisuels dans la Seine-Saint-Denis.* Congrès national des archivistes français (27e: 1985: Limoges, France). Paris, 1986: 14-15.

ARNAULD, Marie-Paule. *Équipement des locaux et matériels.* Congrès national des archivistes français (27e: 1985: Limoges, France). Paris, 1986: 31-32.

Audio-visual archives in the United Kingdom. *ACA Bulletin*. September 1988: 13(1), [2-4].

BERCHE, Claire. *Les implications sur le plan du fonctionnement et du personnel.* Congrès national des archivistes français (27e: 1985: Limoges, France). Paris, 1986: 33-34.

BLANC, Brigitte. Sixième congrès international d'histoire orale (Oxford, 1987). *La Gazette des archives*. 1987: (139), 253-256.

BOURBONNAIS, Michel. Un ambitieux projet de conservation. *L'Archiviste*. Mars/avril 1988: 15(2), 9.

BOURBONNAIS, Michel. Disc conservation state of the art. *The Archivist*. March/April 1988: 15(2), 9.

BOUVIER, Jean-Claude. *Collecte des documents audiovisuels: la production des associations et des chercheurs.* Congrès national des archivistes français (28e: 1986: Paris, France). Paris, 1987: 114-117.

CHANIAC, Régine. Télévision: la mesure de l'audience. *Dossiers de l'audiovisuel.* Novembre/décembre 1988: 22, 11-55.

CHOMEL, Maïc. *Les archives des chaînes publiques de radio.* Congrès national des archivistes français (28e: 1986: Paris, France). Paris, 1987: 208-212.

CHRISTENSEN-SKOELD, Beatrice. The Swedish Library of Talking Books and Braille, TPB. *Phonographic Bulletin*. June 1986: (45), 22-24.

CORNISH, Graham P. Archival collections of audiovisual materials. *Journal of the Society of Archivists*. October 1987: 8(4), 258-260.

CORNISH, Graham P. Audiovisual archives in the United Kingdom. *College and Research Libraries News*. February 1988: 14(1), 17-23.

CROSADO, Doug. A trade unionist looks at archives and records. *Archifacts*. 1987: (3), 5-8.

DUCHEIN, Michel. *Un projet d'instruction relative aux documents sonores.* Congrès national des archivistes français (27e: 1985: Limoges, France). Paris, 1986: 21-30.

FONTAINE, Jean-Marc. *Archives sonores: les implications techniques.* Congrès national des archivistes français (27e: 1985: Limoges, France). Paris, 1986: 56-67.

GAUTHIER-DESVAUX, Élisabeth. *La constitution d'un fonds local d'archives sonores: l'expérience ornaise.* Congrès national des archivistes français (27e: 1985: Limoges, France). Paris, 1986: 12-13.

GAUTHIER-DESVAUX, Élisabeth. *Le traitement archivistique des archives sonores.* Congrès national des archivistes français (27e: 1985: Limoges, France). Paris, 1986: 16-18.

HARRISON, Helen P. Audiovisual archives. *Audiovisual Librarian.* August 1986: 112(3), 133-141.

HARRISON, Helen P. IASA Annual Conference [Amsterdam, Netherlands, 1987]. *Fontes Artis Musical.* January 1988: (35), 45-48.

HOWARTH, Ken. Sound archives in Paris: a lesson to be learned. *Museums Journal.* June 1985: 85(1), 31-33.

International Association of Sound Archives Annual Conference, Stockholm, August 1986. *Phonographic Bulletin.* November 1986: (46), 24-44.

KGABI, D.K. The role of the archivist in oral traditions — the Botswana Case. *Commonwealth Archivists Association Newsletter.* November 1987: (5), 4-6.

KLAUE, Wolfgang. *Les documents audiovisuels en tant qu'archives.* Congrès international des archives (11e: 1988: Paris). Paris, 1988. 5 p.

KOZINE, Yvan. *Technologies actuelles de mémorisation informatique à long terme.* Congrès national des archivistes français (28e: 1986: Paris, France). Paris, 1987: 125-129.

L'HUILLIER, Hervé. Archives, témoignages oraux et histoire des entreprises. Quelques réflexions à la lecture de deux ouvrages récents. *La Gazette des archives.* 1987: (139), 256-260.

MALAVIEILLE, Sophie. *Un fichier central d'archives orales aux Archives nationales.* Congrès national des archivistes français (27e: 1985: Limoges, France). Paris, 1986: 91-97.

MAZIKANA, Peter C. Archives and oral history: overcoming a lack of resources.

Information Development. January 1987: 3(1), 13-16.

MBAYE, Saliou. *Les archives orales.* Congrès international des archives (11e: 1988: Paris). Paris, 1988. 14 p.

MOREAU, Jean-Paul et Denis CARRIER. Bibliographie analytique d'Yves Thériault, 1940-1984. *Revue d'histoire littéraire du Québec et du Canada.* Hiver/printemps 1987: 13, 242-244.

MOSS, William W. et Peter C. MAZIKANA. *Archives, histoire orale et tradition orale: une étude RAMP.* Paris: UNESCO, 1986. 84 p. (PGI-86/WS/2)

NAUD, Gérard. *Orientation pour un centre d'archives audiovisuelles.* Congrès national des archivistes français (27e: 1985: Limoges, France). Paris, 1986: 98-102.

Panorama des archives audiovisuelles: contribution à la mise en œuvre d'une archivistique internationale. Paris: La documentation française, 1986. 298 p.

PETROV, G.D. Les chroniques sonores du Pays des Soviets. *Sovietskje Arkhivy.* 1987: (5), 42-45.

Pourquoi conserver les archives des médias? Rapports et débats de la table ronde tenue en matinée. *La Gazette des archives.* 1988: (140), 9-37.

POZZO DI BORGO, Cécile, Odile RUDELLE et Maurice VAISSE. *Le témoignage oral: choix des témoins, conduite de l'entretien.* Congrès national des archivistes français (28e: 1986: Paris, France). Paris, 1987: 194-197.

PRAX, Hélène. *Les archives informatiques: une approche régionale et départementale.* Congrès national des archivistes français (28e: 1986: Paris, France). Paris, 1987: 149-159.

PUBLIC ARCHIVES CANADA. *Guide to CBC sources at the Public Archives.* Compiled under the direction of Ernest J. Dick. Ottawa: Public Archives Canada, 1987. viii, 125, 141, viii p.

RICHARDSON, G. The music and record libraries of the Canadian Broadcasting Corporation. *Fontes Artis Musical.* October 1987: (34), 211-216.

ROADS, Christopher H. *Les enregistrements de radio et de télévision en tant qu'archives.* Congrès international des archives (11ᵉ: 1988: Paris). Paris, 1988. 8 p.

RODES, Jean-Michel. *Description d'une émission de radio.* Congrès national des archivistes français (28ᵉ: 1986: Paris, France). Paris, 1987: 213-217.

ROUX, Lucie. *L'archivage des documents sonores des radios publiques décentralisées: l'expérience des archives départementales de Belfort.* Congrès national des archivistes français (28ᵉ: 1986: Paris, France). Paris, 1987: 226-231.

SABOURIN, C. Les services de musique de Radio-Canada. *Fontes Artis Musical.* Octobre 1987: (34), 208-210.

SAULNIER, C. Fonds et collections de musique traditionnelle conservés aux Archives de l'Université Laval. *Fontes Artis Musical.* Octobre 1987: (34), 194-197.

SCHULLER, Dietrich. Handling, storage and preservation of sound recordings under tropical and subtropical climatic conditions. *Restaurator.* 1986: 7(1), 14-21.

SIMONI-AUREMBOU, Marie-Rose. *Les entretiens enregistrés à caractère dialectologique et ethnotextuel.* Congrès national des archivistes français (28ᵉ: 1986: Paris, France). Paris, 1987: 198-202.

Sound archives in Sweden. *Phonographic Bulletin.* June 1986: (45), 7-24.

STIELOW, Frederick J. *The management of oral history sound archives.* New York: Greenwood Press, 1986. 158 p.

TOURTIER-BONAZZI, Chantal de. *Les Archives nationales et les sources orales.* Congrès national des archivistes français (27ᵉ: 1985: Limoges, France). Paris, 1986: 86-91.

TOURTIER-BONAZZI, Chantal de. *Bilan du traitement des versements des documents sonores et collecte d'archives orales à la section contemporaine.* Congrès national des archivistes français (27ᵉ: 1985: Limoges, France). Paris, 1986: 83-85.

TOURTIER-BONAZZI, Chantal de. La collecte des témoignages oraux. *La Gazette des archives.* 1987: (139), 249-252.

VIGNES-DUMAS, Claire. Le Centre des archives contemporaines des Archives nationales: les archives audiovisuelles. *La Gazette des archives.* 1988: (141), 67-72.

VOLDMAN, Danièle. *Paroles enregistrées: sources du XXᵉ siècle.* Congrès national des archivistes français (28ᵉ: 1986: Paris, France). Paris, 1987: 184-185.

WALCH, Timothy. *Our family, our town: essays on family and local history sources in the National Archives.* Washington: National Archives and Records Administration, 1987. 223 p.

3.7.1 Acquisition, selection, appraisal and evaluation / Acquisition, sélection et évaluation historique et monétaire

Les entrées d'archives sonores aux Archives nationales, départementales et communales: synthèse. Congrès national des archivistes français (28ᵉ: 1986: Paris, France). Paris, 1987: 189-193.

HARRISON, Helen P. *The archival appraisal of sound recordings and related materials: a RAMP study with guidelines.* Paris: UNESCO, 1987. 86 p. (PGI-87/WS/1)

MOREAU, Jean-Paul. Archives acquires important audio-visual material. *The Archivist.* March/April 1988: 15(2), 14-15.

MOREAU, Jean-Paul. Des trésors archivistiques mis au jour. *L'Archiviste*. Mars/avril 1988: 15(2), 14-15.

POZZO DI BORGO, Cécile, Odile RUDELLE et Maurice VAISSE. *Le témoignage oral: choix des témoins, conduite de l'entretien*. Congrès national des archivistes français (28e: 1986: Paris, France). Paris, 1987: 194-197.

SILVER, Jeremy and Lloyd STICKELLS. Preserving sound recordings at the British Library National Sound Archive. *Library Conservation News*. October 1986: (13), 1-3.

3.7.3 Description and finding aids / Description et instruments de recherche

ODDY, E.C. Characterization of content in historical cylinder recordings. IN ASIS '86: proceedings of the 49th ASIS annual meeting, Chicago, Ill., September 28-October 2, 1986; edited by Julie M. Hurd. Medford, N.J.: Learned Information, 1986: 244-247.

3.7.4 Public service / Service au public

3.7.4.1 Reference and research / Référence et recherche

CONTINI BONACOSSI, Giovanni. Oral sources concerning industrial history. *International Council on Archives. Committee on Business Archives. Bulletin*. 1987: (10), 31-34.

3.7.4.3 Copyright / Droit d'auteur

CALAS, Marie-France. *Problèmes juridiques posés par la consultation et la reproduction des documents sonores: critères de sélection des documents sonores dans une phonothèque*. Congrès national des archivistes français (28e: 1986: Paris, France). Paris, 1987: 218-225.

CHESTERMAN, John and Andy LIPMAN. *The electronic pirates: DIY crime of the century*. London: Routledge, 1988. x, 224 p. (A Comedia book)

FRANCE. MINISTÈRE DE LA CULTURE. DIRECTION DE L'ADMINISTRATION GÉNÉRALE. *Le droit d'auteur et les archives sonores et audio-visuelles*. Congrès national des archivistes français (27e: 1985: Limoges, France). Paris, 1986: 49-55.

3.7.4.4 Security and access / Sécurité et accès

CALAS, Marie-France. *Problèmes juridiques posés par la consultation et la reproduction des documents sonores: critères de sélection des documents sonores dans une phonothèque*. Congrès national des archivistes français (28e: 1986: Paris, France). Paris, 1987: 218-225.

3.7.5 Information processing / Techniques d'information

ROADS, Christopher H. and Lloyd STICKELLS. Neve digital processing desk at the British Library National Sound Archive. *Phonographic Bulletin*. June 1986: (45), 39-44.

3.8 Textual archives / Documents écrits

BELL, Mary Margaret. Preserving local history in Kentucky through microforms. *Microform Review*. Spring 1987: 16(2), 126-129.

CAHILL, Barry. Record keeping in a provincial regiment: the strange case of the loyal Nova Scotia volunteers, 1775-1783. *Archivaria*. Summer 1988: (26), 81-90.

CHAMBERLAND, Nicole. En partance pour le Canada. *L'Archiviste*. Novembre/décembre 1987: 14(6), 14-15.

CHAMBERLAND, Nicole. Sailing for Canada. *The Archivist*. November/December 1987: 14(6), 14-15.

COCHRANE, Shirley G. Manuscripts, manuscripts, manuscripts. *Manuscripts*. Summer 1988: 40(3), 201-209.

DOUGLAS, W.A.B. Archives and Canada's official Air Force history. *Archivaria*. Summer 1988: (26), 154-162.

DOZOIS, Paulette. Sources for the study of the International Labour Organization. *Archivaria*. Winter 1988/89: 27, 125-132.

GHYSSAERT, Jozef. Bijvoegsel aan de catalogus van handschriften van de stedelijke bibliotheek van Brugge. *Archives et bibliothèques de Belgique*. 1986: 57(3/4), 513-529.

HAY, Douglas. Archival research in the history of the law: a user's perspective. *Archivaria*. Summer 1987: (24), 36-46.

HELGERSON, Linda W. *Introduction to scanning technology*. Silver Spring, M.D.: Association for Information and Image Management, 1987. 36 p.

LENDERS, P. La Jointe pour Audition des Comptes: nouvelles pièces d'archives. *Archives et bibliothèques de Belgique*. 1986: 57(3/4), 487-496.

LOMBARDO, Daniel. The use of microform to support the Amherst Local History Project. *Microform Review*. Spring 1987: 16(2), 130-133.

OSTERLUND, Steve. Optical archiving systems. *DEC Professional*. June 1987: 7(7), 66-69, 72.

OTTEN, Klaus. *Integrated document and image management*. Silver Spring, Md.: Association for Information and Image Management, 1987. 66 p.

REYNHOUT, Lucien. Les manuscrits de Bruxelles des Disticha Catonis. *Archives et bibliothèques de Belgique*. 1986: 57(3/4), 462-486.

SAFFADY, William. *Optical disks for data and document storage*. Westport, Ct.: Meckler, 1986. 94 p.

SMART, John. The archival records of Labour Canada. *Archivaria*. Winter 1988/89: 27, 111-124.

SOURINOV, V.M. N.Y. Vavilov sur la documentation des travaux scientifiques et de recherches. *Sovietskje Arkhivy*. 1988: (4), 39-44.

STEPPLER, G.A. Regimental records in the late eighteenth century and the social

history of the British soldier. *Archivaria*. Summer 1988: (26), 7-17.

TAYLOR, Hugh A. "My very act and deed": some reflections on the role of textual records in the conduct of affairs. *The American Archivist*. Fall 1988: 51(4), 456-469.

TERRILL-BREUR, Judith. University publications of America's micropublishing concept for archival material in American history. *Microform Review*. Spring 1987: 16(2), 134-136.

WARNOW-BLEWETT, Joan. Saving the records of science and technology: the role of a discipline history center. *Science and Technology Libraries*. Spring 1987: 29-40.

YOUNG, Rod. Labour archives: an annotated bibliography. *Archivaria*. Winter 1988/89: 27, 97-110.

3.8.1 Acquisition, selection, appraisal and evaluation / Acquisition, sélection et évaluation historique et monétaire

BALLANTYNE, Derek. La DAF à l'ère des ordinateurs. *L'Archiviste*. Juillet/août 1986: 13(4), 20.

BALLANTYNE, Derek. The new tools of the trade: automation in the Federal Archives Division. *The Archivist*. July/August 1986: 13(4), 20.

BLAIS, Gabrielle. Recovering a lost heritage: the case of the Canadian Forestry Service Records. *Archivaria*. Winter 1987-1988: (25), 84-92.

BOCKING, Doug. The records go West: Department of the Interior Records in the Saskatchewan Archives. *Archivaria*. Winter 1987-1988: (25), 107-112.

BOOMS, Hans. Society and the formation of a documentary heritage: issues in the appraisal of archival sources. *Archivaria*. Summer 1987: (24), 69-107.

BROWN, Lauren R. Present at the Tenth Hour: appraising and accessioning the papers of Congresswoman Marjorie S. Holt.

Rare Books & Manuscripts Librarianship. Fall 1987: 2(2), 95-102.

CARROLL, Carman V. From deposit to donation: the National Archives' Acquisitions Strategy for Papers of Cabinet Ministers. *Archivaria.* Winter 1987-1988: (25), 29-43.

CHAMBERLAND, Nicole. En partance pour le Canada. *L'Archiviste.* Novembre/décembre 1987: 14(6), 14-15.

CHAMBERLAND, Nicole. Sailing for Canada. *The Archivist.* November/December 1987: 14(6), 14-15.

COOK, Terry. Legacy in Limbo: an introduction to the records of the Department of the Interior. *Archivaria.* Winter 1987-1988: (25), 73-83.

CUMMING, Judi. Gravel et Associés, avocats. *L'Archiviste.* Mai/juin 1988: 15(3), 12-13.

CUMMING, Judi. Gravel et Associés, law firm. *The Archivist.* May/June 1988: 15(3), 12-13, 15.

DELOTTINVILLE, Peter. Life in an age of restraint: recent developments in labour union archives in English Canada. *Archivaria.* Winter 1988/89: 27, 8-24.

ENDELMAN, Judith E. Looking backward to plan for the future: collection analysis for manuscript repositories. *The American Archivist.* Summer 1987: 50(3), 340-355.

FABIAN, Jurai. Pramenna hodnota memoarovych textov [Source value of memoir texts]. *Slovenska Archivistika.* 1986: 21(1), 73-81.

FISCHER, Ekkehard. Zur Erschliessung und Auswertung von Justizbestaenden im Staatsarchiv Schwerin [On the processing and appraisal of court records in the Schwerin State Archive]. *Archiv Mitteilungen.* 1986: 36(4), 120-123.

FISHBEIN, Meyer H. Reflections on appraising statistical records. *The American Archivist.* May 1987: 50(2), 226-234.

FITZGERALD, S.M.D. Botanical archives: notes for archive selection and classification. *Archives: the Journal of the British Records Association.* April 1988: 18(79), 144-152.

GRAY, David P. A technique for manuscript collection development analysis. *The Midwestern Archivist.* 1987: 12(2), 91-103.

KARAPETIANTS, I.V. Sur le versement des microcopies des rapports scientifiques et de recherches dans les Archives centrales d'État de la documentation scientifique et technique de l'URSS. *Sovietskje Arkhivy.* 1988: (5), 44-48.

LABERGE, Danielle. Information, knowledge and rights: the preservation of archives as a political and social issue. *Archivaria.* Winter 1987-1988: (25), 44-50.

LAVOIE, Andrée. Acquisition: la collection Guy Mauffette. *L'Archiviste.* Mars/avril 1988: 15(2), 16-17.

LAVOIE, Andrée. Acquisition: the Guy Mauffette Collection. *The Archivist.* March/April 1988: 15(2), 16-17.

LEBLANC, André. Tracking the worker's past in Quebec. *Archivaria.* Winter 1988/89: 27, 25-34.

LITALIEN, Raymonde. Acquisition: les documents Ramezay. *L'Archiviste.* Novembre/décembre 1987: 14(6), 10-11.

LITALIEN, Raymonde. Acquisition: Ramezay papers. *The Archivist.* November/December 1987: 14(6), 10-11.

MOMRYK, Myron. J.B. Rudnyckyj and the Bi- and Bi- Commission. *The Archivist.* May/June 1988: 15(3), 18-19.

MOMRYK, Myron. J.B. Rudnyckyj et la Commission sur le bilinguisme et le biculturalisme. *L'Archiviste.* Mai/juin 1988: 15(3), 18-19.

PHILLIPS, Faye. Harper's Ferry revisited: the role of congressional staff archivists in implementing the Congressional Papers Project Report. *Provenance.* Spring 1988: 6(1), 26-44.

ROTA, Anthony. The collecting of twentieth-century literary manuscripts. *Rare Books & Manuscripts Librarianship.* April 1986: 1(1), 39-53.

RUSSELL, Bill. D'hier à demain: le bureau de Londres. *L'Archiviste.* Novembre/décembre 1987: 14(6), 16-18.

RUSSELL, Bill. From the London Office. *The Archivist.* November/December 1987: 14(6), 16-18.

SEGUIN, Gilles. Appraising student academic records. *ACA Archademe.* October 1987: 3(1), 4-6.

SHAEFFER, Roy. The Osgoode Society survey of private legal records in Ontario. *Archivaria.* Summer 1987: (24), 181-185.

SHEPARD, C.J. Court and legal records at the Archives of Ontario. *Archivaria.* Summer 1987: (24), 117-120.

VOSAHLIKOVA, Dana. Nas rozhovor s dr. Emmou Urbankovou o fondech oddeleni rukpoisu a vzacnych tisku Statni knihovny CSR [An interview with Dr. Emma Urbankova about the stock of the Department of Manuscripts and Rare Prints of the State Library of the Czech Socialist Republic]. *Ctenar.* 1986: 38(7), 215-218.

WHYTE, Doug. Excavating the archival legacy of the Department of the Interior: the records of the Mining Lands Branch. *Archivaria.* Winter 1987-1988: (25), 93-106.

WILSON, Tony. The letterbooks of six New Zealand Chief Post Offices, (early 1880s-late 1910s) and their value as social and administrative archives. *Archifacts.* 1987: (3), 9-24.

3.8.2 Arrangement / Classement

FISCHER, Ekkehard. Zur Erschliessung und Auswertung von Justizbestaenden im Staatsarchiv Schwerin [On the processing and appraisal of court records in the Schwerin State Archive]. *Archiv Mitteilungen.* 1986: 36(4), 120-123.

MCCORMACK, Ros. And this is the best view... A new location for the John Oxley Library. *Archives and Manuscripts.* November 1988: 16(2), 119-128.

MUEHLEISEN, Horst. Die Ordnung und Verzeichnung von Militaerakten [Arrangement and listing of military files]. *Archivar.* May 1986: 39(2), 181-188.

SMITH, Colen. A case for the abandonment of "Respect". *Archives and Manuscripts.* November 1986: 14(2), 154-168.

3.8.3 Description and finding aids / Description et instruments de recherche

ALEGBELEYE, G.B.O. A study of the bibliographic control of Methodist church records in Nigeria. *The Indian Archives.* January/June 1985: 34(1), 53-62.

Automating the newspaper clipping files: a practical guide. Washington, D.C.: Special Libraries Association, 1987. 51 p.

BALLANTYNE, Derek. La DAF à l'ère des ordinateurs. *L'Archiviste.* Juillet/août 1986: 13(4), 20.

BALLANTYNE, Derek. The new tools of the trade: automation in the Federal Archives Division. *The Archivist.* July/August 1986: 13(4), 20.

CHAMBERLAND, Nicole. En partance pour le Canada. *L'Archiviste.* Novembre/décembre 1987: 14(6), 14-15.

CHAMBERLAND, Nicole. Sailing for Canada. *The Archivist.* November/December 1987: 14(6), 14-15.

KIMBALL, Margaret J. Workflow for processing manuscripts in automated systems. *Rare Books & Manuscripts Librarianship.* Fall 1986: 1(2), 117-126.

MCCORMACK, Ros. And this is the best view... A new location for the John Oxley Library. *Archives and Manuscripts.* November 1988: 16(2), 119-128.

MUEHLEISEN, Horst. Die Ordnung und Verzeichnung von Militaerakten [Arrangement and listing of military files]. *Archivar.* May 1986: 39(2), 181-188.

RABINS, Joan. Redescription reconsidered: current issues in description and their applications for labour archives. *Archivaria*. Winter 1988/89: 27, 57-66.

SHEPARD, C.J. Court and legal records at the Archives of Ontario. *Archivaria*. Summer 1987: (24), 117-120.

THOMAS, John B. Relator terms for rare book, manuscript, and special collections cataloguing: third edition. *College and Research Libraries News*. October 1987: 48(9), 553-557.

3.8.4 Public service / Service au public

BALLANTYNE, Derek. Histoire de repérer... *L'Archiviste*. Mai/juin 1987: 14(3), 7.

BALLANTYNE, Derek. A new system for researchers. *The Archivist*. May/June 1987: 14(3), 7.

MCCARDLE, Bennett. Les documents des Archives fédérales et le citoyen canadien. *L'Archiviste*. Juillet/août 1986: 13(4), 10-11.

MCCARDLE, Bennett. Federal Archival Records and the Canadian citizen. *The Archivist*. July/August 1986: 13(4), 10-11.

3.8.4.1 Reference and research / Référence et recherche

BALLANTYNE, Derek. Histoire de repérer... *L'Archiviste*. Mai/juin 1987: 14(3), 7.

BALLANTYNE, Derek. A new system for researchers. *The Archivist*. May/June 1987: 14(3), 7.

COPPEJANS-DESMEDT, Hilda. De l'utilité des livres de paye pour la recherche historique. *Conseil international des archives. Comité des archives d'entreprises. Bulletin*. 1988: (11), 69-76.

COPPEJANS-DESMEDT, Hilda. The utility of pay-rolls for historical research. *International Council on Archives. Committee on Business Archives. Bulletin*. 1988: (11), 77.

CREIGHTON, Ken. Using government records. *The Archivist*. July/August 1986: 13(4), 12-13.

CREIGHTON, Ken. Utilisation des documents du gouvernement. *L'Archiviste*. Juillet/août 1986: 13(4), 12-13.

DOUGLAS, W.A.B. Archives and Canada's official Air Force history. *Archivaria*. Summer 1988: (26), 154-162.

DRYDEN, Jean E. Subject headings: the PAASH experience. *Archivaria*. Summer 1987: (24), 173-180.

HAY, Douglas. Archival research in the history of the law: a user's perspective. *Archivaria*. Summer 1987: (24), 36-46.

HEAD, Lyndsay. 'E HOA, E RITI'-friend Ritchie. *Archifacts*. 1988: (2), 21-27.

HEAD, Lyndsay and Buddy MIKAERE. Was 19th Century Maori Society Literate? *Archifacts*. 1988: (2), 17-20.

HOUTMAN-DE SMEDT, Helma. Des documents de comptabilité importants et moins importants dans les archives du XVIIIe siècle. *Conseil international des archives. Comité des archives d'entreprises. Bulletin*. 1988: (11), 83.

HOUTMAN-DE SMEDT, Helma. Useful and less useful bookkeeping documents in 18th century archives. *International Council on Archives. Committee on Business Archives. Bulletin*. 1988: (11), 79-82.

LABERGE, Danielle. Information, knowledge and rights: the preservation of archives as a political and social issue. *Archivaria*. Winter 1987-1988: (25), 44-50.

PELUS, Marie-Louise. Business records and accounts: for a study of Hanseatic commercial enterprises in the 16th and 17th centuries. *International Council on Archives. Committee on Business Archives. Bulletin*. 1988: (11), 91-92.

PELUS, Marie-Louise. Livres et extrait de comptes: pour une étude des entreprises commerciales hanséatiques des XVIe et XVIIe siècles. *Conseil international des archives. Comité des archives d'entreprises. Bulletin*. 1988: (11), 85-90.

RABINS, Joan. Redescription reconsidered: current issues in description and their applications for labour archives. *Archivaria*. Winter 1988/89: 27, 57-66.

SHEPARD, C.J. Court and legal records at the Archives of Ontario. *Archivaria*. Summer 1987: (24), 117-120.

SMITH GRANGER, Diane. Les Archives publiques et la recherche généalogique. *Archives (Revue de l'Association des archivistes du Québec)*. Mars 1987: 18(4), 65-78.

TAYLOR, D.S. Researching collections of public officials: problems and solutions. *Southeastern Librarian*. Fall 1987: 37, 76-78.

WILSON, Tony. The letterbooks of six New Zealand Chief Post Offices, (early 1880s-late 1910s) and their value as social and administrative archives. *Archifacts*. 1987: (3), 9-24.

3.8.4.2 Conferences, displays, diffusion and publications / Conférences, expositions, diffusion et publications

COLES, Laura Millar. The decline of documentary publishing: the role of English-Canadian archives and historical societies in documentary publishing. *Archivaria*. Winter 1986-87: (23), 69-85.

GRISPO, Renato. Uno strumento per ea Ricerca: le pubblicazioni degli archivi di Stato Italiani. *Archives et bibliothèques de Belgique*. 1986: 57(1/2), 185-206.

JAYOT, Franz. L'exportation temporaire d'archives publiques pour cause d'exposition: étude d'un cas. *La Gazette des archives*. 1987: (136), 17-28.

WILSON, Bruce. Identités coloniales — Le Canada de 1760 à 1815. *L'Archiviste*. Novembre/décembre 1988: 15(6), 9.

WILSON, Bruce. New book illustrates richness of National Archives holdings, 1760 to 1815. *The Archivist*. November/December 1988: 15(6), 15.

3.8.4.3 Copyright / Droit d'auteur

FOTHERINGHAM, Richard. Copyright sources for Australian drama and film. *Archives and Manuscripts*. November 1986: 14(2), 144-153.

3.8.4.4 Security and access / Sécurité et accès

CARROLL, Carman V. From deposit to donation: the National Archives' Acquisitions Strategy for Papers of Cabinet Ministers. *Archivaria*. Winter 1987-1988: (25), 29-43.

COOK, Terry. Billions of records: What to keep? What to destroy? Archival appraisal and federal government records. *The Archivist*. March/April 1986: 13(2), 1-3.

COOK, Terry. Conserver ou détruire: comment évaluer les milliards de documents du gouvernement fédéral. *L'Archiviste*. Mars/avril 1986: 13(2), 1-4.

CREIGHTON, Ken. Using government records. *The Archivist*. July/August 1986: 13(4), 12-13.

CREIGHTON, Ken. Utilisation des documents du gouvernement. *L'Archiviste*. Juillet/août 1986: 13(4), 12-13.

The FBI and the farm equipment workers: FBI surveillance records as a source for C10 Union history. *Labour History*. Fall 1986: 27(4), 485-505.

FRUSCIONE, James J. The offline factor: information storage and security. *INFORM: the Magazine of Information and Image Management*. June 1987: 1(6), 20-23.

GREENE, Mark A. Developing a research access policy for student records: a case study at Carleton College. *The American Archivist*. Fall 1987: 50(4), 570-579.

HYAM, Grace Maurice. Accès aux documents. *L'Archiviste*. Mars/avril 1986: 13(2), 1, 4.

HYAM, Grace Maurice. Access to records and manuscripts. *The Archivist*. March/April 1986: 13(2), 1, 3-4.

HYAM, Grace Maurice. Limitations to use: the problem of access to private manuscripts. *Archivaria*. Winter 1986-87: (23), 175-178.

MCCARDLE, Bennett. Les documents des Archives fédérales et le citoyen canadien. *L'Archiviste*. Juillet/août 1986: 13(4), 10-11.

MCCARDLE, Bennett. Federal Archival Records and the Canadian citizen. *The Archivist*. July/August 1986: 13(4), 10-11.

MORDDEL, Anne. Data protection in the United Kingdom. *Records Management Quarterly*. October 1986: 20(4), 58-62.

3.8.5 Information processing / Techniques d'information

Automating the newspaper clipping files: a practical guide. Washington, D.C.: Special Libraries Association, 1987. 51 p.

BLAIS, Gabrielle. Recovering a lost heritage: the case of the Canadian Forestry Service Records. *Archivaria*. Winter 1987-1988: (25), 84-92.

BOCKING, Doug. The records go West: Department of the Interior Records in the Saskatchewan Archives. *Archivaria*. Winter 1987-1988: (25), 107-112.

BORSA, Ivan. Computer aided data processing of Medieval documents in the National Archives of Hungary. *Archives et bibliothèques de Belgique*. 1986: 57(1/2), 83-95.

COOK, Terry. Legacy in Limbo: an introduction to the records of the Department of the Interior. *Archivaria*. Winter 1987-1988: (25), 73-83.

FOSSIER, Lucie and Marie-Josèphe BEAUD. Introducing the Institut de Recherche et d'Histoire des Textes (C.N.R.S.): medieval book and computer. *Computers and the Humanities*. October/December 1986: 20(4), 267-268.

GUILLAUMONT, Agnès and Jean-Luc MINEL. MEDIUM: realities and projects. *Computers and the Humanities*. October/December 1986: 20(4), 269-271.

HAY, Douglas. Archival research in the history of the law: a user's perspective. *Archivaria*. Summer 1987: (24), 36-46.

KIMBALL, Margaret J. Workflow for processing manuscripts in automated systems. *Rare Books & Manuscripts Librarianship*. Fall 1986: 1(2), 117-126.

PIEYNS-RIGO, Paulette. Le notariat franchimontois: traitement informatique des actes notariés (1786-1795). *Archives et bibliothèques de Belgique*. 1988: 59(3/4), 133-148.

POOR, William E. Docu/Master information retrieval system. *Special Libraries*. Summer 1987: 78(3), 170-176.

SISSOKO, Sallou Amadi. Note sur l'informatisation des tables du journal officiel de la république. *ADPA*. 1987: 5(3), 11-22.

WHYTE, Doug. Excavating the archival legacy of the Department of the Interior: the records of the Mining Lands Branch. *Archivaria*. Winter 1987-1988: (25), 93-106.

4. Institutional archives / Archives d'institutions

CONWAY, Paul. Perspectives on archival resources: the 1985 census of archival institutions. *The American Archivist*. Spring 1987: 50(2), 174-191.

DANIELLS, Laurenda. *Grantsmanship and the archivist*. Vancouver: Association of British Columbia Archivists, 1988. 10 p. (A.B.C.A. publications; no. 4)

4.1 Governmental archives / Archives gouvernementales

ARNAULD, Marie-Paule et R. SAVAJOLS. Archives départementales-écoles, opération « relations croisées » en Seine-Saint-Denis. *La Gazette des archives*. 1986: (134-135), 226-229.

AUER, Leopold. Staatennachfolge bei archiven. *Archives et bibliothèques de Belgique*. 1986: 57(1/2), 51-68.

BALON, Brett J. and H. Wayne GARDNER. "It'll never happen here": disaster contingency planning in Canadian urban municipalities. *Records Management Quarterly*. July 1986: 20(3), 26-28.

BROWN, Thomas Elton and Patricia ARONSSON. Government archivists and government automation: the odd couple. *Government Publications Review.* September/October 1986: 13(5), 561-570.

HYAM, Grace Maurice. Accès aux documents. *L'Archiviste.* Mars/avril 1986: 13(2), 1, 4.

KRAUSE, Eric. The Fortress of Louisbourg Archives: the first twenty-five years. *Archivaria.* Summer 1988: (26), 137-148.

MACDONALD, R. Malcolm. Cooperation in local government: the Rome/Floyd Records Program. *Records Management Quarterly.* October 1986: 20(4), 12-14.

RICHEFORT, Isabelle. Un cas particulier de la collecte des archives publiques: les archives des établissements publics nationaux. *La Gazette des archives.* 1986: (134-135), 205-221.

SMART, John. The archival records of Labour Canada. *Archivaria.* Winter 1988/89: 27, 111-124.

4.1.1 Canada

ACA brief to the legislative committee on Bill C-95. *ACA Bulletin.* March 1987: 11(4), [3-5].

BALLANTYNE, Derek. La DAF à l'ère des ordinateurs. *L'Archiviste.* Juillet/août 1986: 13(4), 20.

BALLANTYNE, Derek. Histoire de repérer... *L'Archiviste.* Mai/juin 1987: 14(3), 7.

BALLANTYNE, Derek. A new system for researchers. *The Archivist.* May/June 1987: 14(3), 7.

BALLANTYNE, Derek. The new tools of the trade: automation in the Federal Archives Division. *The Archivist.* July/August 1986: 13(4), 20.

CARROLL, Carman V. Public Archives of Nova Scotia. *ACS Newsletter.* Winter 1988/1989: 10(4), 17.

COOK, Terry. Billions of records: What to keep? What to destroy? Archival appraisal and federal government records. *The Archivist.* March/April 1986: 13(2), 1-3.

COOK, Terry. Conserver ou détruire: comment évaluer les milliards de documents du gouvernement fédéral. *L'Archiviste.* Mars/avril 1986: 13(2), 1-4.

CREIGHTON, Ken. Using government records. *The Archivist.* July/August 1986: 13(4), 12-13.

CREIGHTON, Ken. Utilisation des documents du gouvernement. *L'Archiviste.* Juillet/août 1986: 13(4), 12-13.

DUNAE, Patrick A. The Provincial Archives premiers' papers. *ABCA Newsletter.* Summer 1987: 13(1), 11-12.

EASTWOOD, Terry. Attempts at national planning for archives in Canada, 1975-1985. *The Public Historian.* Summer 1986: 8(3), 74-91.

ESO, Elizabeth. *Promotion and outreach in a community archives.* [Vancouver]: Association of British Columbia Archivists, c1988. 7 p. (A.B.C.A. publications; no. 2)

FECTEAU, Jean-Marie. Les archives judiciaires au criminel et l'historien-né. Problèmes et perspectives. *Archives (Revue de l'Association des archivistes du Québec).* Décembre 1986: 18(3), 56-62.

FORBES, Jamie. *Records management and the Trail City Archives.* [Vancouver]: Association of British Columbia Archivists, c1988. 6 p. (A.B.C.A. publications; no. 5)

GARON, Louis. Les archives gouvernementales aux Archives nationales du Québec: de l'indifférence aux luttes de pouvoir. *Archives (Revue de l'Association des archivistes du Québec).* Mars 1987: 18(4), 22-40.

GARON, Robert. Les archives des organismes publics au Québec. *Bulletin de l'AEC.* Hiver 1988/1989: 10(4), 23-24.

GARON, Robert. Les archives judiciaires au Québec. *Bulletin de l'AEC.* Hiver 1988/1989: 10(4), 22.

HOLMAN, H.T. Having no entries, keeping no books: the records of the Prince Edward Island Fisheries Claims Commission, 1884-1888. *Archivaria.* Summer 1986: (22), 107-113.

HOPKINS, Mark. Computerizing a government records archives — The FEDDOC Experience. *Records Management Quarterly.* July 1986: 20(3), 36-39.

HYAM, Grace Maurice. Access to records and manuscripts. *The Archivist.* March/April 1986: 13(2), 1, 3-4.

ISAAC, Glen. *The arrangement, description, and appraisal of archival map series.* [Vancouver]: Association of British Columbia Archivists, c1988. 7 p. (A.B.C.A. publications; no. 2)

KEIRSTEAD, Robin G. J.S. Matthews and an archives for Vancouver, 1951-1972. *Archivaria.* Winter 1986-87: (23), 86-106.

KOJEVNIKOV, E.M. Sur les Archives du Canada. *Sovietskje Arkhivy.* 1988: (4), 90-96.

KOLISH, Evelyn. Le monde inconnu des archives judiciaires civiles au Québec: problèmes et perspectives de recherche. *Archives (Revue de l'Association des archivistes du Québec).* Décembre 1986: 18(3), 48-55.

KRAEMER, James E. National Postal Museum transferred to Archives, Museum. *Canadian Philatelist.* July/August 1988: 39(4), 254-256.

KRAUSE, Eric. The Fortress of Louisbourg Archives: the first twenty-five years. *Archivaria.* Summer 1988: (26), 137-148.

MCCARDLE, Bennett. Les documents des Archives fédérales et le citoyen canadien. *L'Archiviste.* Juillet/août 1986: 13(4), 10-11.

MCCARDLE, Bennett. Federal Archival Records and the Canadian citizen. *The Archivist.* July/August 1986: 13(4), 10-11.

MACLEOD, Donald. Quaint specimens of the early days: priorities in collecting the Ontario archival record, 1872-1935. *Archivaria.* Summer 1986: (22), 12-39.

MATRAS, Hagit. Jewish collections in the Public Archives of Canada [in Hebrew]. *Yad La-Kore.* September 1986: 22(3/4), 118-127.

New Archives Act for Canada. *ACA Bulletin.* July 1987: 11(6), 1.

New facility recommended for the National Archives of Canada. *ACA Bulletin.* January 1988: 12(3), 1-2.

PAC reorganization. *ACA Bulletin.* July 1987: 11(6), 10-11.

Revitalizing the Archives of Ontario. *ACA Bulletin.* September 1988: 13(1), [15-16].

ROBERTS-MOORE, Judith. The Office of the Custodian of Enemy Property: an overview of the office and its records, 1920-1952. *Archivaria.* Summer 1986: (22), 95-106.

ROSS, Alex. The records of the Hudson's Bay Company Land Department, 1879-1963. *Archivaria.* Summer 1986: (22), 114-119.

Saskatchewan Archives Board. *Saskatchewan History.* Autumn 1987: 40(3), 108.

SMITH, Wilfred I. "Total archives": the Canadian experience. *Archives et bibliothèques de Belgique.* 1986: 57(1/2), 323-346.

SMITH GRANGER, Diane. Les Archives publiques et la recherche généalogique. *Archives (Revue de l'Association des archivistes du Québec).* Mars 1987: 18(4), 65-78.

WALLOT, Jean-Pierre. Les Archives nationales du Canada en 1988-1989. *Bulletin de l'AEC.* Hiver 1988/1989: 10(4), 11-12.

WEILBRENNER, Bernard. Les Archives provinciales du Québec et leurs relations avec les Archives fédérales, 1867-1920. Quatrième partie: une longue torpeur, 1892-1920. *Archives (Revue de l'Association des archivistes du Québec).* Mars 1987: 18(4), 3-21.

WEILBRENNER, Bernard. Au service du public vingt-quatre heures par jour. *Archives et bibliothèques de Belgique.* 1986: 57(1/2), 411-436.

WEINBERG, Gerhard L. Proposed goals for the National Archives. *OAH Newsletter (Organization of American Historians).* November 1987: 15(4), 17.

4.1.2 France

ARNAULD, Marie-Paule et R. SAVAJOLS. Archives départementales-écoles, opération « relations croisées » en Seine-Saint-Denis. *La Gazette des archives.* 1986: (134-135), 226-229.

BABELON, Jean-Pierre. Le Musée de l'histoire de France aux Archives nationales à Paris. *La Gazette des archives.* 1987: (139), 260-265.

BARBIER, J. Le service historique de l'armée de l'air en 1985. *La Gazette des archives.* 1986: (133), 176-177.

BERCHE, Claire. *Les images fixes dans un nouveau département de la couronne parisienne.* Congrès national des archivistes français (28ᵉ: 1986: Paris, France). Paris, 1987: 32-35.

BERCHE, Claire. *La raison de la création d'un secteur audiovisuel en Val-de-Marne.* Congrès national des archivistes français (27ᵉ: 1985: Limoges, France). Paris, 1986: 9-11.

BERTIN-MAGHIT, Jean-Pierre. Le Comité interprofessionnel régional d'épuration de Paris. *La Gazette des archives.* 1987: (136), 29-40.

BILLOUX, Claudine. Les archives des grandes écoles. *La Gazette des archives.* 1987: (136), 41-43.

BLUM, Sylvie. Télévision/spectacle/politique. *Dossiers de l'audiovisuel.* Janvier/février 1988: 17, 61.

BONNIN, Hélène. *Les archives informatiques dans les archives communales.* Congrès national des archivistes français (28ᵉ: 1986: Paris, France). Paris, 1987: 160-161.

BOUVET, Mireille-Bénédicte. *Les archives des stations locales de télévision FR3 dans les archives départementales.* Congrès national des archivistes français (28ᵉ: 1986: Paris, France). Paris, 1987: 89-96.

Le Centre des archives contemporaines des Archives nationales; l'accès au contenu: la base Priam 3. *La Gazette des archives.* 1988: (141), 79-84.

CHOMEL, Maïc. *Les archives des chaînes publiques de radio.* Congrès national des archivistes français (28ᵉ: 1986: Paris, France). Paris, 1987: 208-212.

CLAIR, Sylvie. Le Centre des archives d'outre-mer. *La Gazette des archives.* 1988: (142-143), 5-17.

CONCHON, Michèle. L'archivage des fichiers informatiques: bilan de la mise en œuvre de Constance (1982-1988). *La Gazette des archives.* 1988: (141), 61-66.

CONCHON, Michèle. *L'archivage des fichiers magnétiques des administrations centrales bilan et perspectives de « Constance ».* Congrès national des archivistes français (28ᵉ: 1986: Paris, France). Paris, 1987: 130-148.

COUEDELO, Rose-Anne, Jean-Pierre DEFRANCE et Perrine CANAVAGGIO. *Bilan de l'enquête effectuée par la section des missions sur les archives audiovisuelles des administrations centrales.* Congrès national des archivistes français (27ᵉ: 1985: Limoges, France). Paris, 1986: 79-82.

COUEDELO, Rose-Anne. Présentation des missions. *La Gazette des archives.* 1987: (137-138), 103-112.

DEFRANCE, Jean-Pierre. Les archives audiovisuelles des services centraux de l'État. *La Gazette des archives.* 1987: (137-138), 150-161.

DEFRANCE, Jean-Pierre. *Bilan pour les Archives nationales des pratiques de collecte et de traitement des archives audiovisuelles des services centraux de l'État.* Congrès national des archivistes français

(28ᵉ: 1986: Paris, France). Paris, 1987: 97-106.

DETHAN, G. Le service des archives diplomatiques en 1985. *La Gazette des archives*. 1986: (133), 171-176.

DEVOS, J.-C. et M.A. HEPP. Le service historique de l'armée de terre en 1985. *La Gazette des archives*. 1986: (133), 172-175.

DU BOISROUVRAY, Xavier. *Les images fixes dans les archives départementales: l'exemple de la Loire-Atlantique*. Congrès national des archivistes français (28ᵉ: 1986: Paris, France). Paris, 1987: 26-31.

DUCHEIN, Michel. La clef du trésor: l'évolution des instruments de recherche d'archives du Moyen Age à nos jours d'après des exemples français. *Archives et bibliothèques de Belgique*. 1986: 57(1/2), 109-126.

DUCHEIN, Michel. Législation et structures administratives des Archives de France, 1970-1988. *La Gazette des archives*. 1988: (141), 7-18.

DUMONT, Jacques. Les techniques de la télévision. *Dossiers de l'audiovisuel*. Mars/avril 1987: 12, 13-54.

Les entrées d'archives sonores aux Archives nationales, départementales et communales: synthèse. Congrès national des archivistes français (28ᵉ: 1986: Paris, France). Paris, 1987: 189-193.

ERMISSE, Gérard. Les Archives nationales de France et leur public. *Janus*. 1988: (1), 26-28.

ERMISSE, Gérard. The National Archives of France and its public. *Janus*. 1988: (1), 13-14.

L'essor des archives communales. *La Gazette des archives*. 1988: (141), 139-168.

L'établissement cinématographique et photographique des armées. Congrès national des archivistes français (28ᵉ: 1986: Paris, France). Paris, 1987: 77-82.

FARCIS, Daniel. La mission des Archives nationales auprès du ministère de l'Inté-

rieur. *La Gazette des archives*. 1987: (137-138), 113-131.

FAUVEL-ROUIF, Denise. L'Institut français d'histoire sociale: ses archives manuscrites et imprimées. *La Gazette des archives*. 1986: (133), 161-165.

GAUTHIER-DESVAUX, Élisabeth. *La constitution d'un fonds local d'archives sonores: l'expérience ornaise*. Congrès national des archivistes français (27ᵉ: 1985: Limoges, France). Paris, 1986: 12-13.

HOURIEZ, Élisabeth. Bibliographie des inventaires, répertoires et guides d'archives publiés en 1986. *La Gazette des archives*. 1987: (136), 77-82.

L'informatique au CARAN. *La Gazette des archives*. 1988: (141), 128-136.

L'informatique au service des fonds clos: réflexions à partir des expériences faites aux Archives nationales. *La Gazette des archives*. 1988: (141), 118-127.

KORCHIA, Robert. *Les collections des archives photographiques*. Congrès national des archivistes français (28ᵉ: 1986: Paris, France). Paris, 1987: 44-48.

KOWALEWSKI, Anne-Françoise. Le Centre des archives contemporaines des Archives nationales: nouveaux aspects des bibliothèques. *La Gazette des archives*. 1988: (141), 85-86.

LACHOWSKI, Michel. La formation professionnelle aux métiers de l'audiovisuel. *Problèmes audiovisuels*. Janvier 1985: 23, 1-48.

LE MARESQUIER, E. Le service historique de la marine en 1985. *La Gazette des archives*. 1986: (133), 175-176.

LE PEUTREC, Christian. Journaux télévisés. *Dossiers de l'audiovisuel*. Janvier/février 1987: 11, 12-55.

MALAVIEILLE, Sophie. *Un fichier central d'archives orales aux Archives nationales*. Congrès national des archivistes français (27ᵉ: 1985: Limoges, France). Paris, 1986: 91-97.

MAROTEAUX, Vincent. Informatique et archives contemporaines, une approche nouvelle. *La Gazette des archives.* 1987: (137-138), 144-149.

MENIER, Marie-Antoinette. Cent ans dans l'histoire des archives de la colonisation. *La Gazette des archives.* 1987: (139), 207-222.

MEROT, Catherine et Christine LANGE. Le Centre des archives contemporaines des Archives nationales: la chaîne archivistique. *La Gazette des archives.* 1988: (141), 72-79.

MORELLE, Laurent. Les missions et la recherche. *La Gazette des archives.* 1987: (137-138), 178-187.

NATHAN-TILLOY, Michèle. *La collecte des documents audiovisuels dans les archives départementales.* Congrès national des archivistes français (28e: 1986: Paris, France). Paris, 1987: 83-88.

NAUD, Gérard. *Orientation pour un centre d'archives audiovisuelles.* Congrès national des archivistes français (27e: 1985: Limoges, France). Paris, 1986: 98-102.

NAUD, Gérard. Le traitement des archives au Centre des archives contemporaines des Archives nationales: le Centre des archives contemporaines dans le système archivistique français. *La Gazette des archives.* 1988: (141), 57-61.

OTT, Florence. Le centre rhénan d'archives et de recherche économiques. *La Gazette des archives.* 1986: (134-135), 222-226.

PASTOUREAU, Mireille. Maps at the Bibliothèque nationale: a collection of collections. *The Map Collector.* Autumn 1987: 40, 8-16.

PELLETIER, Catherine. Les études archivistiques de la Section des missions. *La Gazette des archives.* 1987: (137-138), 132-143.

PELLETIER, Monique. Geography for all: the founding of the department of maps and plans at the Bibliothèque natio-nale. *The Map Collector.* Autumn 1987: 40, 2-6.

PETILLAT, Christine et Anne-Claude LAMUR-DAUDREU. Le traitement des archives contemporaines dans les administrations centrales. *La Gazette des archives.* 1988: (141), 35-56.

PIEJUT, Geneviève. Feuilletons et séries. *Dossiers de l'audiovisuel.* Novembre/décembre 1987: 16, 51.

PRAX, Hélène. *Les archives informatiques: une approche régionale et départementale.* Congrès national des archivistes français (28e: 1986: Paris, France). Paris, 1987: 149-159.

RICHEFORT, Isabelle. Un cas particulier de la collecte des archives publiques: les archives des établissements publics nationaux. *La Gazette des archives.* 1986: (134-135), 205-221.

RICHEFORT, Isabelle. Les instruments de recherche élaborés par les missions. *La Gazette des archives.* 1987: (137-138), 165-177.

ROUX, Lucie. *L'archivage des documents sonores des radios publiques décentralisées: l'expérience des archives départementales de Belfort.* Congrès national des archivistes français (28e: 1986: Paris, France). Paris, 1987: 226-231.

SALAUN, Jean-Michel. Sport et télévision. *Dossiers de l'audiovisuel.* Mars/avril 1988: 18, 11-55.

SCHMITT, Frantz. *Le service des archives du film.* Congrès national des archivistes français (28e: 1986: Paris, France). Paris, 1987: 74-76.

TOURTIER-BONAZZI, Chantal de. *Les Archives nationales et les sources orales.* Congrès national des archivistes français (27e: 1985: Limoges, France). Paris, 1986: 86-91.

TOURTIER-BONAZZI, Chantal de. *Bilan du traitement des versements des documents sonores et collecte d'archives orales à la section contemporaine.* Congrès national des archivistes français

(27e: 1985: Limoges, France). Paris, 1986: 83-85.

VIGNES-DUMAS, Claire. Le Centre des archives contemporaines des Archives nationales: les archives audiovisuelles. *La Gazette des archives.* 1988: (141), 67-72.

VOISIN, Jean-Claude. *Comment traiter un patrimoine photographique: l'exemple des archives communales de Montbéliard.* Congrès national des archivistes français (28e: 1986: Paris, France). Paris, 1987: 36-43.

WELFELE, Odile. Information et formation du personnel des administrations centrales et des établissements publics nationaux. *La Gazette des archives.* 1987: (137-138), 162-164.

4.1.3 Great Britain / Grande-Bretagne

BECKLEY, Susan. Archive therapy in Carmarthenshire: some further developments. *Journal of the Society of Archivists.* April 1987: 8(3), 199-201.

BEECH, Geraldine. Cartography and the State: the British Land Registry Experience. *Journal of the Society of Archivists.* October 1988: 9(4), 190-196.

BERRY, E.K. The Local Government Act 1985 and the archive services of the Greater London Council and the metropolitan county councils. *Journal of the Society of Archivists.* April 1988: 9(2), 119-147.

BERRY, Elizabeth. The West Yorkshire Archive Service: the development of a unified service 1974-1983 and its work to 1986. *Journal of the Society of Archivists.* October 1987: 8(4), 247-257.

BLOOMFIELD, B. The India Office Library and Records. IN Encyclopedia of library and information science. New York: Dekker, 1985: 226-230.

BOWEN, Laurel G. The Manuscripts Department of the Illinois State Historical Library: the 1980s. *Illinois Libraries.* October 1987: 69(8), 582.

CLEMENTS, D.W.G. Preservation microfilming and substitution policy in the British Library. *Microform Review.* February 1988: 17(1), 17-22.

CLUBB, Clare M. The archives of the city and guilds of London Institute. *Journal of the Society of Archivists.* October 1986: 8(2), 124-126.

COCHRANE, C. Regional film archives in Great Britain: the report of a study tour. *Leabharlann.* 1987: 2ND, SER. 4 NO. 2, 35-44.

CORNISH, Graham P. Audiovisual archives in the United Kingdom [first report from the National Archival Collections of Audiovisual Materials Forum]. *Audiovisual Librarian.* May 1988: 14, 17-23.

FAGAN, Michele L. Practical aspects of conducting research in British libraries and archives. *RQ (Request Inquiries).* Spring 1987: 26(3), 370-376.

FITZGERALD, S.M.D. Botanical archives: notes for archive selection and classification. *Archives: the Journal of the British Records Association.* April 1988: 18(79), 144-152.

HARVEY, Charles. Business records at the Public Record Office. *Business Archives.* November 1986: (52), 1-17.

HURST, Warwick. Pre-Raphaelites and others: the Mitchell Library, State Library of New South Wales. *Journal of the Society of Archivists.* October 1988: 9(4), 173-175.

KIRK, Simon. The University of Leicester Archives Project. *Journal of the Society of Archivists.* October 1986: 8(2), 120-123.

KITCHING, Christopher. The history of record keeping in the United Kingdom to 1939: a select bibliography. *Journal of the Society of Archivists.* April 1988: 9(2), 88-100.

LEARY, William H. Preservation microfilming at the National Archives. *Microform Review.* Fall 1987: 16(4), 286-290.

LESTER, Robert E. Filming "The Oriental Question". *Microform Review.* May 1988: 17(2), 94-96.

ROBERTSON, Peter, ed. But we are fortunately able to carry on: letters from PAC's London Office, 1940. *Archivaria.* Summer 1988: (26), 176-177.

WILLIAMS, Bernard. Optical disks at the Public Records Office. *Information Media & Technology.* September 1987: 20(5), 204-205.

4.1.4 United States / États-Unis

ANDERS, Roger M. Our heritage in documents: the president and the atomic bomb: who approved the Trinity Nuclear Test. *Prologue: Quarterly of the National Archives.* 1988: 20(4), 268-282.

Archives II: a new building for the National Archives. *SAA Newsletter.* September 1988: 8-9.

Archivist's Perspective. Studying the constitution in the National Archives Field Branches. *Prologue: Journal of the National Archives.* Fall 1987: 19(3), 190-196.

ARNOLD III, Robert W. The Albany Answer: pragmatic and tactical considerations in local records legislative efforts. *The American Archivist.* Fall 1988: 51(4), 475-479.

BAILEY, Martha J. Microfilming state agriculture and forestry documents: program of the National Agricultural Library. *Microform Review.* May 1988: 17(2), 72-75.

BAUMANN, Roland M. The administration of access to confidential records in State archives: common practices and the need for a model law. *The American Archivist.* Fall 1986: 49(4), 349-369.

BOWEN, Laurel G. Illinois and the National Survey of Congressional Papers. *Illinois Libraries.* October 1987: 69(8), 547.

BRADSHER, James Gregory. A brief history of the growth of Federal Government records, archives and information 1789-1985. *Government Publications Review.* July/August 1986: 13, 491-505.

BRADSHER, James Gregory. Discussion forum: federal records and archives. *Government Information Quarterly.* 1987: 4(2), 127-134.

BRADSHER, James Gregory. Federal field archives: past, present, and future. *Government Information Quarterly.* 1987: 4(2), 151-166.

BRADSHER, James Gregory. National Archives and Records Administration. IN Bowker Annual of Library and Book Trade Information, 33rd ed. Bowker, 1988: 97-101.

BRADSHER, James Gregory. Researchers, archivists, and the access challenge of the FBI Records in the National Archives. *The Midwestern Archivist.* 1986: 11(2), 95-110.

BRETON, Arthur J. The critical first step: in situ handling of large collections. *The American Archivist.* Fall 1986: 49(4), 455-458.

BROWN, Lauren R. Present at the Tenth Hour: appraising and accessioning the papers of Congresswoman Marjorie S. Holt. *Rare Books & Manuscripts Librarianship.* Fall 1987: 2(2), 95-102.

BROWN, Thomas Elton. Archives law and machine-readable data files: a look at the United States. *ADPA.* 1986: 5(2), 37-42.

BUNCE, Peter W., W. Kenneth SHANKS and Shirley J. BURTON. More of trials, tribes, and topographers: an update on the holdings of the National Archives-Chicago Branch. *Illinois Libraries.* October 1987: 69(8), 590.

BURKE, Frank G.. You don't have to live in Washington to visit the National Archives. *Prologue: Journal of the National Archives.* Winter 1986: 18(4), 220-221.

BURTON, Shirley J. Documentation of the United States at war in the 20th century: an archivist's reflections on sources, themes and access. *The Midwestern Archivist.* 1988: XIII(1), 17-25.

BUTLER, Randall. The Los Angeles Central Library: "nightmare, part II". *Conservation Administration News*. January 1987: (28), 1-2.

CANAVAGGIO, Perrine. La conservation des archives présidentielles aux États-Unis. *La Gazette des archives*. 1986: (133), 123-142.

COCHRANE, Shirley G. Manuscripts, manuscripts, manuscripts. *Manuscripts*. Summer 1988: 40(3), 201-209.

COKER, Kathy Roe. Lessons learned and to be learned in inter-governmental appraisal. *Provenance*. Fall 1987: 5(2), 1-13.

Court holds that Privacy Act requires federal agencies to maintain accurate records. *Information Hotline*. May 1986: 18(5), 1, 13-14.

DALY, John. The Illinois State Archives, 1981-1986. *Illinois Libraries*. October 1987: 69(8), 578.

DALY, John. State Archives and metropolitan records: the case of Chicago. *The American Archivist*. Fall 1988: 51(4), 470-474.

DEPEW, John N. A statewide disaster preparedness and recovery program for Florida libraries. *Conservation Administration News*. April 1988: (33), 6, 13.

DIBBLE, Thomas G. *A guide to court records management*. Williamsburg, Va.: National Center for State Courts, 1986. xi, 94 p. (NCSC R-101)

ELDER, Sean. Just the facts, Ma'am: San Francisco's archivist, Gladys Hansen, debunks myths and resurrect buried thruth. *Image*. September 28, 1986: 15-16.

ENDELMAN, Judith E. and Joel WURL. The NHPRC/Mellon Foundation fellowship in archives administration: structured training on the job. *The American Archivist*. Summer 1988: 51(3), 286-297.

HACKMAN, Larry J. Cuomo transfers record management to New York State Archives. *SAA Newsletter*. March 1987: 8.

HACKMAN, Larry J. A perspective on American archives. *The Public Historian*. Summer 1986: 8(3), 10-28.

HALLER, Uli. Variations in the processing rates on the Magnuson and Jackson Senatorial Papers. *The American Archivist*. Winter 1987: 50(1), 100-109.

HEFNER, Loretta L. The change masters: organizational development in a State Archives. *The American Archivist*. Fall 1988: 51(4), 440-454.

HOOTEN, Bill. Archiving the archives. *Computerworld*. 24 August 1987: 21(34), 63.

HUBENER, Hal. Sunshine state showpieces: alligator-skin bindings in Florida Archives. *Provenance*. Fall 1988: 6(2), 42-43.

HUDSON, Alice C. and Maude D. COLE. The cartographic treasures in the New York Public Library, Astor, Lennox and Tilden Foundations. *The Map Collector*. Summer 1988: 43, 2-10.

INGRAM, John E. Preservation of library and archival collections at Colonial Williamsburg. *Conservation Administration News*. April 1988: (33), 1-2.

JOYCE, William L. The evolution of the concept of special collections in American research libraries. *Rare Books & Manuscripts Librarianship*. Spring 1988: 3(1), 19-29.

LOWELL, Howard P. Elements of a state archives and records management program. *Records Management Quarterly*. October 1987: 21(4), 3-14, 23.

MADDEN, Dennis D. *Offsite storage at the Nebraska State Archives: learning by strategy, trial, and error*. [Vancouver]: Association of British Columbia Archivists, [1988]. [7] p. (A.B.C.A. Publications; no. 6)

MILLER, Page Putnam. Fighting for a qualified, nonpartisan U.S. archivist: what we learned. *SAA Newsletter*. September 1988: 12.

NATIONAL ARCHIVES AND RE-CORDS SERVICE. *Guide to records retention requirements.* Washington, D.C.: National Archives and Records Service, Office of the Federal Register, 1986. 355 p.

National policy statement on our documentary heritage [draft statement]. *SAA Newsletter.* January 1987: 6.

NELSON, Anna Kasten. The 1985 report of the Committee on the Records of Government: an assessment. *Government Information Quarterly.* 1987: 4(2), 143-150.

New IRS record retention requirements. *Modern Office Technology.* January 1987: 31(1), 33-34.

1987 Local Government Records Bill [state of New York]. *Record.* Spring 1987: 5(1), 1, 4.

PARON, Gerardo. National Center for film and video preservation. *Conservation Administration News.* April 1988: (33), 7.

PETERSON, Trudy Huskamp. Archives fédérales, vie privée et personnages publics aux États-Unis. *Janus.* 1987: (2), 3-19.

PETERSON, Trudy Huskamp. Federal records, privacy and public officials in the United States. *Janus.* 1987: (2), 3-17.

POLITES, Angeline. The Documentary Heritage Trust of the United States: newest ally in the effort to preserve America's memory. *Conservation Administration News.* April 1988: (33), 8, 20-21.

POTTER, Constance. Research at the National Archives [NARA]. *Perspectives [American Historical Association Newsletter].* March 1987: 25(3), 15-18.

Privacy Act: privacy act system notices. Washington, D.C.: General Accounting Office, General Government Div., 1987. 17 p.

The Quiet Revolution: managing New York's local government records in the information age. Albany: N.Y. State Archives and Records Administration, 1988.

QUINN, Patrick M. Archival developments in Illinois. *Illinois Libraries [Special issue].* October 1987: 69(8), 533-606.

SCHULZ, Constance B. Analysis of the marketplace for educated archivists: state archives as a case study. *The American Archivist.* Summer 1988: 51(3), 320-329.

SOCIETY OF AMERICAN ARCHIVISTS. Archival census: first analysis. IN The Bowker Annual of Library and Book Trade Information. 32nd ed. Bowker, 1987: 390-396.

The Strange and convoluted history of the Nixon material: a retrospective, part I. *SAA Newsletter.* January 1987: 11-14.

Too close for comfort? A Reagan Library flap. *Newsweek.* February 23, 1987: 109(8), 30.

U.S. OFFICE OF MANAGEMENT AND BUDGET. *Managing Federal Information Resources: Annual Report under the Paperwork Reduction Act of 1980.* 6th ed. Washington, D.C.: The Office, July 1988. 63 p.

VEIT, Fritz. *Presidential libraries and collections.* New York: Greenwood Press, 1987. xvii, 152 p.

WEILL, Georges. La préservation des documents d'archives. À propos de deux enquêtes américaines récentes. *La Gazette des archives.* 1988: (140), 64-70.

WHEALAN, Ronald E. Microfilmed records in the John Fitzgerald Kennedy Library. *Microform Review.* October 1988: 17(4), 197-201.

WILSON, Don W. Prologue in perspective. The National Archives: new challenges, new opportunities. *Prologue: Journal of the National Archives.* Winter 1987: 19(4), 220-221.

WILSON, Don W. Prologue in perspective: National Archives II. *Prologue: Quarterly of the National Archives.* 1988: 20(2), 76-77.

WILSON, Don W. Prologue in perspective: serving the American people.

Prologue: Journal of the National Archives. Spring 1988: 20(1), 4-5.

4.1.5 Others / Autres

AGAFONOVA, E.A. et G.E. SOMINITCH. Les documents des Archives centrales historiques d'État de l'URSS sur l'activité des institutions d'archives en 1918-1922. *Sovietskje Arkhivy.* 1988: (3), 44-47.

AKERS, Robert C. Florence to the eighties: the Data and Archival Damage Control Centre. *Conservation Administration News.* April 1987: (29), 4-5.

ALEGBELEYE, G.B.O. Archival development in Nigeria. *Janus.* 1988: (2), 9-11.

ALEGBELEYE, G.B.O. Archives administration and records management in Nigeria: up the decades from amalgamation. *Records Management Quarterly.* July 1988: 22(3), 26-30.

ALEGBELEYE, G.B.O. Le développement des archives au Nigeria. *Janus.* 1988: (2), 26-28.

ALLERSTRAND, Sven. Arkivet foer Ljud och Bild (ALB) — The National Archives of Recorded Sound and Moving Images. *Phonographic Bulletin.* June 1986: (45), 7-11.

ALONSO, Vicenta Cortez. Archival education in Spain. *The American Archivist.* Summer 1988: 51(3), 330-335.

ALSBERG. P.A. The Israel Archives Law: a retrospect after 30 years. *Archives et bibliothèques de Belgique.* 1986: 57(1/2), 13-49.

ANDROSSOVA, M.E. Le classement des documents cinématographiques et photographiques des Archives d'État. *Sovietskje Arkhivy.* 1988: (6), 33-37.

ARAD, A. Indexing from "non-structured" input. *ADPA.* 1987: 5(3), 29-46.

Arsstatistk 1985 [Annual statistics 1985]. *Nordisk Arkivnyt.* 1986: 31(1), 10-18.

AUER, Leopold. Africa, Asia and Oceania in the Austrian State Archives. *Informa-tion Development.* January 1987: 3(1), 17-19.

AZEVEDO, Carmen Lucia de, Luciano FIGUEIREDO and Maria Regina HIPPOLITO. MAPA data base — Brazilian public administration memory. *ADPA.* 1986: 5(2), 69-77.

BABICKA, Vacslav. Archiv ministerstva unitra a archivy na slovensku 1918-1938 [Archives of the Ministry of Interior and archives in Slovakia]. *Slovenska Archivistika.* 1986: 21(1), 54-72.

BACK, Birgit Arfwidsson. Les archives en Zambie. *Janus.* 1988: (2), 33-36.

BACK, Birgit Arfwidsson. Archives in Zambia. *Janus.* 1988: (2), 16-18.

BACK, Birgit Arfwidsson. Les archives municipales dans les pays nordiques. *Janus.* 1988: (2), 22-25.

BACK, Birgit Arfwidsson. Municipal archives in the Nordic countries. *Janus.* 1988: (2), 5-8.

BALAZS, Peter. Ungarns Archivwesen nach 1945. *Archives et bibliothèques de Belgique.* 1987: 58(3/4), 383-409.

BARRITT, Marjorie Rabe. Archival training in the land of Muller, Feith, and Fruin: the Dutch National Archives School. *The American Archivist.* Summer 1988: 51(3), 336-344.

BATTYE LIBRARY. J.S. Battye Library of West Australian History. *Archives and Manuscripts.* November 1986: 14(2), 111-128.

BELOVA, T.V. et K.G. TCHERNENKOV. L'utilisation des documents des archives de la R.F.A.: critique et bibliographie. *Sovietskje Arkhivy.* 1988: (5), 99.

Berichte der Fachgruppen der Verein deutscher Archivare ueber ihre Arbeitssitzungen auf dem 58 Deutschen Archivtag [Reports of the various sections of the Association of German Archivists on their meetings at the 58th Congress of German Archivists]. *Archivar.* February 1987: 40(1), 77-88.

BERTRAND, Jean-Wilfrid. Les Archives nationales d'Haiti: près de deux siècles d'histoire, un nouveau départ. *La Gazette des archives*. 1988: (142-143), 25-35.

BLOUIN, Francis X., Jr. Moscow State Historico-Archival Institute and archival education in USSR. *The American Archivist*. Fall 1988: 51(4), 501-511.

BOAG, P.W. The state of NZ Archives in the 1980s — the administrative viewpoint. *Archifacts*. 1987: (2), 14-23.

BOLOTENKO, George. The current state of Soviet archives. *Archivaria*. Winter 1988/89: 27, 186-193.

BOOMS, Hans. Die archivgesetzgebung in der Bundesrepublik Deutschland. *Archives et bibliothèques de Belgique*. 1986: 57(1/2), 69-81.

BORSA, Ivan. Computer aided data processing of Medieval documents in the National Archives of Hungary. *Archives et bibliothèques de Belgique*. 1986: 57(1/2), 83-95.

BOUDANOV, O.A., V.R. KLEIN et V.V. TSAPLINE. Sur le perfectionnement des formes d'organisation des activités des Archives centrales d'État de l'économie nationale de l'URSS et des Archives centrales d'État de la documentation scientifique et technique de l'URSS. *Sovietskje Arkhivy*. 1987: (4), 52-54.

BRACHMANN-TEUBNER, Elisabeth and Wolfgang MERKER. 40 Jahre Zentrales Staatsarchiv: Archivarbeit im Dienste des Friedens und des Sozialismus [40 years of a Central State Archive: archive work in the service of peace and socialism]. *Archiv Mitteilungen*. 1986: 36(2), 44-51.

BRIDGES, Edwin C. Can state archives meet the challenges of the eighties? *Records Management Quarterly*. April 1986: 20(2), 15-21, 52.

BRIDGES, Edwin C. The Soviet Union's Archival Research Centre: observations of an American visitor. *The American Archivist*. Fall 1988: 51(4), 486-500.

A Brief introduction of the Chinese Archives Society. *Janus*. 1986: 3, 14-15.

BURLACU, Ioana. Les Archives de Roumanie après 1945. *Archives et bibliothèques de Belgique*. 1987: 58(3/4), 431-441.

BUTLER, Randall. Grass Valley's empire mine: a conservation challenge for the mining frontier. *Conservation Administration News*. July 1988: (34), 1-2.

BYKOVA, T.A. Sur la documentation du développement social des entreprises. *Sovietskje Arkhivy*. 1988: (5), 39-44.

CHRISTENSEN-SKOELD, Beatrice. The Swedish Library of Talking Books and Braille, TPB. *Phonographic Bulletin*. June 1986: (45), 22-24.

Les chroniques de l'édification archivistique en URSS [1962-1979]. *Sovietskje Arkhivy*. 1988: (1), 45-48.

Les chroniques de l'édification archivistique en URSS [1980-1987]. *Sovietskje Arkhivy*. 1988: (2), 48-51.

COLLIER, Rosemary. Ten years on: the Archives and Records Association of New Zealand. *Archifacts*. 1987: (2), 10-14.

COLLIER, Rosemary. Will action follow Acton? *Archifacts*. 1986: (4), 14-16.

COLQUHOUN, David. War art at National Archives. *Archifacts*. 1988: (2), 57-64.

La conférence nationale des responsables et spécialistes du Service d'archives d'État de l'URSS sur le perfectionnement de l'organisation du travail dans les conditions de la transparence. *Sovietskje Arkhivy*. 1988: (2), 3-27.

CROCKETT, Margaret A. A German local history centre: the Mannheim Stadtarchiv. *Journal of the Society of Archivists*. October 1986: 8(2), 117-119.

DAJIC, Mirjana. Les archives en Yougoslavie. *Archives et bibliothèques de Belgique*. 1987: 58(3/4), 483-496.

Le Décret du Conseil des Commissaires du peuple de la R.S.F.S.R. « Sur la conservation et la destruction des archives ». *Sovietskje Arkhivy.* 1988: (1), 41-44.

Der 58 Deutsche Archivtag 1986 in Muenchen. Vortraege, Berichte, Referate [The 58th Congress of German Archivists 1986 in Munich. Reports, Lectures, Seminar papers. *Archivar.* February 1987: 40(1), 1-22.

DE SILVA, G.P.S.H. Sri Lanka Archives: a brief account of its contents and an examination of its patterns of use. *Archives et bibliothèques de Belgique.* 1986: 57(1/2), 97-108.

DURANTI, Luciana. Education and the role of the archivist in Italy. *The American Archivist.* Summer 1988: 51(3), 346-355.

DURANTI, Luciana. Records management in Italy. *The American Archivist.* Fall 1986: 49(4), 459-462.

ERMISSE, Gérard et Paule RENÉ-BAZIN. Deux archivistes au pays des soviets: Paris-Moscou-Aschkhabad, 24 août-6 septembre 1987. *La Gazette des archives.* 1988: (142-143), 36-49.

FIALA, Tomas. Archives in Czechoslovakia after 1945. *Archives et bibliothèques de Belgique.* 1987: 58(3/4), 443-462.

FILIPOVA, Velicka. État actuel de l'archivistique en Bulgarie. *Archives et bibliothèques de Belgique.* 1987: 58(3/4), 375-381.

FISCHER, Ekkehard. Zur Erschliessung und Auswertung von Justizbestaenden im Staatsarchiv Schwerin [On the processing and appraisal of court records in the Schwerin State Archive]. *Archiv Mitteilungen.* 1986: 36(4), 120-123.

FOTHERINGHAM, Richard. Copyright sources for Australian drama and film. *Archives and Manuscripts.* November 1986: 14(2), 144-153.

FRANZ, Eckhart G. Archive im Dienst der Offentlichkeit: die Wanderausstellungen der Hessischen Staatsarchive. *Archives et bibliothèques de Belgique.* 1986: 57(1/2), 173-184.

FRASER, Alison. Records officers and the Acton Report, or, What's in it for me? *Archifacts.* 1986: (4), 13-14.

FRITZ, Walter. Das oesterreichische Filmarchiv [The Austrian Film Archive]. *Scrinium.* 1986: (34), 162-167.

Georgia's Archives. *SGA Newsletter.* Fall 1988: 20(3), 2-9.

GOBEL, Erik. Det dansk-norske arkivsporgsmal: Loosning i sigte [The Danish-Norwegian archive question: solution in sight]. *Nordisk Arkivnyt.* 1986: 31(2), 31-32.

GRAHN, Gerlinde. Die Auswertung des Archivgutes beim Aufbau der Grundlagen des Sozialismus und im Kampf um den Sieg der sozialistischen Produktionsverhaeltnisse (1949-1961/62). [Appraisal of archive material in the development of the foundations of socialism and in the struggle for victory in socialist productivity quotas (1949-1961/62)]. *Archiv Mitteilungen.* 1986: 36(2), 52-5

GRISPO, Renato. Uno strumento per ea Ricerca: le pubblicazioni degli archivi di Stato Italiani. *Archives et bibliothèques de Belgique.* 1986: 57(1/2), 185-206.

GROHMANN, Ingrid. Zur Einfuehrung des Ordnungsmodells fuer das Archivgut des Bestandstyps "Kreistag und Rat des Kreises" in den Kreisarchiven der DDR [On the introduction of the arrangement for the archive class "Regional assemblies and regional councils" in East German regional archives]. *Archiv Mitteilungen.* 1986: 36(4), 116-118.

GUNE, V.T. Marathi records at the Historical Archives, Goa, Panaji. *The Indian Archives.* January/June 1985: 34(1), 1-13.

HART, Beverly, Stephen ELLIS and Ian PRITCHARD. The appraisal and scheduling of government records: a new approach by the Australian Archives. *The American Archivist.* Fall 1987: 50(4), 591-597.

HEREDIA HERRERA, Antonia. Archivos e informatica: un proyecto de mecnizacion documental en Espana [Archives and information science: a project for automated documentation in Spain]. *Information Development*. April 1988: 4(2), 91-93.

HEROLD, Wolfgang and Detlef MAGNUS. Veranstaltungen zum 30 jaehrigen Bestehen der Facshule fuer Archivwesen "Franz Mehring" [Events to celebrate 30 years of the Franz Mehring Archive School]. *Archiv Mitteilungen*. 1986: 36(1), 27-28.

HUTCHISON, Anne. Gathering Westland's Archives. *Archifacts*. 1988: (2), 40-46.

Les institutions d'archives du pays [U.R.S.S.] sur la voie de l'accélération et de la restructuration. *Sovietskje Arkhivy*. 1988: (1), 3-20.

JAITNER, K.J. The European Community Historical Archives in Florence. *Journal of the Society of Archivists*. October 1988: 9(4), 176-180.

JOUKOVA, M.P. et Z.P. KHODAKOVA. Les listes des sources des accroissements des Archives d'État sont les bases de l'amélioration de la composition du Fonds d'archives photographiques d'État de l'URSS. *Sovietskje Arkhivy*. 1988: (6), 28-32.

KALNY, Adolf. Zpracovani obrazovych dokumentu v trebonskem archivie [Processing of iconographic documents in the Archives of Trebon]. *Archivni Casopis*. 1986: 36(3), 141-149.

KAMBA, Angeline S. Archive repatriation in Southern Africa. *Information Development*. April 1988: 4(2), 79-85.

KAMBA, Angeline S. Archives and national development in the Third World. *Information Development*. April 1987: 3(2), 108-113.

KAMBA, Angeline S. The impact of the National Archives of Zimbabwe Act 1986 on records management in Zimbabwe. *Commonwealth Archivists Association Newsletter*. November 1987: (5), 10-13.

KARAPETIANTS, I.V. Sur le versement des microcopies des rapports scientifiques et de recherches dans les Archives centrales d'État de la documentation scientifique et technique de l'URSS. *Sovietskje Arkhivy*. 1988: (5), 44-48.

KARTOUS, Peter and Frantisek SEDLAK. Die methodologie des publizierens von Quellen aus dem 18.-19. Jahrhundert. *Archives et bibliothèques de Belgique*. 1986: 57(1/2), 221-243.

KARTOUS, Peter. Hlavne ulohy slovenskeho archivnictva v rokoch 1986-1990 [Main tasks of Slovak archives for the period 1986-1990]. *Slovenska Archivistika*. 1986: 21(1), 3-10.

KETELAAR, Éric. Une brève introduction à la Société des archives en Chine. *Janus*. 1986: 3, 13-14.

KETELAAR, Éric. Centralisation, décentralisation et les archives aux Pays-Bas. *Janus*. 1986: 3, 15-19.

KETELAAR, Eric. Centralization, decentralization and the archives in the Netherlands. *Janus*. 1986: 3, 16-25.

KHARBOVA, Elena. Komplektuvaneto na arkhivniya fond v Bulgarskiya istoricheski arkhiv [Historical archives of Bulgaria at the National Library]. *Bibliotekar (Sofia)*. June 1986: 33(6), 21-24.

KHARTCHENKO, V.I. Le perfectionnement de l'appareil administratif et de la gestion des documents en Ukraine (1925-1930). *Sovietskje Arkhivy*. 1987: (5), 52-56.

KHORKHORDINA, T.I. De l'histoire des Archives nationales de Cuba. *Sovietskje Arkhivy*. 1988: (5), 90-96.

KIOBE, Lumenga-Neso. Les Archives nationales du Zaïre. *Janus*. 1988: (2), 29-30.

KIOBE, Lumenga-Neso. The National Archives of Zaïre. *Janus*. 1988: (2), 12-13.

KISS, Jeno. Learned libraries in Hungary after 1945. *Archives et bibliothèques de Belgique*. 1987: 58(3/4), 497-514.

KISTNER, Hans-Juergen and Ruediger OSTERMANN. Zur Aufbereitung historischer Archivdaten mit statistischen Methoden am Beispiel der Stadt Kamen [Handling and analysing of historical archive data by means of statistical methods — some examples of the city of Kamen]. *Archivar*. February 1987: 40(1), 87-94.

KLASINC, Peter. The Archives Centre for Professional and Technical Questions at Maribor (Yugoslavia). *Janus*. 1988: (1), 5-8.

KLASINC, Peter. Le Centre des archives pour les questions professionnelles et techniques à Maribor (Yougoslavie). *Janus*. 1988: (1), 17-20.

KLUGE, Reinhard et Diethelm WEIDEMANN. The archival system of the German Democratic Republic: its history, structure, objectives with reference to records on India therein. *The Indian Archives*. January/June 1985: 34(1), 15-32.

KOHL, Margret. Erfahrungen aus der Bearbeitung eines Grossbestandes der sozialistischen Epoche im Zentralen Stattsarchiv, dargestellt am Beispiel Staatliche Plankommission [Experiences in processing a major collection from the socialist era in the Central State Archive, illustrated by the example of the State Planning Committee]. *Archiv Mitteilungen*. 1986: 36(3), 82-86.

KOLOTOV, O.B. La succession au travail et la collaboration des archives administratives et d'État [en russe]. *Sovietskje Arkhivy*. 1987: (1), 26-33.

KUBICZEK, Barbara et Maria LEWANDOWSKA. Les archives d'État en République populaire de Pologne. *Archives et bibliothèques de Belgique*. 1987: 58(3/4), 411-430.

LAING, Josie. Maps or misfits. *Archifacts*. 1988: (2), 28-31.

LEONTIEVA, O.G. Sur les accroissements des archives d'État par les documents des kolkhozes et sovkhozes. *Sovietskje Arkhivy*. 1988: (5), 81-83.

LIENERT, Marina. Gedanken zur archivwissenschaftlichen Berwertung der medizinischen Betreuungsdokumentation im Gesundheitswesen der DDR [Thoughts of the archival appraisal of medical care documentation within East Germany's health programme]. *Archiv Mitteilungen*. 1986: 36(2), 65-71.

LILBURN, Rachel. Developing local authority archives in the Auckland region. *Archifacts*. 1986: (3), 9-12.

Local archives: current statutory provisions. *Archifacts*. 1986: (3), 12-13.

LOVELL-SMITH, Brian. Notes on the Canterbury Museum Map Collection. *Archifacts*. 1988: (2), 31.

MCBAIN, J. The Scottish Film Archive. *Audiovisual Librarian*. May 1987: 13, 88-90.

MACMILLAN, Bryony. The DSIR Herbarium at Lincoln. *Archifacts*. 1988: (2), 35-40.

MAREE, Johann and Anneke MARAIS. Famous collectors, book collections and the state of the art of preservation of library materials in South Africa. *Archives et bibliothèques de Belgique*. 1987: 58(1/2), 209-226.

MARR, Cathy. New Zealand government records management review: information can be managed, the Acton Report. *Archifacts*. 1986: (4), 11-12.

MBAYE, Saliou. Archives et recherche au Sénégal (1976-1984). *Archives et bibliothèques de Belgique*. 1986: 57(1/2), 295-308.

MICHAUD, Marius. Bibliothèques et archives privées: l'exemple des fonds privés de la Bibliothèque nationale suisse. *Arbido-R*. 1987: 2(1), 8-9.

MILOSEVIC, Milos. Archives de Yougoslavie. *Janus*. 1988: (1), 21-25.

MILOSEVIC, Milos. Archives in Yugoslavia. *Janus*. 1988: (1), 9-12.

MIREAULT, Manon. Les services éducatifs d'archives en Belgique wallonne. *Archives (Revue de l'Association des archivistes du Québec).* Décembre 1987/ mars 1988: 19(3/4), 10-22.

MORDDEL, Anne. Records management in Switzerland. *Records Management Quarterly.* July 1988: 22(3), 36, 47.

MUSEMBI, Musila. Archives development in Kenya. *Information Department.* October 1986: 2(4), 218-222.

MWIYERIWA, Steve. The developments of archives in Africa: problems and prospects. IN Aspects of African librarianship: a collection of writings; compiled and edited by Michael Wise. New York: Mansell, 1985: 222-263.

NDIAYE, Ahmeth. Les archives en Afrique occidentale francophone. Bilan et perspectives. *La Gazette des archives.* 1987: (139), 223-232.

NJOVANA, Samuel. Cours de gestion des documents au Zimbabwe. *Janus.* 1988: (2), 31-32.

NJOVANA, Samuel. Zimbabwe, national certificate in records management. *Janus.* 1988: (2), 14-15.

NOESSING, Josef. Das Suedtiroler Landesarchiv [The state archive of South Tyrol]. *Scrinium.* 1986: (34), 153-161.

NORBERG, Erik. ADP and archives in the Swedish Armed Forces. *ADPA.* 1986: 5(2), 43-52.

O'BRIEN, A.P. Establishing local authority archives. *Archifacts.* 1986: (3), 7-9.

PCHENITCHNYI, A.P. De l'histoire de la gestion des archives en URSS 1918-1941. *Sovietskje Arkhivy.* 1988: (3), 18-26.

PEBALL, Kurt. Der Neubau des Oesterreichischene Staatsarchivs [The new building of the Austrian State Archive]. *Scrinium.* 1986: (34), 135-143.

PERTI, R.K. *Le recrutement des spécialistes.* Congrès international des archives (11e: 1988: Paris). Paris, 1988. 5 p.

PETIT, Roger. Les affiches aux archives de l'État. *Archives et bibliothèques de Belgique.* 1988: 59(3/4), 111-125.

PETROV, G.D. Les chroniques sonores du Pays des Soviets. *Sovietskje Arkhivy.* 1987: (5), 42-45.

POKROVSKI, M. L'importance politique des archives. *Sovietskje Arkhivy.* 1988: (3), 11-15.

PONOMAREVA, V.I. et L.I. SOLODOVNIKOVA. Sur l'activité d'information des institutions d'archives du pays. *Sovietskje Arkhivy.* 1988: (5), 21-29.

Pour le 70e anniversaire du décret de V.I. Lénine sur les archives: l'arrêté du Conseil des Commissaires du peuple de la R.S.F.S.R. du 27 mars 1919. *Sovietskje Arkhivy.* 1987: (5), 46.

Pour le 70e anniversaire du décret de V.I. Lénine sur les archives: les chroniques de l'édification archivistique en URSS [1930-1941]. *Sovietskje Arkhivy.* 1987: (5), 47-49.

PRITCHARD, Colleen. Survey of business records. *Archives and Manuscripts.* November 1987: 15(2), 139-148.

RAFAJ, Pavel. Podil archivu na plncni volebnich programu Narodni fronty CSR [Sharing of archives in the implementation of the election programmes of the National Front of the Czech Socialist Republic. *Archivni Casopis.* 1986: 36(2), 69-71.

RICCI, I.M. and M. CARASSI. Adapting an ancient archives building in Turin. *Information Development.* January 1988: 4(1), 37-40.

ROESSLER, Monika. Erste Erfahrungen mit dem Archivpass im Staatsarchiv Schwerin [Initial experiences from using the archives control pass in Schwerin State Archives]. *Archiv Mitteilungen.* 1986: 36(4), 118-119.

ROGERS, Frank. Archival sources for New Zealand's medical history. *Archifacts.* 1988: (1), 19-24.

ROGERS, Frank. Western Pacific and Western Pacific High Commission Archives. *Archifacts*. March 1986: (1), 10-12.

ROSCHLAU, Gertrud and Volker ERNST. Thematische Inventare im Militaerarchiv der DDR [Thematic inventories in the East German Military Archive]. *Archiv Mitteilungen*. 1986: 36(4), 130-131.

RUMSCHOETTEL, Hermann, [et al.]. Archive in Muenchen: zum 58. Deutschen Archivtag und 13. Tag der Landesgeschichte [Archives in Munich: on the 58th German Archive Conference and the 13th Regional History Conference]. *Archivar*. July 1986: 39(3), 269-292.

RUMSCHOETTEL, Hermann. Der 57. Deutsche Archivtag 1985 in Hannover: Vortraege Berichte, Referate-Rationalisierung im Archivwesen-Moeglichkeiten und Grenzen [The 57th German Archive Conference 1985 in Hanover: lectures, reports, talks — rationalisation in archives — possibilities and limitations. *Archivar*. February 1986: 39(1), 5-20.

SBAITI, A.A. Archives automation at the Arab Fund for Economic and Social Development. *ADPA*. 1987: 5(3), 23-27.

SCADDEN, Ken. Maps — mainstream or misfits. *Archifacts*. 1988: (2), 32-34.

SCHOULLER, Jacques, Sylvia FILLING et David BATAZZI. L'archivage sur microfilm à Codes-à-Barres au parlement européen: la Base ARCO (archives courrier officiel). *Archives et bibliothèques de Belgique*. 1987: 58(1/2), 313-330.

SEIBEL, C. Sheldon. A superfund assessment from the records perspective. *Records Management Quarterly*. January 1986: 20(1), 28-34.

SHEIKK, Atique Zafar. The National Archives of Pakistan. IN South Asian Studies: papers presented at a colloquium 24-26 April 1985, edited by Albertine Gaur. London: British Library, 1986: 210-215.

SISSOKO, Sallou Amadi. Note sur l'informatisation des tables du journal officiel de la république. *ADPA*. 1987: 5(3), 11-22.

SLADEK, Oldrich. Podnikove archivnictui CSR v petiletce

1981-1985 [Business archives in the Czech Socialist Republic in the 1981-1985 Five-year plan period]. *Archivni Casopis*. 1986: 36(3), 129-133.

SMITH, Kenneth E. Vale David MacMillan (1925-1987). *Archives and Manuscripts*. November 1988: 16(2), 87-89.

70 ans du décret de Lénine du 1er juin 1918 sur les archives: la brochure de Petrograd sur les archives (1919). *Sovietskje Arkhivy*. 1988: (4), 27-30.

SOMINITCH, G.E. Le travail avec les microfiches dans les Archives centrales historiques de l'URSS. *Sovietskje Arkhivy*. 1988: (5), 79-80.

Sound archives in Sweden. *Phonographic Bulletin*. June 1986: (45), 7-24.

SPANG, Paul. Une page commune dans l'histoire des archives de la Belgique et du Luxembourg: le partage des archives du Grand-duché de Luxembourg après le traité de Londres du 19 avril 1839. *Archives et bibliothèques de Belgique*. 1986: 57(1/2), 347-369.

STAROSTINE, E.V. La provenance d'un principe de fonds du classement des documents. *Sovietskje Arkhivy*. 1988: (6), 18-28.

State archives. IN Buller, N. Libraries and library services in Portugal. Halifax, N.S.: Dalhousie University, School of Library and Information Studies, 1988: 75-79.

STRACHAN, S.R. The protection of local archives notice. *Archifacts*. 1986: (3), 14-18.

Svensk arsstatistik 1985 [Swedish annual statistics 1985]. *Nordisk Arkivnyt*. 1986: 31(2), 39-41.

SYMONDSON, B. Records disposal schedules, Aukland City Council, an introductory statement. *Archifacts*. 1988: (3), 17-19.

TARANOV, I.T. Le développement ultérieur des Archives est le souci des Soviets des députés du peuple [en russe]. *Sovietskje Arkhivy*. 1987: (3), 40-46.

THIAM, Mbaye. Pour une approche globale de la fonction archives en Afrique de l'Ouest francophone. *La Gazette des archives*. 1988: (142-143), 18-24.

THURSTON, Anne. The Zanzibar Archives Project. *Information Development*. October 1986: 2(4), 223-226.

TURNER, Éric. *Problèmes spéciaux dans les pays tropicaux*. Congrès international des archives (11e: 1988: Paris). Paris, 1988. 6 p.

UDINA, Federico. Espana y el consejo internacional de archivos (1950-1984). *Archives et bibliothèques de Belgique*. 1986: 57(1/2), 371-379.

UHL, Bodo, [et al.]. Berichte der Fachgruppen ueber ihre Arbeitssitzungen auf dem 57. Deutschen Archivtag [Reports from the specialist groups on their working sessions during the 57th German Archive Conference]. *Archivar*. February 1986: 39(1), 59-70.

ULATE-SEGURA, Bodil. *Access to the archives of United Nations agencies: a RAMP study with guidelines*. Paris: United Nations Educational, Scientific and Cultural Organization, 1987. 123 p.

UNION OF SOVIET SOCIALIST REPUBLICS. MAIN ARCHIVAL ADMINISTRATION. *Basic rules for the work of the USSR State Archives*. Moscow: Main Archival Administration at the USSR, Council of Ministers, 1984. xv, 352 p.

VAGANOV, F.M. Archival affairs in the USSR. *The American Archivist*. Fall 1988: 51(4), 481-485.

VAGANOV, F.M. Archivistique en U.R.S.S. *Archives et bibliothèques de Belgique*. 1987: 58(3/4), 463-482.

VAGANOV, F.M. Das Archivwesen in der UdSSR [Archives work in the USSR]. *Archivar*. February 1986: 39(1), 69-82.

VAGANOV, F.M. La vitalité des principes léninistes de l'édification des archives. *Sovietskje Arkhivy*. 1988: (3), 3-10.

VAN DER SAAG, Bert J. Automatic data processing in a municipal record office: managing information by micro-computers using Ask Sam (the text based management system). *ADPA*. 1987: 5(3), 47-59.

VOLKOVA, I.V. et N.A. KARPOUNOVA. Sur l'établissement des catalogues des documents dans les Archives d'Etat. *Sovietskje Arkhivy*. 1988: (5), 29-38.

VOSAHLIKOVA, Dana. Nas rozhovor s dr. Emmou Urbankovou o fondech oddeleni rukpoisu a vzacnych tisku Statni knihovny CSR [An interview with Dr. Emma Urbankova about the stock of the Department of Manuscripts and Rare Prints of the State Library of the Czech Socialist Republic]. *Ctenar*. 1986: 38(7), 215-218.

WALLOT, Jean-Pierre. A fascinating visit to the archives of the USSR. *The Archivist*. January/February 1987: 14(1), 14-15.

WALLOT, Jean-Pierre. Une visite fascinante des archives en URSS. *L'Archiviste*. Janvier/février 1987: 14(1), 14-15.

WARDS, I. National Archives in the past decade. *Archifacts*. 1987: (2), 3-8.

WEBER, Dieter and Margaret POELLEN. Gesetzliche Bestimmungen und Verwaltungsvorschriften fuer das staatliche Archivwesen und zur Archivpflege in der Bundesrepublik Deutschland [Legal restrictions and administrative requirements for state archive work and archive care in West Germany]. *Archivar*. May 1986: 39(2), 187-196.

WELLENS, Robert. Le département des archives contemporaines aux archives générales du royaume à Bruxelles. *Archives et bibliothèques de Belgique*. 1988: 59(3/4), 219-236.

WHITAKER, Albert H. *The New Massachusetts Archives facility: a study in planning and process*. Albany: NAGARA, 1988.

WHITTICK, Christopher and Margaret WHITTICK. CAS: a Dutch solution to records appraisal. *Journal of the Society of Archivists*. October 1986: 8(2), 111-116.

WISE, Joseph. An American look at micrographics in Japan. *IMC Journal*. 1987: 23(3), 22-23.

WOLFSHOERNDL, Vladimir. Povercnictvo poohospodarstva 1945-1960 [Commissionary of Agriculture 1945-1960]. *Slovenska Archivistika*. 1986: 21(1), 31-53.

YASUZAWA, Shuichi and M. ANDO. Japanese archives at the dawn of a new age. *Information Development*. January 1988: 4(1), 33-36.

ZIZHI, Feng. *Les choix technologiques des pays en voie de développement*. Congrès international des archives (11e: 1988: Paris). Paris, 1988. 4 p.

4.2 Business archives / Archives d'entreprises

ARMSTRONG, John and Stephanie JONES. *Business documents: their origins, sources and uses in historical research*. London: Mansell, 1987. xvi, 251 p.

BOOKER, John. The historical records of Lloyds Bank: an exercise in classification. *Business Archives*. May 1987: (53), 9-19.

CONNORS, Thomas. The labour archivist and the "labour question": two steps forward, one step back. *The Midwestern Archivist*. 1987: 12(2), 61-72.

COPPEJANS-DESMEDT, Hilda. De l'utilité des livres de paye pour la recherche historique. *Conseil international des archives. Comité des archives d'entreprises. Bulletin*. 1988: (11), 69-76.

COPPEJANS-DESMEDT, Hilda. The utility of pay-rolls for historical research. *International Council on Archives. Committee on Business Archives. Bulletin*. 1988: (11), 77.

CRESPO, Carmen. La conservation des documents et son application aux archives d'entreprises. *Conseil international des archives. Comité des archives d'entreprises. Bulletin*. 1988: (11), 27-32.

CRESPO, Carmen. Document conservation and its application to business archives. *International Council on Archives. Committee on Business Archives. Bulletin*. 1988: (11), 23-27.

DASCHER, Ottfried. Les Archives économiques régionales. *Conseil international des archives. Comité des archives d'entreprises. Bulletin*. 1988: (11), 44-45.

DASCHER, Ottfried. Regional economic archives. *International Council on Archives. Committee on Business Archives. Bulletin*. 1988: (11), 43-44.

DASCHER, Ottfried. Social history. Recent developments and contemporary perspectives. *International Council on Archives. Committee on Business Archives. Bulletin*. 1987: (10), 1-4.

DAVIES, Vanessa. The Archive and Library of Adam International Review. *Libraries Bulletin (University of London)*. April/June 1986: (37), 5-7.

DEPAUW, Claude. Les archives de la filature Motte & Cie à Mouscron. *Archives et bibliothèques de Belgique*. 1988: 59(3/4), 69-77.

DIXON, Diana. Bibliography [business archives]. *Business Archives*. November 1988: (56), 45-58.

DOLBEC, Michelle. Archives d'entreprise: Hydro-Québec. *Bulletin de l'AEC*. Hiver 1988/1989: 10(4), 18.

ECKER, Ulrich. Les archives de Fribourg en Brisgau et les relations publiques. *Janus*. 1987: (1), 10-12.

ECKER, Ulrich. The archives of Freiburg and public relations. *Janus*. 1987: (1), 13-15.

GARAY, K.E. The Saturday Night Archive. *Library Research News*. Spring 1988: 12(1), 1-133.

GARAY, K.E. The Saturday Night Archive. *Library Research News*. Fall 1988: 12(2), 1-155.

GARLAND, Sue. The Kent Business Archives Survey: a case study. *Business Archives*. May 1988: (55), 49-60.

GRAY, David P. *Records management for parishes and schools*. Richardton, N.D.: Diocesen of Bismarck, 1985. 44 p.

HAMON, Maurice. Archives d'entreprises, histoire industrielle et histoire sociale. *Conseil international des archives. Comité des archives d'entreprises. Bulletin*. 1987: (10), 5-12.

HAMON, Maurice. Les bâtiments économiques d'archives. *Conseil international des archives. Comité des archives d'entreprises. Bulletin*. 1988: (11), 33-34.

HAMON, Maurice. Economical storage facilities for business archives. *International Council on Archives. Committee on Business Archives. Bulletin*. 1988: (11), 34-35.

HARVEY, Charles. Business records at the Public Record Office. *Business Archives*. November 1986: (52), 1-17.

HILDESHEMEIR, Françoise. *The Processing of Architects' records a case study: France*. Paris: Unesco, 1987. 74 p. (PGI-86/WS/13)

HIVES, Christopher L. The future of business archives in North America. *Business Archives*. November 1986: (52), 27-36.

HIVES, Christopher L. History, business records, and corporate archives in North America. *Archivaria*. Summer 1986: (22), 40-57.

HOUTMAN-DE SMEDT, Helma. Des documents de comptabilité importants et moins importants dans les archives du XVIIIe siècle. *Conseil international des archives. Comité des archives d'entreprises. Bulletin*. 1988: (11), 83.

HOUTMAN-DE SMEDT, Helma. Useful and less useful bookkeeping documents in 18th century archives. *International Council on Archives. Committee on Business Archives. Bulletin*. 1988: (11), 79-82.

HYE, Franz-Heinz. Les archives de Innsbruck et les relations publiques. *Janus*. 1987: (1), 6-7.

HYE, Franz-Heinz. The Archives of Innsbruck and public relations. *Janus*. 1987: (1), 8-9.

IGUARTUA, José E. Les dossiers du personnel et l'histoire des travailleurs: l'exemple de l'Alcan au Saguenay. *Archives (Revue de l'Association des archivistes du Québec)*. Mars 1987: 18(4), 56-64.

JANSEN, Chris F.M. Gestion des documents et conservation des documents d'archives de sociétés. *Conseil international des archives. Comité des archives d'entreprises. Bulletin*. 1988: (11), 17-21.

JANSEN, Chris F.M. Records management and preservation of business records. *International Council on Archives. Committee on Business Archives. Bulletin*. 1988: (11), 9-16.

KLOS, Miroslav. Ucelovy objekt podnikoveho archivu Tatry Koprivnice [Structure of the Business Archives of Tatra Koprivnice]. *Archivni Casopis*. 1986: 36(2), 83-87.

L'HUILLIER, Hervé. Archives, témoignages oraux et histoire des entreprises. Quelques réflexions à la lecture de deux ouvrages récents. *La Gazette des archives*. 1987: (139), 256-260.

MCCLYMONT, Jill. The Dunedin City Council Archives. *Archifacts*. 1986: (4), 3-9.

MILLER, Peter. Business and legal archives: the Hocken Library's Experience. *Archifacts*. 1986: (3), 19-22.

MOORE, Idella. Undertaking a microfilming project. A case study. *Business Archives*. May 1987: (53), 21-29.

MORTON, Anne. The old company in a new age: 20th century records in the Hudson's Bay Company Archives. IN Glaciological data; Twelfth Northern Libraries Colloquy, 5-9 June 1988. August 1988: 307-313.

NOKES, Jane. The value of archives: selling the program. *Archives and Manuscripts.* May 1988: (1), 31-41.

PELUS, Marie-Louise. Business records and accounts: for a study of Hanseatic commercial enterprises in the 16th and 17th centuries. *International Council on Archives. Committee on Business Archives. Bulletin.* 1988: (11), 91-92.

PELUS, Marie-Louise. Livres et extrait de comptes: pour une étude des entreprises commerciales hanséatiques des XVIe et XVIIᵉ siècles. *Conseil international des archives. Comité des archives d'entreprises. Bulletin.* 1988: (11), 85-90.

PRITCHARD, Colleen. Survey of business records. *Archives and Manuscripts.* November 1987: 15(2), 139-148.

RETTER, David C. Business and legal records at the Alexander Turnbull Library. *Archifacts.* 1986: (3), 23-25.

RIKHEIM, Brita. Business archives as source material to social history. *International Council on Archives. Committee on Business Archives. Bulletin.* 1987: (10), 13-16.

RIKHEIM, Brita. Préservation d'archives d'entreprises — moyens de préservations d'archéologie industrielle et des archives d'entreprises. *Conseil international des archives. Comité des archives d'entreprises. Bulletin.* 1988: (11), 49-51.

RIKHEIM, Brita. Preservation of business archives — possibilities for preservation: industrial archaeology and business archives. *International Council on Archives. Committee on Business Archives. Bulletin.* 1988: (11), 47-49.

RIKHEIM, Brita. Verneplan for industriarkiver [Preservation plan for industrial records]. *Nordisk Arkivnyt.* 1986: 31(1), 3.

ROSS, Alex. The records of the Hudson's Bay Company Land Department, 1879-1963. *Archivaria.* Summer 1986: (22), 114-119.

RUMM, John C. Working through the records: using business records to study workers and the management of labour. *Archivaria.* Winter 1988/89: 27, 67-96.

SACLIER, Michael. Social history and business history in Australia. *International Council on Archives. Committee on Business Archives. Bulletin.* 1987: (10), 17-22.

SKUPSKY, Donald S. *Recordkeeping requirements: the first practical guide to help you control your records... what you need to keep and what you can safely destroy.* Denver, Colo.: Information Requirements Clearinghouse, 1988. xviii, 323 p.

SLADEK, Oldrich. Podnikove archivnictui CSR v petiletce 1981-1985 [Business archives in the Czech Socialist Republic in the 1981-1985 Five-year plan period]. *Archivni Casopis.* 1986: 36(3), 129-133.

SMITH, D.R.A. Mickey Mouse index: indexing and cataloguing the Walt Disney Archives. *Indexer.* April 1987: 15, 154-156.

SMITH, D.R.A. Preserving the history of Mickey Mouse. *AB Bookman's Weekly.* 23 May 1988: 81, 2185-2190.

SMITH, George D. Managing the corporate memory. *INFORM : the Magazine of Information and Image Management.* June 1988: 2(6), 8.

STOCKFORD, Bridget. Company archives in print: producing a company brochure. *Business Archives.* May 1987: (53), 31-38.

TEDDE, Pedro. La collecte des archives en regard des besoins des historiens d'entreprises. *Conseil international des archives. Comité des archives d'entreprises. Bulletin.* 1988: (11), 53.

TEDDE, Pedro. The ways we collect records — do they coincide with the needs of business historians? *International*

Council on Archives. Committee on Business Archives. Bulletin. 1988: (11), 51-52.

TORTELLA, Teresa. The Bank of Spain. International Council on Archives. Committee on Business Archives. Bulletin. 1988: (11), 3-7.

TORTELLA, Teresa. La Banque d'Espagne. Conseil international des archives. Comité des archives d'entreprises. Bulletin. 1988: (11), 1-3.

TURTON, Alison. Business archives principles and practice, a select bibliography. Business Archives. May 1987: (53), 51-57.

ULFSPARRE, Anna Christina. Practical solutions for the preservation of business archives. International Council on Archives. Committee on Business Archives. Bulletin. 1988: (11), 37-40.

ULFSPARRE, Anna Christina. Solutions pratiques pour la préservation d'archives d'entreprises: quelques aspects. Conseil international des archives. Comité des archives d'entreprises. Bulletin. 1988: (11), 40-41.

WRATTEN, Nigel. Setting up a records centre: some practical advice. Business Archives. May 1987: (53), 39-49.

XIUXIAN, Zhou. Les archives devraient servir les structures économiques actuelles. Conseil international des archives. Comité des archives d'entreprises. Bulletin. 1988: (11), 56-57.

XIUXIAN, Zhou. Archives should serve the current economic construction. International Council on Archives. Committee on Business Archives. Bulletin. 1988: (11), 55-56.

4.3 Religious archives / Archives religieuses

AEBERSOLD, Rolf, [et al.]. Bibliographie archivistique 1985/1986. Arbido-R. 1988: 3(2), 53-56.

Archives of the United Church of Canada. ACS Newsletter. Winter 1988/1989: 10(4), 15-16.

BAKER, Ron. Beulah Alliance Church Archives: a model for the arrangement and description of local church archives of the Christian and Missionary Alliance in Canada. Edmonton: R. Baker, 1986. 1 v.

BOULFATA, Issa J. The Arabic Manuscript Collection at Hartford Seminary. Pakistan Library Bulletin. June 1986: 17(2), 16-20.

DUFFY, Mark J. The archival bridge: history, administration, and the building of church tradition. Historical Magazine of the Protestant Episcopal Church. December 1986: 55, 275-287.

ERICKSEN, Paul A. Letting the world in: anticipating the use of religious archives for the study of non religious subjects. The Midwestern Archivist. 1987: 12(2), 83-90.

GERRARD BROWNE, Valerie. Loyola University of Chicago Archives. Illinois Libraries. October 1987: 69(8), 587.

GRAY, David P. Records management for parishes and schools. San Diego: Association of Catholic Diocesan Archivists, 1987.

KLIPPENSTEIN, Lawrence. Mennonite archives in Canada. ACA Bulletin. November 1988: 13(2), 1-2.

LANGE, Janet M. The Dirksen Congressional Center: A Better Kind of Memorial. Illinois Libraries. October 1987: 69(8), 577.

LYNCH, James R. Brethren Historical Library and Archives. Illinois Libraries. October 1987: 69(8), 567.

MACDONALD, Wilma. Anglican archives in Rupert's Land. Archivaria. Summer 1986: (22), 246-251.

O'TOOLE, James M. Things of the Spirit: documenting religion in New England. The American Archivist. Fall 1987: 50(4), 500-517.

Parish archives handbook: guidelines for the care and preservation of parochial records. Auckland: Provincial Archives Committee of the Anglican Church in New Zealand, 1986. 42 p.

Religious archives in the United States and Canada: a bibliography. Compiled by the SAA Religious Archives Section. Chicago: Society of American Archivists, 1984. 17 p.

SANFILIPPO, Matteo. L'Archivio segreto vaticano et le fonds de la première délégation apostolique permanente au Canada (1899-1902). *Cultures du Canada français*. 1988: 5, 219-226.

SHUSTER, Robert D. The Archives of the Billy Graham Center. *Illinois Libraries*. October 1987: 69(8), 566.

SWEENEY, Shelley. Sheep that have gone astray? Church record keeping and the Canadian archival system. *Archivaria*. Winter 1986-87: (23), 54-68.

TREANOR, John J. The Archdiocese of Chicago's Archives and Records Center. *Illinois Libraries*. October 1987: 69(8), 570.

VAN DE WIEL, Constant. Kerkelyjk Archiefwezen historiek en Huidige Wet geving. *Archives et bibliothèques de Belgique*. 1986: 57(1/2), 381-409.

WATELET-CHERTON, Anne. Les archives de l'évêché de Namur: contribution à l'histoire d'un dépôt d'archives diocésain. *Archives et bibliothèques de Belgique*. 1988: 59(3/4), 37-45.

WITTMAN, Elisabeth. The Archives of the Lutheran Church in America On the Eve of the Evangelical Lutheran Church in America. *Illinois Libraries*. October 1987: 69(8), 589.

4.4 University and college archives / Archives d'universités et de collèges

BARKER, Kevin. Past tense [UBC archives]. *Chronicle*. Spring 1988: 18-20.

BAUMANN, Roland M. Oberlin College and the movement to establish an archives, 1920-1966. *The Midwestern Archivist*. 1988: 13(1), 27-38.

BOULFATA, Issa J. The Arabic Manuscript Collection at Hartford Seminary. *Pakistan Library Bulletin*. June 1986: 17(2), 16-20.

CAREFOOT, Lillian. School archives: saving our collective memories. *School Libraries in Canada*. Fall 1986: 7(1), 45-46.

CLOUD, Patricia D. Fitting in: the automation of the archives at Northwestern University. *Provenance*. Fall 1987: 5(2), 14-26.

CLOUD, Patricia D. The Northwestern University Archives. *Illinois Libraries*. October 1987: 69(8), 595.

CLUBB, Clare M. The archives of the city and guilds of London Institute. *Journal of the Society of Archivists*. October 1986: 8(2), 124-126.

DE GRAFF, Kathryn. DePaul University Archives. *Illinois Libraries*. October 1987: 69(8), 576.

DENTON, A.W. The archive database manager: managing a college's archives. *Learning Resources Journal*. February 1988: 4(1), 34-46.

DUNN, Lucia S. The New Trier Township High School Archives. *Illinois Libraries*. October 1987: 69(8), 592.

FUNSTON-MILLS, S. and W.G. MCKINNIE. Archives in the School Library Resource Centre: getting started. *Emergency Librarian*. May/June 1988: 15, 17-21.

GARRISON, Ellen. L'il Abner revisited: The Archives of Appalachia and regional multicultural education. *The American Archivist*. May 1987: 50(2), 236-238.

The Guelph Collegiate and Vocational Institute Archives: statement of policy and procedures. *Emergency Librarian*. May/June 1988: 15, 22-23.

HEROLD, Wolfgang and Detlef MAGNUS. Veranstaltungen zum 30 jaehrigen Bestehen der Facshule fuer Archivwesen "Franz Mehring" [Events to celebrate 30 years of the Franz Mehring Archive School]. *Archiv Mitteilungen*. 1986: 36(1), 27-28.

HOLDEN, Harley P. Athens and Sparta: the archivist and resource allocators. *Provenance.* Fall 1987: 5(2), 37-46.

JANSON, Gilles. Les archives universitaires au Québec. *Bulletin de l'AEC.* Hiver 1988/1989: 10(4), 19-21.

JOYCE, William L. The evolution of the concept of special collections in American research libraries. *Rare Books & Manuscripts Librarianship.* Spring 1988: 3(1), 19-29.

KISS, Jeno. Learned libraries in Hungary after 1945. *Archives et bibliothèques de Belgique.* 1987: 58(3/4), 497-514.

KOCH, David V. The University Archives of Southern Illinois University at Carbondale. *Illinois Libraries.* October 1987: 69(8), 598.

LOSIER, Cynthia F. Fredericton High School Archives Project. *School Library — Media News.* October 1987: 16(1), 5-6.

MAREE, Johann and Anneke MARAIS. Famous collectors, book collections and the state of the art of preservation of library materials in South Africa. *Archives et bibliothèques de Belgique.* 1987: 58(1/2), 209-226.

PENNEY, Christine L. The Manuscript Collections of the University of Birmingham Library. *Archives (UK).* October 1986: 17(76), 27-32.

PILGER, Rick. The Timms Centre [University of Alberta Archives]. *New Trail.* Winter 1988: 15-19.

Recueil de délais de conservation des documents des collèges d'enseignement général et professionnel. Montréal: Fédération des cégeps, 1986. 1 v. (pag. multiple)

SANDERS, Robert L. The company index: information retrieval thesaurus for organizations and institutions. *Records Management Quarterly.* April 1986: 20(2), 3-14.

SCHIWY, Angela. W.A.C. Bennett Papers: personal, political and provincial records, 1959-1979. *ABCA Newsletter.* Summer 1987: 13(1), 8-10.

SHERMAN, Sarah. A case study: the archivist as activist at the Northwestern University Library's Women's Collection. *Provenance.* Spring 1987: 5(1), 31-38.

SHERVINGTON, Christine. Automating records management. *Archives and Manuscripts.* November 1986: 14(2), 129-143.

STREIT, Samuel Allen. All that glitters: fund raising for special collections in academic libraries. *Rare Books & Manuscripts Librarianship.* Spring 1988: 3(1), 31-41.

TOUGH, Alistair. The present position in university-based repositories. *Journal of the Society of Archivists.* April 1988: 9(2), 78-80.

The University Archives Office at the University of Waterloo... *Focus.* January/ February 1986: 21(1), 8.

WOOD, Thomas J. Archives and Manuscript Collections at Sangamon State University. *Illinois Libraries.* October 1987: 69(8), 597.

WURZBURGER, Marilyn. Current security practices in college and university special collections. *Rare Books & Manuscripts Librarianship.* Spring 1988: 3(1), 43-57.

4.5 Others / Autres

Les archives du monde du travail. *La Gazette des archives.* 1988: (141), 171-180.

BACK, Birgit Arfwidsson. Les archives municipales dans les pays nordiques. *Janus.* 1988: (2), 22-25.

BACK, Birgit Arfwidsson. Municipal archives in the Nordic countries. *Janus.* 1988: (2), 5-8.

BOULET-WERNHAM, Monique. Les ressources manuscrites et sonores du CRCCF. *Cultures du Canada français.* 1985: 2, 83-88.

B.C. Teachers' Federation organizes a strike archives. *BCLA Reporter.* July 1986: 30(4), 10.

BUTLER, Randall. Earthquake! The experience of two California libraries.

Conservation Administration News. January 1988: (32), 1-2, 23-24.

CHARNEUX, Jacques. Lettres et correspondants (1536-1801) dans les archives du Château de Mirwart (Saint-Hubert). *Archives et bibliothèques de Belgique.* 1988: 59(3/4), 21-35.

COOPER, Sarah. The politics of protest collections: developing social action archives. *Provenance.* Spring 1987: 5(1), 8-16.

CORNISH, Graham P. Audiovisual archives in the United Kingdom. *College and Research Libraries News.* February 1988: 14(1), 17-23.

DAY, David A. An inventory of manuscript scores at the Royal Opera House, Convent Garden. *Notes.* March 1988: 44(3), 456-462.

DAYS, D.C. Archival documentation of the history of geoscience. IN Geoscience Information Society. Meeting (22nd: 1987: Phoenix, Ariz.). Collections for the future: archivists, curators, historians, bibliographers speak... Alexandria, Va.: Geoscience Information Society, 1988: 7-17.

DELAET, Jean-Louis. Les archives de la ville de Charleroi. *Archives et bibliothèques de Belgique.* 1988: 59(3/4), 47-55.

DENIS, Philippe, Françoise ROSART et Guy ZELIS. Le Groupe Coordination Traces: une expérience de sauvegarde de la documentation des organisations sociales. *Archives et bibliothèques de Belgique.* 1988: 59(3/4), 63-68.

DE SILVA, G.P.S.H. Sri Lanka Archives: a brief account of its contents and an examination of its patterns of use. *Archives et bibliothèques de Belgique.* 1986: 57(1/2), 97-108.

DIBBLE, Thomas G. *A guide to court records management.* Williamsburg, Va.: National Center for State Courts, 1986. xi, 94 p. (NCSC R-101)

FILLION, Chantale. L'organisation des archives dans les bureaux de profession-nels. Enquête réalisée à Montréal. *Archives (Revue de l'Association des archivistes du Québec).* Automne 1988: 20(2), 21-43.

FITZGERALD, S.M.D. Botanical archives: notes for archive selection and classification. *Archives: the Journal of the British Records Association.* April 1988: 18(79), 144-152.

GILDEMEISTER, Glen. The Earl W. Hayter Regional History Center at Northern Illinois University. *Illinois Libraries.* October 1987: 69(8), 593.

HACKMAN, Larry J. and Joan WARNOW-BLEWETT. The documentation strategy process: a model and case study. *The American Archivist.* Winter 1987: 50(1), 12-47.

HILDESHEMEIR, Françoise. *The Processing of Architects' records a case study: France.* Paris: Unesco, 1987. 74 p. (PGI-86/WS/13)

HILLER, I. The Central Library of the University of Forestry and the Wood Industry [i.e. science] as a public collections centre of the university. *IATUL Quarterly.* Summer 1987: 1, 174-181.

HOBBS, Brenda. "Automating the lifecycle — a municipal perspective". IN Proceedings: Conference of the Association of Canadian Archivists (1987: McMaster University). Hamilton, Ont., 1987. 7 p.

HUTCHISON, Anne. Gathering Westland's Archives. *Archifacts.* 1988: (2), 40-46.

JOHNSON, Timothy J. The Covenant Archives and Historical Library. *Illinois Libraries.* October 1987: 69(8), 574.

JOHNSON, Timothy J. The Swedish American Archives of Greater Chicago. *Illinois Libraries.* October 1987: 69(8), 600.

KATES, Christine J.N. The Osgoode Society: preservation of legal records. *Law Society Gazette.* March 1987: 21(1), 58-70.

KEIRSTEAD, Robin G. Hospital archives: professional challenge. *ABCA Newsletter.* Winter 1987: 12(5), 9-11.

KEIRSTEAD, Robin G. J.S. Matthews and an archives for Vancouver, 1951-1972. *Archivaria.* Winter 1986-87: (23), 86-106.

KENWORTHY, Mary Anne, [et al.]. *Preserving field records: archival techniques for archaeologists and anthropologists.* Philadelphia: University Museum, University of Pennsylvania, 1985. x, 102 p.

KISS, Jeno. Learned libraries in Hungary after 1945. *Archives et bibliothèques de Belgique.* 1987: 58(3/4), 497-514.

KNOWLTON, Elizabeth. Documenting the Gay Rights Movement. *Provenance.* Spring 1987: 5(1), 17-30.

LAINE, Edward W. Kallista Perintoa-Precious Legacy!: Finnish-Canadian archives, 1882-1985. *Archivaria.* Summer 1986: (22), 75-94.

LOVELL-SMITH, Brian. Notes on the Canterbury Museum Map Collection. *Archifacts.* 1988: (2), 31.

MCCLYMONT, Jill. The Dunedin City Council Archives. *Archifacts.* 1986: (4), 3-9.

MACE, Angela. *The Royal Institute of British Architects: a guide to its archive and history.* With an essay by Robert Thorne. London: New York: Mansell Publishing Limited, 1986. 378 p.

MACMILLAN, Bryony. The DSIR Herbarium at Lincoln. *Archifacts.* 1988: (2), 35-40.

MAHER, William J. The Illini Archives in the 1980s. *Illinois Libraries.* October 1987: 69(8), 584.

MICHELSON, Avra. Description and reference in the age of automation. *The American Archivist.* Spring 1987: 50(2), 192-208.

MOLGAT, Anne. Canadian women's movement archives. *CCWH Newsletter.* Fall 1988: 1-3.

MOORE, Karl. The Illinois Regional Archives: putting the past in our grasp. *Illinois Libraries.* September 1987: 69(7), 525.

MOTLEY, Archie. The Chicago Historical Society. *Illinois Libraries.* October 1987: 69(8), 572.

NOËL, Ginette. Les archives municipales et la recherche: la réalité à la Ville de Québec. *Archives (Revue de l'Association des archivistes du Québec).* Mars 1987: 18(4), 41-55.

NORBERG, Erik. ADP and archives in the Swedish Armed Forces. *ADPA.* 1986: 5(2), 43-52.

OAKES, Kathleen. Sci-Tech meeting. *Archives and Manuscripts.* November 1986: 14(2), 169-172.

PAGÉ, Lucie. Les archives de l'Ontario français conservées au Centre de recherche en civilisation canadienne-française. *Cultures du Canada français.* 1988: 5, 227-232.

PAGÉ, Lucie. Les archives du CRCCF. *Cultures du Canada français.* 1985: 2, 94-96.

PAGÉ, Lucie. Les archives du CRCCF. *Cultures du Canada français.* 1986: 3, 95-98.

PAGÉ, Lucie. Les archives du CRCCF. *Cultures du Canada français.* 1987: 4, 98-102.

PAGÉ, Lucie. Les archives iconographiques de l'Ontario français. *Cultures du Canada français.* 1985: 2, 79-82.

PARKS, Stephen. *The Elizabethan Club of Yale University and its library.* New Haven: Yale University Press, 1986. 280 p. (The Elizabethan Club series; v. 8)

POTHIER, Bernard. Archival material at the Canadian War Museum. *Archivaria.* Summer 1988: (26), 149-153.

Pourquoi conserver les archives des médias? Rapports et débats de la table ronde tenue en matinée. *La Gazette des archives.* 1988: (140), 9-37.

RÉMILLARD, Juliette. Le Centre de recherche Lionel-Groulx. *Bulletin de l'AEC*. Hiver 1988/1989: 10(4), 24-25.

SCHAEFFER, Roy. The Law Society of Upper Canada Archives. *Law Society Gazette*. March 1987: 21(1), 48-57.

SHERMAN, Sarah. A case study: the archivist as activist at the Northwestern University Library's Women's Collection. *Provenance*. Spring 1987: 5(1), 31-38.

SPADONI, Carl. The contribution of librarianship to Medical Archives. *Bibliotheca Medica Canadiana*. 1987: 9(1), 53-66.

THIBODEAU, S.G. For the records: federal geoscientist and the National Archives. IN Geoscience Information Society. Meeting (22nd: 1987: Phoenix, Ariz.). Collections for the future: archivists, curators, historians, bibliographers speak... Alexandria, Va.: Geoscience Information Society, 1988: 9-25.

THOMAS, Bettye Collier. Towards black feminism: the creation of the Bethune Museum-Archives. *Special Collections*. Spring/Summer 1986: 43-66.

VAN DER SAAG, Bert J. Automatic data processing in a municipal record office: managing information by micro-computers using Ask Sam (the text based management system). *ADPA*. 1987: 5(3), 47-59.

VERDEBOUT, Luc. Le fonds d'archives musicales de la collégiale Saint-Vincent-de-Soignies. *Archives et bibliothèques de Belgique*. 1988: 59(3/4), 209-217.

WALSH, Mark. Documenting our side of the Detroit River: the Municipal Archives, Windsor Public Library. *Archivaria*. Summer 1986: (22), 238-245.

WESTERBERG, Kermit B. Swenson Swedish Immigration Research Center. *Illinois Libraries*. October 1987: 69(8), 601.

5. Technical services / Services techniques

ABT, Jeffrey. Objectifying the book: the impact of science on books and manuscripts. *Recent Trends in Rare Book Librarianship*. Summer 1987: 23-38.

BANNASCH, Hermann. Dokumentenverantwortung — aktuelle Aspekte aus der Sicht der Archive "Safekeeping documents — actual problems from the point of view of archives". *Nachrichten für Dokumentation*. June 1988: 39, 145-150.

DESMARAIS, Norman. CD/Private+: easy access to private company information. *Optical Information Systems*. September/October 1988: 8(5), 248-259.

HOLDEN, Jill R.J. *Opportunities in the United States for Education in Book and Paper Conservation and Preservation*. January 1988. 25 p.

Imaging. *Records and Retrieval Report*. December 1988: 4(10), 1-14.

MANASSE, P.M. and H.A. SANDERS. Conservering in het IISG: beleids-en organisatorische aspecten "Conservation at the International Institute for Social History: policy and organizational aspects". *Open*. April 1987: 19, 206-212.

THOMAS, D.L. *Conservation et sécurité des fonds et collections d'archives: une étude RAMP accompagnée de principes directeurs*. Paris: Unesco, 1988. iv, 45 p. (PGI-86/WS/23)

5.1 Preservation / Préservation

ADELSTEIN, Peter Z. and James M. REILLY. The Image Permanence Institute: new preservation resource. *INFORM: the Magazine of Information and Image Management*. October 1987: 1(10), 37-39.

AKERS, Robert C. Florence to the eighties: the Data and Archival Damage Control Centre. *Conservation Administration News*. April 1987: (29), 4-5.

AMMERMAN, Dean. Salvaging damaged microfilm. *AIIM Conference Daily*. April 30, 1987: 67-68.

ANDERSON, Hazel and John E. MCINTYRE. *Planning manual for disaster control in Scottish libraries and records offices.* Edinburgh: National Library of Scotland, 1985. 75 p.

BALON, Brett J. and H. Wayne GARDNER. Disaster contingency planning: the basic elements. *Records Management Quarterly.* January 1987: 21(1), 14-16.

BALON, Brett J. and H. Wayne GARDNER. Disaster planning for electronic records. *Records Management Quarterly.* July 1988: 22(3), 20-25, 30.

BALON, Brett J. and H. Wayne GARDNER. "It'll never happen here": disaster contingency planning in Canadian urban municipalities. *Records Management Quarterly.* July 1986: 20(3), 26-28.

BANKS, Joyce M. *Directives régissant la conservation préventive.* Éd. rév. Ottawa: Comité chargé de la conservation et de la préservation des documents de bibliothèque, Bibliothèque nationale du Canada, 1987. 45 p.

BANKS, Joyce M. *Guidelines for preventive conservation.* Rev. ed. Ottawa: Committee on Conservation/Preservation of Library Materials, National Library of Canada, 1987. 45 p.

BAUTSCH, Gail. What you don't know can hurt you. *Records Management Quarterly.* October 1986: 20(4), 20-24.

BAYNES-COPE, A.D. Ethics and the conservation of archival documents. *Journal of the Society of Archivists.* October 1988: 9(4), 185-187.

BLOODWORTH, J.G. and M.J. PARKINSON. The display of parchment and vellum. *Journal of the Society of Archivists.* April 1988: 9(2), 65-68.

BRICHFORD, Maynard J. A brief history of the physical protection of archives. *Conservation Administration News.* October 1987: (31), 10, 21.

BUCHANAN, Sally. *Disaster planning: preparedness and recovery for libraries and archives.* Paris: Unesco, 1988. vi, 187 p. (PGI-88/WS/6)

BULGAWICZ, Susan and Charles E. NOLAN. Disaster planning and recovery: a regional approach. *Records Management Quarterly.* January 1987: 21(1), 14-16.

BUTLER, Randall. The Inland Empire Libraries Disaster Response Network. *Conservation Administration News.* July 1988: (34), 8-9.

BYRNES, Margaret M. and Nancy E. ELKINGTON. Containing preservation microfilming costs at the University of Michigan Library. *Microform Review.* Winter 1987: 16(1), 37-39.

CALMES, Alan. The importance of containers for the preservation of paper archives. *Archives et bibliothèques de Belgique.* 1987: 58(1/2), 33-44.

CALMES, Alan. Theory and practice of paper preservation for archives. *Restaurator.* 1988: 9(2), 96-111.

CALMES, Alan. To archives and preserve: a media primer. *INFORM: the Magazine of Information and Image Management.* May 1987: 1(5), 14-17, 33.

CANNING, Bonnie. Backup and redundancy for automated records systems. *Administrative Management.* September 1987: 48(9), 41.

CARLISLE, Van G. Avoiding electronic media disasters. *Records Management Quarterly.* January 1986: 20(1), 42-43.

CARSON, Eugene. Distributed access to administrative systems. *Cause/Effect.* September 1987: 10(5), 6-12.

CLAPP, Anne F. *Curatorial care of works of art on paper: basic procedures for paper preservation.* New York: Nick Lyons Books, 1987. x, 191 p.

CLEMENTS, D.W.G. *Preservation and conservation of library documents: a UNESCO/IFLA/ICA enquiry into the current state of the world's patrimony.* Paris: UNESCO, 1987. 32 p. PGI-87/WS/15.

COOKE, Donald F. Map storage on CD-ROM. *Byte*. July 1987: 129-130, 132, 134-136, 138.

COPPENS, Chris. De "International Paper Conservation Conference", Oxford 14-18 April 1986: enkele aantekeningen. *Archives et bibliothèques de Belgique*. 1986: 57(3/4), 497-505.

CRAIG-BULLEN, Catherine. Rescuing paper from the ravages of time. *The Archivist*. January/February 1986: 13(1), 14-15.

CRAIG-BULLEN, Catherine. Support en danger. *L'Archiviste*. Janvier/février 1986: 13(1), 14-15.

CREWS, Patricia Cox. A comparison of clear versus yellow ultraviolet filters in reducing fading of selected dyes. *Studies in Conservation*. May 1988: 33(2), 87-93.

CRIBBS, Margaret A. Photographic conservation: an update. *Records Management Quarterly*. July 1988: 22(3), 17-19.

CUNHA, George M. *Methods of evaluation to determine the preservation needs in libraries and archives: a RAMP study with guidelines*. Paris: Unesco, 1988. iv, 75 p.

CUNNINGHAM, Veronica Colley. The preservation of newspaper clippings. *Special Libraries*. Winter 1987: 78(1), 41-46.

DEPEW, John N. A statewide disaster preparedness and recovery program for Florida libraries. *Conservation Administration News*. April 1988: (33), 6, 13.

DEWHITT, Benjamin L. Long-term preservation of data on computer magnetic media: part 1. *Conservation Administration News*. April 1987: (29), 7, 19, 28.

Don't stuff your backup tapes in a box and stash them in a cave. *Infosystems*. August 1987: 34(8), 18.

DUFOUR, Frank et Gilbert TAIEB. *Techniques de l'enregistrement et problèmes de conservation des bandes magnétiques*. Congrès national des archivistes français (28ᵉ: 1986: Paris, France). Paris, 1987: 203-207.

DVORIASHINA, Z.P. Biodamage protection of book collections in the USSR. Some aspects of organization of insect control. *Restaurator*. 1987: 8(4), 182-188.

ENGLAND, Claire and Karen EVANS. *Disaster management for libraries planning and process*. [Ottawa]: Canadian Library Association, 1988. xi, 207 p.

FAVIER, Lucie. Le colmatage des lacunes des papiers anciens aux Archives nationales: automatisation du calcul de la quantité de pâte à papier à utiliser. *Archives et bibliothèques de Belgique*. 1987: 58(1/2), 111-120.

FEINDT, W. Massenrestaurierung. Das beispiel buckeburg und die künftige entwicklung. *Archives et bibliothèques de Belgique*. 1987: 58(1/2), 121-134.

FENSTERMANN, Duane W. Recommendations for the preservation of photographic slides. *Conservation Administration News*. October 1987: (31), 7.

FIELD, Jeffrey. Long-term preservation of data on computer magnetic media: part II. *Conservation Administration News*. July 1987: (30), 4, 24.

FIELD, Jeffrey. The NEH Office of Preservation, 1986-1988. *Microform Review*. October 1988: 17(4), 187-189.

FLIEDER, Françoise. Méthodes mécaniques utilisées en France pour la restauration du papier. *Archives et bibliothèques de Belgique*. 1987: 58(1/2), 135-144.

FOX, Lisa L. *A core collection in preservation*. Chicago: ALA/RTSD, 1988. 15 p.

GAVREL, Sue. Preserving machine-readable archival records: a reply to John Mallinson. *Archivaria*. Summer 1986: (22), 153-155.

GELLER, L.D. In-house conservation and the general practice of archival science. *Archivaria*. Summer 1986: (22), 163-167.

GERTZ, Janet. The University of Michigan brittle book microfilming program: a case study. *Microform Review*. Winter 1987: 16(1), 37-39.

GRAHAM-BELL, Maggie. *Preventive conservation: a manual.* 2nd ed. Victoria: British Columbia Museums Association, 1986. 87 p. (Handbook; no. 2)

HAGEN, Carlos B. A sequel to Disaster Planning Analysis Study: seismic dangers at the UCLA Map Library. *Western Association of Map Libraries. Information Bulletin.* June 1987: 18(3), 221-222.

HENDERSON, Cathy. Curator or conservator: who decides on what treatment? *Rare Books & Manuscripts Librarianship.* Fall 1987: 2(2), 103-107.

HERTHER, N.K. Between a rock and a hard place: preservation and optical media. *Database.* April 1987: 10, 122-124.

HOFFMAN, Annie and Bryan BAUMANN. Disaster recovery: a prevention plan for NWNL. *Records Management Quarterly.* April 1986: 20(2), 40-44.

HORNE, Stephen A. *Way to go! Crating artwork for travel.* Hamilton, N.Y.: Gallery Association of New York State, 1985. 55 p.

HOWATT-KRAHN, Ann. East, West and the paths to conservation. *Muse.* Spring/April 1987: 38-43.

HOWATT-KRAHN, Ann. L'Orient, l'Occident et les voies de la conservation. *Muse.* Printemps/avril 1987: 5(1), 44-49.

INGRAM, John E. Preservation of library and archival collections at Colonial Williamsburg. *Conservation Administration News.* April 1988: (33), 1-2.

Introducing the conservation information network. *Archival Informatics Newsletter.* Winter 1988/1989: 2(4), 70-73.

An Introduction to the preservation of information on paper-film-magnetic and optical media. Silver Spring, Md.: Association for Information and Image Management, [1984?]. 51 p.

JIRAT-WASIUTYNSKI, Thea. Caring for works on paper. Part IV: care of watercolours. *Canadian Collector.* January/February 1987: 22(1), 30-33.

JONES, Roger. Barrow lamination: the North Carolina State Archives Experience. *The American Archivist.* Summer 1987: 50(3), 390-396.

KAEBNICK, Gregory. Microfilm and the Benedictine tradition: Hill Monastic Manuscript Library preserves the past. *INFORM: the Magazine of Information and Image Management.* October 1987: 1(10), 34-35.

KANSAS CITY AREA ARCHIVISTS. *Keeping your past: a basic guide to the care and preservation of personal papers.* Kansas City, Mo.: Kansas City Area Archivists, 1987. 25 p.

KANTOR, Paul B. *Costs of preservation microfilming at research libraries: a study of four institutions.* Washington, D.C.: Council on Library Resources Inc., 1986. 32 p.

KEANE, Edward T. The archiving microform. *Micro-notes.* Spring 1987: 15(2), 15.

KERNS, Ruth B. A positive approach to negatives: preserving photographs via microfilm technology. *The American Archivist.* Winter/Spring 1988: 51(1/2), 111-114.

KOCKAERTS, Roger. Les problèmes de photoconservation en archives. *Archives et bibliothèques de Belgique.* 1988: 59(3/4), 97-110.

KONRAD, Dietmar. Konservierung von spezialpapieren. *Archives et bibliothèques de Belgique.* 1987: 58(1/2), 183-191.

KUHN, Hermann. *Conservation and restoration of works of art and antiquities.* London: Butterworths, 1986. 262 p.

KUYK, Robert Egeter van. La recommandation pour la sauvegarde et la conservation des images en mouvement, huit ans après. *Janus.* 1988: (3), 34-38.

KUYK, Robert Egeter van. Recommandations for the preservation and conservation of moving images, eight years on. *Janus.* 1988: (3), 31-34.

LAURENCIC, Tamara. *Storage and preservation of paper records*. Australia: Library Board of Queensland, 1987. 60 p.

MCCARTHY, Paul H. and R. Bruce PARHAM. Photomicrofiche: a conservation and research tool. *Microform Review*. Spring 1987: 16(2), 118-125.

MCDONALD, Peter. Color microfilm: new possibilities. *Microform Review*. August 1988: 17(3), 146-149.

MCINTYRE, Katherine. Preserving our paper heritage: evaluation and disposal of treasures — Part 2. *Canadian Collector*. January/February 1987: 22(1), 20-21.

MADDEN, Dennis D. *Offsite storage at the Nebraska State Archives: learning by strategy, trial, and error*. [Vancouver]: Association of British Columbia Archivists, [1988]. [7] p. (A.B.C.A. Publications; no. 6)

MALLINSON, John C. Preserving machine-readable archival records for the millenia. *Archivaria*. Summer 1986: (22), 147-155.

MAREE, Johann and Anneke MARAIS. Famous collectors, book collections and the state of the art of preservation of library materials in South Africa. *Archives et bibliothèques de Belgique*. 1987: 58(1/2), 209-226.

MARSH, F.J. *Problems of archival/book restoration: report prepared for the Government of the Republic of Guyana by the United Nations Educational, Scientific and Cultural Organization*. Paris: Unesco, 1985. i, 24 p.

MARTINEK, Frantisek. Novy pristup k reseni otazek fyzicke pece o archivalie [A new approach to solutions of problems involved in the physical care of archival documents]. *Archivni Casopis*. 1986: 36(3), 149-153.

MATTHEWS, Fred W. Sorting a mountain of books. *Library Resources and Technical Services*. January/March 1987: 31(1), 88, 94.

MERRILL-OLDHAM, Jan. A brief preservation bibliography. *Conservation Administration News*. July 1987: (30), 9.

MILLER, David. Evaluating CD-ROMSs: to buy or not to buy? *Database*. June 1987: 36-42.

MONTORI, Carla J. and Karl E. LONGSTRETH. The preservation of library materials, 1987: a review of the literature. *Library Resources and Technical Services*. July 1988: 32(3), 235-247.

MORAN, Robert. Courting midrange calamities. *Computer & Communications Decisions*. August 1987: 19(11), 69-72, 74-76.

MORENTZ, James W. Computerizing libraries for emergency planning. *Special Libraries*. Spring 1987: 78(2), 100-104.

MOUNT, Ellis, editor. *Preservation and conservation of sci-tech materials*. New York: Haworth Press, 1987. 171 p.

MURRAY, Toby. Disaster planning and recovery: don't get caught with your plans down. *Records Management Quarterly*. April 1987: 21(2), 12-30, 41.

New security copy paper has implications for archivist [nocopi paper]. *ACA Bulletin*. January 1987: 11(3), 5.

Optical disk may preserve millions of National Archives documents. *Infosystems*. July 1987: 34(7), 14.

Parish archives handbook: guidelines for the care and preservation of parochial records. Auckland: Provincial Archives Committee of the Anglican Church in New Zealand, 1986. 42 p.

PARKER, Thomas A. *Study on integrated pest management for libraries and archives*. Paris: Unesco, 1988. vi, 119 p.

PARON, Gerardo. National Center for film and video preservation. *Conservation Administration News*. April 1988: (33), 7.

PASSAGLIA, E. *Characterization of microenvironments and the degradation of archival records: a research program*. Gaithersburg, Md.: National Bureau of

Standards (IMSE), Polymers Div., 1987. 129 p.

PENNSYLVANIA STATE UNIVERSITY LIBRARIES. PRESERVATION COMMITTEE. Guaranteeing a library for the future. The final report of the Preservation Committee of the Pennsylvania State University Libraries. *Restaurator.* 1987: 8(4), 151-181.

POLIAKOVA, J.V. La protection des documents d'archives contre la détérioration biologique. *Sovietskje Arkhivy.* 1988: (2), 68-73.

POLITES, Angeline. The Documentary Heritage Trust of the United States: newest ally in the effort to preserve America's memory. *Conservation Administration News.* April 1988: (33), 8, 20-21.

Pour le perfectionnement ultérieur de la conservation des documents du Fonds d'archives d'État dans les Archives administratives [en russe]. *Sovietskje Arkhivy.* 1987: (2), 40-47.

The Preservation of newspaper clippings: Veronica Colley Cunningham. *Special Libraries.* Winter 1987: 78(1), 41-46.

PRESLOCK, Karen. Publications. *Conservation Administration News.* July 1987: (30), 16-17.

PRESLOCK, Karen. Publications. *Conservation Administration News.* October 1987: (31), 18-19.

PRESLOCK, Karen. Publications. *Conservation Administration News.* January 1988: (32), 17.

PRESLOCK, Karen. Publications. *Conservation Administration News.* April 1988: (33), 18, 21.

PRESLOCK, Karen. Publications. *Conservation Administration News.* July 1988: (34), 14, 22.

PRESLOCK, Karen. Publications. *Conservation Administration News.* October 1988: (35), 20.

REICHER, Leslie Arden. 9 to 5: the textbook disaster: a case for disaster prepared-

ness. *Conservation Administration News.* July 1986: (26), 6, 10.

RHODES, Barbara J. *Hell and high water: a disaster information sourcebook.* New York: METRO, 1988. 58 p.

RICCI, I.M. and M. CARASSI. Adapting an ancient archives building in Turin. *Information Development.* January 1988: 4(1), 37-40.

ROHM, Wendy Goldman. "That's all that's left!". *Infosystems.* February 1987: 34(2), 42, 45, 46, 48.

SARETZKY, Gary D. Photographic conservation: part II. *Conservation Administration News.* July 1988: (34), 4, 9.

SCHAM, A.M. *Managing special collections.* New York: Neal-Schuman, 1987. 201 p.

SCHNARE, Robert E. and Marilyn D. CURTIS. Fire aftermath and the recovery process. *Conservation Administration News.* October 1988: (35), 1-2, 22.

SCHNARE, Robert E. Publications. *Conservation Administration News.* July 1986: (26), 18-20.

SCHNARE, Robert E. Publications. *Conservation Administration News.* January 1987: (28), 18-21.

SCHNARE, Robert E. Publications. *Conservation Administration News.* April 1987: (29), 24-25, 28.

SCHUR, Susan E. Conservation terminology: a review of past & current nomenclature of materials, part III. *Technology and Conservation.* 1988: 9(3/4), 40-41.

SÉGUIN, Gilles. Met Life helps University preserve historical records. *Ontario Association of Archivists Newsletter.* Spring 1988: 4(4), [2].

SMITH, Clive. Starting a conservation programme. *Archives and Manuscripts.* May 1987: 15(1), 41-47.

SOPKO, Sandra. Fire and humidity: data safes protect against both. *The Office.* October 1987: 106(4), 72, 74.

SPORCK, John H. Without a records recovery plan, start from square one. *Office.* June 1987: 105(6), 57-58.

STANGE, Eric. Millions of books are turning to dust: can they be saved? *New York Times.* March 29, 1987: 3, 38.

STEKATCHEVA, E.V. Sur la possibilité de l'utilisation de la gelée pour la lutte contre les parasites des documents d'archives. *Sovietskje Arkhivy.* 1988: (4), 59-62.

STONER, Joyce Hill. Getty Museum invests in conservation. *Museum News.* April 1986: 64(4), 36-39.

STRONG, Gary E. Rats! Oh no, not rats! *Special Libraries.* Spring 1987: 78(2), 105-111.

SULLIVAN, Robert C. Five decades of microforms at the Library of Congress. *Microform Review.* August 1988: 17(3), 155-158.

TAYLOR, Hugh A. The enemy is us: archival conservation in Canada. *ACA Bulletin.* January 1988: 12(3), 4-5.

TAYLOR, Hugh A. The enemy is us: archival conservation in Canada. *Council of Nova Scotia Archives Newsletter.* Winter 1988: (8), 10.

TAYLOR, Hugh A. Strategies for the future: the preservation of archival materials in Canada. *Conservation Administration News.* April 1987: (29), 1-3.

THOMAS, D.L. *Conservation et sécurité des fonds et collections d'archives: une étude RAMP accompagnée de principes directeurs.* Paris: Unesco, 1988. iv, 45 p. (PGI-86/WS/23)

THOMAS, D.L. *Survey on national standards on paper and ink to be used by the administration for records creation: a RAMP study with guidelines.* Paris: United Nations Educational, Scientific and Cultural Organization, 1987. 58 p.

THOMPSON, Robert J. Disaster recovery is silly! *Data Management.* February 1987: 46.

USDIN, Steve. Like it or not, plan for a disaster recovery. *Office.* March 1987: 105(3), 90-92.

The Use of permanent paper for biomedical literature. Summary of the proceedings of the National Library of Medicine Board of Regents Hearing (Bethesda, Maryland, January 27, 1987). Bethesda, Md.: National Library of Medicine (DHHS/NIH), 1987. 18 p.

VAGANOV, F.M. *La conservation des nouvelles archives.* Congrès international des archives (11e: 1988: Paris). Paris, 1988. 27 p.

VAISEY, David. The Maurice Bond memorial lecture 1987: archivists, conservators, and scientists: the preservation of the nations's heritage. *Archives: the Journal of the British Records Association.* April 1988: 18(79), 131-143.

VINAS, V. and R. VINAS. *Las tecnicas tradicionales de restauracion: un estudio del RAMP.* Paris: Unesco, 1988. iii, 72 p. (PGI-88/WS/17)

VOSSLER, Janet L. The human element of disaster recovery. *Records Management Quarterly.* January 1987: 21(1), 10-12.

VSA-GILDUNGSAUSSCHUSS. Die Ausleihe von Archivalen für Ausstellungen, das Photokopieren und die Gebührenerhebung in den Archiven der Schweiz und des Fürstentums Liechtenstein. *Arbido-R.* 1987: 2(3), 74-79.

WALSH, Betty. Conservation notes: photographic enclosures II: choosing enclosures that meet your needs. *ACA Bulletin.* January 1987: 11(3), [4-5].

WARNOW-BLEWETT, Joan. Saving the records of science and technology: the role of a discipline history center. *Science and Technology Libraries.* Spring 1987: 29-40.

WEILL, Georges. La préservation des documents d'archives. À propos de deux enquêtes américaines récentes. *La Gazette des archives.* 1988: (140), 64-70.

WESTBROOK, Lynn. *Paper preservation: nature, extent & recommendations.* Champaign, Ill.: University of Illinois, Graduate School of Library and Information Science, 1985. 75 p. (Occasional Paper, No. 171)

WHITEHEAD, Janet C. and DiAnn CONYERS. Survival in a computer environment — the synergistic approach. *Records Management Quarterly.* January 1988: 22(1), 8-14.

WOOD LEE, Mary. *Prevencion y tratamiento del moho en las colecciones de bibliotecas, con particular referencia a las que padecen climas tropicales: un estudio del RAMP.* Paris: Unesco, 1988. v, 57 p. (PGI-88/WS/9)

WRIGHT, Sandra and Peter YURKIW. The collections survey in the Federal Archives and Manuscript Divisions of the Public Archives of Canada: a progress report on conservation programme planning. *Archivaria.* Summer 1986: (22), 58-74.

ZIZHI, Feng. *Les choix technologiques des pays en voie de développement.* Congrès international des archives (11e: 1988: Paris). Paris, 1988. 4 p.

5.1.1 Building requirements / Installations

ARNAULD, Marie-Paule. *Équipement des locaux et matériels.* Congrès national des archivistes français (27e: 1985: Limoges, France). Paris, 1986: 31-32.

ARYA, A.S. *Protection of educational buildings against earthquakes: a manual for designers and builders.* Bangkok: Unesco, 1987. 67 p. (Educational Building Report; 13)

BENOÎT, Gérard et Danièle NEIRINCK. *Les moyens de conservation les plus économiques dans les bâtiments d'archives des pays industriels et tropicaux.* Paris: Unesco, 1987. [54] p. (PGI-87/WS/18)

BUTLER, Randall. Earthquake! The experience of two California libraries. *Conservation Administration News.* January 1988: (32), 1-2, 23-24.

BUTLER, Randall. The Los Angeles Central Library: "nightmare, part II". *Conservation Administration News.* January 1987: (28), 1-2.

CATAPANO, Fred T. The invisible partner: building management in museum operations. *Museum News.* June 1986: 64(5), 9-16.

DAVID, Jonathan. Light in museums. *Museums Journal.* March 1986: 85(4), 203-215.

HAMON, Maurice. Les bâtiments économiques d'archives. *Conseil international des archives. Comité des archives d'entreprises. Bulletin.* 1988: (11), 33-34.

HAMON, Maurice. Economical storage facilities for business archives. *International Council on Archives. Committee on Business Archives. Bulletin.* 1988: (11), 34-35.

HANSOTTE, Georges. Le nouveau bâtiment des archives de l'État à Liège. *Archives et bibliothèques de Belgique.* 1988: 59(3/4), 91-95.

JACKSON, Celia and Sylvia JAMES. Commercial off site storage for archives. *Business Archives.* May 1987: (53), 1-7.

MCCORMACK, Ros. And this is the best view... A new location for the John Oxley Library. *Archives and Manuscripts.* November 1988: 16(2), 119-128.

MARÉCHAL, Michel et Alexandre VOYEVODA. Les bâtiments d'archives modulaires économiques. *La Gazette des archives.* 1988: (140), 70-75.

New facility recommended for the National Archives of Canada. *ACA Bulletin.* January 1988: 12(3), 1-2.

PACIFICO, Michele F. A new building for the National Archives. *OAH Newsletter (Organization of American Historians).* November 1988: 16(4), 16.

PEBALL, Kurt. Der Neubau des Oesterreichischene Staatsarchivs [The new building of the Austrian State Archive]. *Scrinium.* 1986: (34), 135-143.

PENNSYLVANIA STATE UNIVERSITY LIBRARIES. PRESERVATION COMMITTEE. Guaranteeing a library for the future. The final report of the Preservation Committee of the Pennsylvania State University University Libraries. *Restaurator*. 1987: 8(4), 151-181.

PFERSCHY, Gerhard. Probleme der Adaptierung von Altbauten fuer Archivzwecke [The problems of adapting old buildings for archive purposes]. *Scrinium*. 1986: (34), 144-152.

SCHUELER, Winfied. Der Neubau des Hessischen Hauptstaatsarchivs in Wiesbaden [The new building for the Hesse Principal State Archive in Wiesbaden]. *Archivar*. May 1986: 39(2), 157-166.

THOMAS, David. Archive buildings: international comparisons. *Journal of the Society of Archivists*. January 1988: 9(1), 38-44.

WHITAKER, Albert H. *The New Massachusetts Archives facility: a study in planning and process*. Albany: NAGARA, 1988.

WRATTEN, Nigel. Setting up a records centre: some practical advice. *Business Archives*. May 1987: (53), 39-49.

5.1.2 Air conditioning and air purification / Climatisation et purification de l'air

CRESPO, Carmen. La conservation des documents et son application aux archives d'entreprises. *Conseil international des archives. Comité des archives d'entreprises. Bulletin*. 1988: (11), 27-32.

CRESPO, Carmen. Document conservation and its application to business archives. *International Council on Archives. Committee on Business Archives. Bulletin*. 1988: (11), 23-27.

MOUROMTSEV, V.A. et M.M. PROSVIRNIKOV. L'indicateur à distance de la température dans les dépôts d'archives. *Sovietskje Arkhivy*. 1987: (5), 83-85.

OPREA, Florea. Measures of control and hygiene of records in repositories. *Archives et bibliothèques de Belgique*. 1987: 58(1/2), 299-312.

PASSAGLIA, E. *Characterization of microenvironments and the degradation of archival records: a research program*. Gaithersburg, Md.: National Bureau of Standards (IMSE), Polymers Div., 1987. 129 p.

PENNSYLVANIA STATE UNIVERSITY LIBRARIES. PRESERVATION COMMITTEE. Guaranteeing a library for the future. The final report of the Preservation Committee of the Pennsylvania State University Libraries. *Restaurator*. 1987: 8(4), 151-181.

STAZICKER, Elizabeth. Climatic control: a hopeless bewilderment? *Journal of the Society of Archivists*. April 1987: 8(3), 171-173.

WOOD LEE, Mary. *Prevencion y tratamiento del moho en las colecciones de bibliotecas, con particular referencia a las que padecen climas tropicales: un estudio del RAMP*. Paris: Unesco, 1988. v, 57 p. (PGI-88/WS/9)

5.1.3 Storage conditions / Conditions d'entreposage

AMBROSIO, Johanna. Micrographics remains a viable medium. *Government Computer News*. March 27, 1987: 6(6), 40.

ANDERSON, Sigrid and G.W. LARSON. A study of environmental conditions associated with customer keeping of photographic prints. *Journal of Imaging Technology*. 1987: 13(2), 49-54.

BUTTERFIELD, Fiona J. The potential long-term effects of gamma irradiation on paper. *Studies in Conservation*. November 1987: 32(4), 181-191.

CALMES, Alan. The National Archives' charters monitoring system. *Conservation Administration News*. October 1987: (31), 6.

CANNING, Bonnie. Technology marches on. *Administrative Management*. January 1987: 48(1), 55.

CRAIG-BULLEN, Catherine. Rescuing paper from the ravages of time. *The Archivist*. January/February 1986: 13(1), 14-15.

CRAIG-BULLEN, Catherine. Support en danger. *L'Archiviste*. Janvier/février 1986: 13(1), 14-15.

CRESPO, Carmen. La conservation des documents et son application aux archives d'entreprises. *Conseil international des archives. Comité des archives d'entreprises. Bulletin*. 1988: (11), 27-32.

CRESPO, Carmen. Document conservation and its application to business archives. *International Council on Archives. Committee on Business Archives. Bulletin*. 1988: (11), 23-27.

CRIBBS, Margaret A. Photographic conservation: an update. *Records Management Quarterly*. July 1988: 22(3), 17-19.

Don't stuff your backup tapes in a box and stash them in a cave. *Infosystems*. August 1987: 34(8), 18.

DVORIASHINA, Z.P. Biodamage protection of book collections in the USSR. Some aspects of organization of insect control. *Restaurator*. 1987: 8(4), 182-188.

FAVIER, Jean. *Les documents graphiques et photographiques: analyse et conservation*. Travaux du Centre de recherche sur la conservation des documents graphiques, 1984-1985. Paris: Archives nationales, 1986. 242 p.

FOSTER, Ken. Conserver pour demain. *L'Archiviste*. Mai/juin 1987: 14(3), 14-15.

FOSTER, Ken. New branch dedicated to conservation. *The Archivist*. May/June 1987: 14(3), 14-15.

HAGEN, Remon. Further improvements in the permanence of cibachrome materials under adverse display conditions. *Journal of Imaging Technology*. 1986: 12(3), 160-162.

Is the future of records on cards? *Records and Retrieval Report*. February 1987: 3(2), 12-15.

JACKSON, Celia and Sylvia JAMES. Commercial off site storage for archives. *Business Archives*. May 1987: (53), 1-7.

JONES, G. William. Nitrate film: dissolving images of the past. *Conservation Administration News*. October 1987: (31), 1-2, 12.

LAROSE, Michèle. Colloque international sur la conservation. *L'Archiviste*. Novembre/décembre 1987: 14(6), 18.

LAROSE, Michèle. International Conservation Symposium in 1988. *The Archivist*. November/December 1987: 14(6), 18.

Listing of commercial off-site records centers. *Records and Retrieval Report*. September 1986: 2(7), 6-22.

MCINTOSH, Melinda C. Sabbatical report: results of a survey of library microform facilities. *Microform Review*. Winter 1987: 16(1), 41-51.

O'FARRELL, William S. Cold storage for colour film. *The Archivist*. March/April 1988: 15(2), 18.

O'FARRELL, William S. Entreposage au froid. *L'Archiviste*. Mars/avril 1988: 15(2), 18.

Off-site storage of records. *Records and Retrieval Report*. September 1986: 2(7), 1-5.

OPREA, Florea. Measures of control and hygiene of records in repositories. *Archives et bibliothèques de Belgique*. 1987: 58(1/2), 299-312.

Optical disk systems. *Records and Retrieval Report*. January 1987: 3(1), 1-15.

PASSAGLIA, E. *Characterization of microenvironments and the degradation of archival records: a research program*. Gaithersburg, Md.: National Bureau of Standards (IMSE), Polymers Div., 1987. 129 p.

REINHARDT, Victor. Storing PCB film. *INFORM: the Magazine of Information and Image Management.* October 1988: 2(9), 32-34.

SOPKO, Sandra. Fire and humidity: data safes protect against both. *The Office.* October 1987: 106(4), 72, 74.

STANGE, Eric. Millions of books are turning to dust: can they be saved? *New York Times.* March 29, 1987: 3, 38.

STEHKAEMPER, Hugo. Natural air conditioning of stacks. *Restaurator.* 1988: 9(4), 163-177.

THOMAS, D.L. *Study on control of security and storage of holdings: a RAMP study with guidelines.* Paris: United Nations Educational, Scientific and Cultural Organization, 1987. 62 p.

TURNER, James. Unrolling maps for flat storage. *Archivaria.* Winter 1987-1988: (25), 171-176.

TURNER, Jeffrey H. The suitability of diazo film for long term storage. *Microform Review.* August 1988: 17(3), 142-145.

WEIHS, Jean. *Accessible storage of non-book materials.* Phoenix: Onyx Press, 1984. 101 p.

WHITMORE, Paul M. and Glen R. CASS. The ozone fading of traditional Japanese colorants. *Studies in Conservation.* February 1988: 33(1), 29-40.

WHITMORE, Paul M., [et al.]. The ozone fading of traditional natural organic colorants on paper. *Journal of the American Institute for Conservation.* Spring 1987: 26(1), 45-58.

5.1.4 Storage materials / Matériel d'entreposage

AMBROSIO, Johanna. Moving the mountain: automating high-density paper storage. *Today's Office.* September 1987: 22(4), 33-37.

BENDER, Avi. Full text search and image retrieval. *IMC Journal.* 1987: 23(4), 28-30.

BOURKE, Thomas A. Retrospect and prospect: micrographics evolution in research libraries. *INFORM: the Magazine of Information and Image Management.* October 1987: 1(10), 28-30.

BOZEVICH, Ken. Storage conversion: consider the alternatives. *INFORM: the Magazine of Information and Image Management.* August 1987: 1(8), 10, 14.

CALMES, Alan. The importance of containers for the preservation of paper archives. *Archives et bibliothèques de Belgique.* 1987: 58(1/2), 33-44.

CALMES, Alan. *Preservation of permanently valuable information on paper, film, tape and disk.* Washington, D.C.: National Archives and Records Administration, 1987. 8 p.

CALMES, Alan. To archives and preserve: a media primer. *INFORM: the Magazine of Information and Image Management.* May 1987: 1(5), 14-17, 33.

CANNING, Bonnie. Les disques optiques au bureau. *IMC Journal.* 1987: 23(5), 11-12.

CANNING, Bonnie. Optical disk systems: pros and cons. *Administrative Management.* March 1987: 48(3), 51.

CANNING, Bonnie. Optical disks in the office. *IMC Journal.* 1987: 23(5), 9-10.

CANNING, Bonnie. Records automation: micrographics addresses records automation challenge. *Administrative Management.* April 1988: 49(3), 38.

CITARELLA, Judith and Lynne LEAHY. Integrated CAR takes charge at Barclay's Bank. *INFORM: the Magazine of Information and Image Management.* July 1987: 1(7), 26-28.

CLITES, Lorraine and William TUTTLE. Industrial document management: an optical system. *INFORM: the Magazine of Information and Image Management.* August 1987: 1(8), 30-33.

COOKE, Donald F. Map storage on CD-ROM. *Byte.* July 1987: 129-130, 132, 134-136, 138.

CRAVEN, Paul Taylor. Optical records management: application development in action. *INFORM: the Magazine of Information and Image Management.* February 1987: 1(2), 35-39.

CRIBBS, Margaret A. Photographic conservation: an update. *Records Management Quarterly.* July 1988: 22(3), 17-19.

DAVIS, Douglas L. Optical archiving: where are we now and where do we go from here? *Optical Information Systems.* January/February 1987: 7(1), 66-71.

DESMARAIS, Norman. Information management on a compact silver disc. *Optical Information Systems.* May/June 1987: 7(3), 193-204.

DOLLAR, Charles M. Trends in new computer technology. *ADPA.* 1986: 5(2), 25-35.

Financial markets: Filenet automates the flow. *INFORM: the Magazine of Information and Image Management.* July 1987: 1(7), 22-25.

FLUTY, Steve. Online reduction innovation at Chemical Bank. *INFORM: the Magazine of Information and Image Management.* July 1987: 1(7), 6-7.

FRASE, H. Michael. Videomicrographics: multi-media image management. *INFORM: the Magazine of Information and Image Management.* April 1987: 1(4), 26-29.

GRIGSBY, Mason. The integration and use of write-once optical information systems automation (DDA) right decision. *IMC Journal.* 1987: 23(4), 9-13.

GRIGSBY, Mason. Write-one optical disk systems in the automated office. *Records Management Quarterly.* July 1986: 20(3), 30-34.

HELGERSON, Linda W. *Introduction to scanning technology.* Silver Spring, Md.: Association for Information and Image Management, 1987. 36 p.

HELGERSON, Linda W. Optical storage peripherals: the right format. *INFORM:*

the *Magazine of Information and Image Management.* February 1987: 1(2), 14-16, 18-19.

HOLDER, Carol. Protecting your image: microform storage and security. *INFORM: the Magazine of Information and Image Management.* October 1987: 1(9), 18-21.

HOOTEN, Bill. Archiving the archives. *Computerworld.* 24 August 1987: 21(34), 63.

HORNE, Stephen A. *Way to go! Crating artwork for travel.* Hamilton, N.Y.: Gallery Association of New York State, 1985. 55 p.

HUBENER, Hal. Sunshine state showpieces: alligator-skin bindings in Florida Archives. *Provenance.* Fall 1988: 6(2), 42-43.

Information and image management industry: job descriptions. Silver Spring, Md.: Association for Information and Image Management, 1987. 30 p.

Information management sourcebook. Silver Spring, Md.: Association for Information and Image Management, 1987. 430 p.

JOHNSON, Don S. Creeping towards the paperless office. *Administrative Management.* October 1987: 48(10), 5.

The Leading edge of CALS. *INFORM: the Magazine of Information and Image Management.* September 1987: 1(9), 30.

LYNCH, Clifford A. Optical storage media, standards and technology life-cycle management. *Records Management Quarterly.* January 1986: 20(1), 44-54.

MCDONALD, Evelyn. Report says microform is cheapest storage medium. *Government Computer News.* 9 October 1987: 6(20), 54.

MARQUARDT, Leigh R. Priorities in bank document management. *INFORM: the Magazine of Information and Image Management.* July 1987: 1(7), 34-35.

MARTIN, Craig. Video technology in the computer industry. *International Journal of Micrographics and Video Technology.* 1986: 15(3/4), 185-198.

Media storage. *Information Center.* April 1987: 3(4), 7.

MILLER, David. Evaluating CD-ROMSs: to buy or not to buy? *Database.* June 1987: 36-42.

Mobile storage shrinks space while expanding capacity. *Administrative Management.* February 1988: 49(1), 12.

MORLEY, Jeanine. Mobile storage systems glide toward greater efficiency. *Today's Office.* November 1988: 23(6), 16-23.

MROZ, Terry. The phased box at the CCA: a revised model. *Conservation Administration News.* January 1988: (32), 6-7.

NIKOLAISON, Ray. Two directions in the future of micrographics. *The Office.* October 1987: 106(4), 54, 56.

NOVINGER, Walter B. Optical storage: a conversion perspective. *INFORM: the Magazine of Information and Image Management.* September 1987: 1(9), 22-23.

Optical disk may preserve millions of National Archives documents. *Infosystems.* July 1987: 34(7), 14.

An Optical disk primer. *Records and Retrieval Report.* October 1987: 3(8), 1-16.

OSTERLUND, Steve. Optical archiving systems. *DEC Professional.* June 1987: 7(7), 66-69, 72.

OTTEN, Klaus. *Integrated document and image management.* Silver Spring, Md.: Association for Information and Image Management, 1987. 66 p.

PAZNIK, Megan Jill. Optical disks vs. micrographics. *Administrative Management.* April 1988: 49(3), 18-23.

PFEIFFER, Ken. The paper challenge and progressive records management. *INFORM: the Magazine of Information and Image Management.* April 1987: 1(4), 18-20, 24, 44.

SAFFADY, William. Optical disks: an overview. *AIIM Conference Daily.* April 29, 1987: 10, 20, 30.

SAFFADY, William. *Optical disks for data and document storage.* Westport, Ct.: Meckler, 1986. 94 p.

SCALA, Bea. Telco conversion: from paper records to online information system. *INFORM: the Magazine of Information and Image Management.* March 1987: 1(3), 20-23.

SCELI, W. Clair. Document management systems today and tomorrow. *AIIM Conference Daily.* April 28, 1987: 5, 20.

SÉGUIN, Gilles. Met Life helps University preserve historical records. *Ontario Association of Archivists Newsletter.* Spring 1988: 4(4), [2].

SHAW, Abigail. Integrating document storage: an end user's view. *INFORM: the Magazine of Information and Image Management.* May 1987: 1(5), 34-37.

Solving the paper problem: an introduction to document processing. Sunnyvale, Calif.: Interfile, [1987?]. 8 p.

SPILKER, Chris. Medical imaging: merging picture archives and communications. *INFORM: the Magazine of Information and Image Management.* February 1987: 1(2), 24-27.

Storing paper. *Records and Retrieval Report.* September 1987: 3(7), 1-12.

THOMA, G., [et al.]. Design consideration affecting throughput in an optical disk-based document storage system. IN ASIS '87: Proceedings of the 50th ASIS annual meeting, Boston, Mass., Oct. 4-8, 1987. Medford, N.J.: Learned Information, 1987: 225-233.

WAEGEMANN, C. Peter, ed. Integrating information carriers. *Records and Retrieval Report.* March 1988: 4(3), 1-16.

WALSH, Betty. Conservation notes: photographic enclosures II: choosing enclosures that meet your needs. *ACA Bulletin.* January 1987: 11(3), [4-5].

Will optical disks ever forget? *The Economist*. 28 September 1987: 9(39), 90-91.

WILLIAMS, Bernard. Optical disks at the Public Records Office. *Information Media & Technology*. September 1987: 20(5), 204-205.

ZAGAMI, Robert W. State-of-the-art report on micrographics and optical disks. *Administrative Management*. April 1987: 48(4), 24-29.

5.2 Copying / Reproduction

Au royaume du traitement de l'image; les gestionnaires du groupe commerce sont devenus des pionniers dans l'implantation d'un système de conservation des dossiers à base de pochettes et de pellicule 16 mm. *Le Bureau*. Septembre/octobre 1987: 23(5), 44-45.

BELL, Mary Margaret. Preserving local history in Kentucky through microforms. *Microform Review*. Spring 1987: 16(2), 126-129.

EDWARDS, Ian C. Optical storage developments — write-once media. *Electronic and Optical Publishing Review*. March 1987: 7(1), 16-20.

KUDER, James E. Organic active layer materials for optical recording. *Journal of Imaging Science*. March/April 1988: 32(2), 51-56.

LIPPIN, Paula. Reprographic successes you can duplicate. *Modern Office Technology*. April 1987: 32(4), 70, 74, 78, 82.

LOMBARDO, Daniel. The use of microform to support the Amherst Local History Project. *Microform Review*. Spring 1987: 16(2), 130-133.

Les lutrins de demain: actes du forum technique organisé sur le thème « archives, images et électronique ». *La Gazette des archives*. 1986: (134-135), 230-256.

MARTIN, Wayne. Colour micrographics and mapping today. *SLA. Geography & Map Division. Bulletin*. June 1988: (152), 36-38.

Papier duplicateur fabriqué en Finlande. *Le Bureau*. Mai/juin 1987: 23(3), 13.

SAVIERS, Shannon Smith. Reflections on CD-ROM: bridging the gap between technology and purpose. *Special Libraries*. Fall 1987: 78(4), 288-294.

SUBT, Sylvia S.Y. Xerographic quality control. *INFORM: the Magazine of Information and Image Management*. July 1987: 1(7), 10-11, 47.

VSA-GILDUNGSAUSSCHUSS. Die Ausleihe von Archivalen für Ausstellungen, das Photokopieren und die Gebührenerhebung in den Archiven der Schweiz und des Fürstentums Liechtenstein. *Arbido-R*. 1987: 2(3), 74-79.

5.2.1 Microfilming / Microfilmage

ADELSTEIN, Peter Z. and James M. REILLY. The Image Permanence Institute: new preservation resource. *INFORM: the Magazine of Information and Image Management*. October 1987: 1(10), 37-39.

AMBROSIO, Johanna. Micrographics remains a viable medium. *Government Computer News*. March 27, 1987: 6(6), 40.

AMMERMAN, Dean. Salvaging damaged microfilm. *AIIM Conference Daily*. April 30, 1987: 67-68.

ANDORS, Alice. Micrographics service in the information age. *INFORM: the Magazine of Information and Image Management*. June 1987: 1(6), 26-29.

Au royaume du traitement de l'image; les gestionnaires du groupe commerce sont devenus des pionniers dans l'implantation d'un système de conservation des dossiers à base de pochettes et de pellicule 16 mm. *Le Bureau*. Septembre/octobre 1987: 23(5), 44-45.

BAILEY, Martha J. Microfilming state agriculture and forestry documents: program of the National Agricultural Library. *Microform Review*. May 1988: 17(2), 72-75.

BALON, Brett J. Microfilm systems: silver recovery is money recovery. *Records*

Management Quarterly. April 1987: 21(2), 31-32.

BAO-SEN, Ge. The development of microfilming technology in China. *IMC Journal*. November/December 1988: 24(6), 13-15.

BARR, Jean. Choosing a microfilm based technology. *Records Management Quarterly*. January 1987: 21(1), 32-37.

BARR, Robert D. Microfilm or optical disk: the choice is between systems, not media. *IMC Journal*. March/April 1988: 24(2), 7-8.

BELL, Mary Margaret. Preserving local history in Kentucky through microforms. *Microform Review*. Spring 1987: 16(2), 126-129.

BIDA, Michael C. Scanning, OCR devices complement microfilm in solving data entry bottlenecks. *AIIM Conference Daily*. April 30, 1987: 5, 14, 39.

BOLNICK, Franklin I. and Susan LAW. Managing concept: putting system design to work. *INFORM: the Magazine of Information and Image Management*. January 1987: 1(1), 12-15, 44.

BORDAS, Richard. The CAD-microfilm connection: linking for productivity. *INFORM: the Magazine of Information and Image Management*. January 1988: 2(1), 28-29.

BORDAS, Richard. Engineering document management systems: today's reality is becoming tomorrow's foundation. *IMC Journal*. March/April 1988: 24(2), 43-45.

BOTTOMLEY, Michael. Microforms: an annotated bibliography. *Business Archives*. May 1988: (55), 61-64.

BOURKE, Thomas A. Retrospect and prospect: micrographics evolution in research libraries. *INFORM: the Magazine of Information and Image Management*. October 1987: 1(10), 28-30.

BOURKE, Thomas A. Spaulding and Materazzi revisited: a ten year retrospect. *Microform Review*. August 1988: 17(3), 130-136.

BRATHAL, Daniel A. and Mark LANGEMO. *Planning conversions to micrographic systems*. Prairie Village, Ks.: ARMA International, 1987. vii, 31, 51 p.

BROWN, Marlene. Image retrieval keeps PM in touch with public. *Government Computer News*. 9 October 1987: 6(20), 44, 48.

BUCK, W.G. (Wally). Silver duplicating. *Micro-notes*. Spring 1987: 15(2), 21.

BURMOVA-VELTCHEVA, Maya I. et Janna S. KRAITCHEVA. *Les microformes en tant qu'archives*. Congrès international des archives (11e: 1988: Paris). Paris, 1988. 6 p.

BYER, Richard J., ed. Densitometry: measuring for quality control. *INFORM: the Magazine of Information and Image Management*. January 1988: 2(1), 7-9, 42.

BYRNE, Sherry. Guidelines for contracting microfilming services. *Microform Review*. Fall 1986: 15(4), 253-264.

BYRNES, Margaret M. and Nancy E. ELKINGTON. Containing preservation microfilming costs at the University of Michigan Library. *Microform Review*. Winter 1987: 16(1), 37-39.

CAR systems in records management-1988. *Records and Retrieval Report*. September 1988: 4(7), 1-11.

'CAR' systems valuable tool to modern office automation. *Micro-notes*. Summer 1987: 15(3), 15, 30.

CARPENTIER, Louise. Quebec government publications in microform. *Microform Review*. December 1988: 17(5), 260-261.

CLEMENTS, D.W.G. Preservation microfilming and substitution policy in the British Library. *Microform Review*. February 1988: 17(1), 17-22.

CONWAY, Paul. IPI reports new microfilm permanence research. *SAA Newsletter*. September 1988: 7.

COURTOT, Marilyn and Sigrid ANDERSON. *Micrographics standards and related items*. Silver Spring, Md.: Association for Information and Image Management, 1987. 29 p.

COURTOT, Marilyn. Vaults of granite and steel: a journey through the genealogical storage complex of the Mormon Church. *INFORM: the Magazine of Information and Image Management*. July/August 1988: 2(7), 22-25.

COUVELIS, Joyce. Optimizing records management at Foodmaker, Inc. *INFORM: the Magazine of Information and Image Management*. January 1988: 2(1), 18-21.

CRUSE, Larry. MIMI, the map and graphic information index to major microform sets. *Microform Review*. Fall 1986: 15(4), 224-227.

CUNNINGHAM, Roger B. Microcomputer-based CAR system increases electronic filing flexibility. *Micro-notes*. Winter 1986: 15(1), 12, 22.

CURRIE, Jack. International Development Research Centre (IDRC) assists government of Trinidad and Tobago to improve land registration information system. *Micro-notes*. Summer 1987: 15(3), 16-17, 20.

DICKEY, Sam. New directions in micrographics. *Today's Office*. August 1987: 22(3), 34-38.

ENIN, G.P., [et al.]. Rukopis'i mikrofisha [Manuscript and microfiche]. *Sovetskoe Bibliotekovedenie*. 1986: (1), 90-98.

FABREGUETTES, Catherine. L'ABC du CD: où en est le CD-ROM? *Bulletin des bibliothèques de France*. 1987: 32(2), [150]-159.

FELDHAUSEN, Mark. Microfilm retrieval enhanced by CAR. *INFORM: the Magazine of Information and Image Management*. October 1987: 1(10), 40.

FIELD, Jeffrey. The NEH Office of Preservation, 1986-1988. *Microform Review*. October 1988: 17(4), 187-189.

FLUBACHER, F. Shirley. Old-line bank's approach to new records management. *The Office*. December 1987: 106(6), 15-19.

FLUTY, Steve. Growth management: American Express goes the distance. *INFORM: the Magazine of Information and Image Management*. January 1987: 1(1), 34-36.

FLUTY, Steve. Streamlining the flow: information management at CBS. *INFORM: the Magazine of Information and Image Management*. January 1987: 1(1), 32-33, 45-46.

FRANK, John W. Micrographics and optical disk — friends or foes? *IMC Journal*. July/August 1988: 24(4), 7-9.

GERTZ, Janet. The University of Michigan brittle book microfilming program: a case study. *Microform Review*. Winter 1987: 16(1), 37-39.

La gestion des documents: trouver un chèque parmi tant d'autres [Recordak Reliant 550]. *Le Bureau*. Juillet/août 1986: 10-11.

GOLDBERG, Michael. The conversion challenge. *INFORM: the Magazine of Information and Image Management*. September 1988: 2(8), 11-12, 36.

Goodbye micrographics — welcome back microfilm? *Information Media & Technology*. March 1987: 20(2), 61.

GRAFF, Michael W. Avoid tomorrow's disaster with today's microfilm. *INFORM: the Magazine of Information and Image Management*. June 1988: 2(6), 12-13.

Grain inspection service simplifies records with fiche. *Government Computer News*. 9 October 1987: 6(20), 50.

GRANAT, Burton (Bud). Microfilm service: market savvy for the future. *INFORM: the Magazine of Information and Image Management*. June 1987: 1(6), 14-15.

GRAY, Edward. To film or not to film: that is the question — an essay. *International*

Journal of Micrographics and Video Technology. 1986: 15(3/4), 177-183.

GRECO, Edgar J. Microfilm will help bridge technologies of integrated systems, artificial intelligence. *IMC Journal.* 1987: 23(1), 21-22.

GWINN, Nancy E. *Preservation microfilming: a guide for librarians and archivists.* Chicago: American Library Association, 1987. xxix, 207 p.

HAMILTON, Sybille. Insurance applications. *IMC Journal.* 1987: 23(1), 41-43.

HENDLEY, Anthony M. The development of microfilm in engineering applications. *IMC Journal.* March/April 1988: 24(2), 18-20.

HENDRICKS, Klaus B. Notes on microfilm. *Archivaria.* Winter 1986-87: (23), 179-184.

HIGGINS, Kevin B. Optical disk and micrographic document management system. *Micro-notes.* September 1986: 14(3), 5-6.

HOLDER, Carol. Protecting your image: microform storage and security. *INFORM: the Magazine of Information and Image Management.* October 1987: 1(9), 18-21.

HOOPER, Patricia. The move to microform: a converting experience. *INFORM: the Magazine of Information and Image Management.* June 1987: 1(6), 16-19.

HOSE, John. An introduction to COM. *Micro-notes.* Summer 1987: 15(3), 10-11.

HUNTER, Gregory S. Microcomputing and micrographic control. *INFORM: the Magazine of Information and Image Management.* October 1987: 1(10), 22-23.

HUSSEY, Harold E. COM for the Pepsi generation. *AIIM Conference Daily.* April 28, 1987: 10, 31.

Imaging. *Records and Retrieval Report.* December 1988: 4(10), 1-14.

KAEBNICK, Gregory. Microfilm and the Benedictine tradition: Hill Monastic Manuscript Library preserves the past.

INFORM: the Magazine of Information and Image Management. October 1987: 1(10), 34-35.

KANTOR, Paul B. *Costs of preservation microfilming at research libraries: a study of four institutions.* Washington, D.C.: Council on Library Resources Inc., 1986. 32 p.

KEANE, Edward T. The archiving microform. *Micro-notes.* Spring 1987: 15(2), 15.

KER, Neil. Gold toning the Domesday Book gives better than archival permanence. *Microform Review.* Fall 1987: 16(4), 300-302.

KER, Neil. Preparing your archives for the next 20,000 years. *International Journal of Micrographics and Video Technology.* 1986: 15(3/4), 223-226.

KERNS, Ruth B. A positive approach to negatives: preserving photographs via microfilm technology. *The American Archivist.* Winter/Spring 1988: 51(1/2), 111-114.

KRAMER, C.M. Micrographics: small is beautiful, cost-effective and efficient. *Micro-notes.* Spring 1987: 15(2), 5, 7.

LACY, John A. The future of document management: the "fourth stage" and beyond. *AIIM Conference Daily.* April 30, 1987: 5, 14, 16.

Latest technology and beyond - sought as Caja Galicia improves information access. *IMC Journal.* March/April 1988: 24(2), 9-11.

LEARY, William H. Preservation microfilming at the National Archives. *Microform Review.* Fall 1987: 16(4), 286-290.

LESTER, Robert E. Filming "The Oriental Question". *Microform Review.* May 1988: 17(2), 94-96.

LINDER, C.E. (Ted). COM services offer records-keeping alternative. *Micro-notes.* Spring 1987: 15(2), 13.

LOMBARDO, Daniel. The use of microform to support the Amherst Local History

Project. *Microform Review*. Spring 1987: 16(2), 130-133.

LUEBBE, Mary. Update on Canadian government documents in microform. *Microform Review*. December 1988: 17(5), 254-259.

LYNCH, Clifford A. and Edwin B. BROWNRIGG. Conservation, preservation and digitization. *College and Research Libraries News*. July 1986: 47(4), 379-382.

MCCARTHY, Paul H. and R. Bruce PARHAM. Photomicrofiche: a conservation and research tool. *Microform Review*. Spring 1987: 16(2), 118-125.

MCCLELLAN, William M. Microformatted music indexes. *Microform Review*. Winter 1987: 16(1), 21-31.

MCDONALD, Evelyn. Report says microform is cheapest storage medium. *Government Computer News*. 9 October 1987: 6(20), 54.

MCDONALD, Peter. Color microfilm: new possibilities. *Microform Review*. August 1988: 17(3), 146-149.

MCGING, Angela and Anne PICOT. The conservation of building plans project. *Archives and Manuscripts*. November 1988: 16(2), 97-118.

MAKI, John. Automating image management: the software factor. *INFORM: the Magazine of Information and Image Management*. May 1988: 2(5), 33-34.

Managing engineering drawings in the Department of National Defence. *Micronotes*. Winter 1986: 15(1), 10.

MARTIN-MERAS, Luisa. Cartographic materials in microform at the Museo Naval, Madrid. *Microform Review*. February 1988: 17(1), 14-16.

Microfilm or optical disc: choose the system. *The Office*. October 1987: 106(4), 130.

Micrographics at the Royal Bank. *Micronotes*. September 1986: 14(3), 10-11.

MILES, Charles S. Micrographic services enjoy market surge. *INFORM: the Magazine of Information and Image Management*. June 1988: 2(6), 14.

MOORE, Idella. Undertaking a microfilming project. A case study. *Business Archives*. May 1987: (53), 21-29.

MORGAN, D.A. New capabilities with dry silver recording materials. *Journal of Imaging Technology*. February 1987: 13(1), 4-7.

NIKOLAISON, Jeanne. Passport Services automates records process to provide rapid service to customers. *IMC Journal*. May/June 1988: 24(3), 33-36.

NIKOLAISON, Ray. Two directions in the future of micrographics. *The Office*. October 1987: 106(4), 54, 56.

NOVAMEDIA CORP. Why vesicular duplicating film. *Micro-notes*. Spring 1987: 15(2), 14-15.

Oakville Fire Department computerizes microfiche. *Micro-notes*. Spring 1987: 15(2), 10, 23.

PASS, Herman W. and Wayne W. WARTIAN. Automated document flow at McDonnell Douglas. *INFORM: the Magazine of Information and Image Management*. January 1988: 2(1), 23-27.

PAZNIK, Megan Jill. Optical disks vs. micrographics. *Administrative Management*. April 1988: 49(3), 18-23.

PELLETIER, Monique and Jean-Marie ARNOULT. Reproduction on microfiche of the ancient cartographic holdings of the Bibliothèque nationale, Paris sets. *Microform Review*. Fall 1986: 15(4), 221-227.

PENDERGRAFT, Lee. "I want to start a microfilm program". *Microfilm Services & Systems*. April/June 1987: 10-11.

PENNINGTON, Mike. Microfiche streams files at USDA. *INFORM: the Magazine of Information and Image Management*. November 1987: 1(11), 37-39.

PHILLIPS, Trudy M. Managing choice: single and multivendor options. *INFORM: the Magazine of Information and Image Management*. January 1987: 1(1), 20-23.

POPIUL, Jacklyn. The modern manager and the people/productivity balance. *INFORM: the Magazine of Information and Image Management*. April 1987: 1(4), 30-33.

POWER, William. Caseload automation with micrographics. *INFORM: the Magazine of Information and Image Management*. March 1988: 2(3), 8-9.

Princeton microform guide. Princeton, N.J.: Princeton Microfilm Corp., 1987-1988. 189 p.

PTACEK, William P. Microfilm, microfilmers and the future. *INFORM: the Magazine of Information and Image Management*. July/August 1988: 2(7), 8-11.

RAMSAY, Nancy C. Using optical disk in non-image applications. *Optical Information Systems*. July/August 1988: 8(4), 164-168.

Records management, cost effective efficiency is here. *Modern Office Technology*. January 1987: 31(1), 100-110, 112-114.

REILLY, James M., [et al.]. Stability of black-and-white photographic images, with special reference to microfilm. *Microform Review*. December 1988: 17(5), 270-278.

REILLY, James M., [et al.]. When clouds obscure silver film's lining: IPI research points to new care and handling for silver film. *INFORM: the Magazine of Information and Image Management*. September 1988: 2(8), 16-20, 37-38.

Retrieval terminals will be a key component in microfilm access systems of the future. *AIIM Conference Daily*. April 30, 1987: 16.

RODRIGUEZ, Manuel and Jeffrey C. SCHOWEN. System management from start to finish. *INFORM: the Magazine of Information and Image Management*. January 1987: 1(1), 26-31, 45-46.

ROWH, Mark C. Records management systems are better than ever before. *The Office*. October 1987: 106(4), 92-93.

RUBIN, Jack. Science finds new uses for ancient art of micrography. *Government Computer News*. 9 October 1987: 6(20), 56.

SCELI, W. Clair. Micrographics and/or optical disk? Ideas to help you make the right decision. *IMC Journal*. 1987: 23(4), 44-49.

SCHOULLER, Jacques, Sylvia FILLING et David BATAZZI. L'archivage sur microfilm à Codes-à-Barres au parlement européen: la Base ARCO (archives courrier officiel). *Archives et bibliothèques de Belgique*. 1987: 58(1/2), 313-330.

SEIBEL, C. Sheldon. A superfund assessment from the records perspective. *Records Management Quarterly*. January 1986: 20(1), 28-34.

SETTANNI, Joseph Andrew. Information management is a matter of records. *Office Systems*. January 1987: 4(1), 50, 52, 54, 57.

SETTANNI, Joseph Andrew. Micrographics is here to stay. *IMC Journal*. 1987: 23(1), 50-53.

SHAFFER, Norman J. Maps on microfiche: a success story at the Library of Congress. *INFORM: the Magazine of Information and Image Management*. November/December 1988: 2(10), 21-22.

SOMINITCH, G.E. Le travail avec les microfiches dans les Archives centrales historiques de l'URSS. *Sovietskje Arkhivy*. 1988: (5), 79-80.

SPAULDING, George. An HMO chooses CAR. *IMC Journal*. 1987: 23(1), 31-33.

SPENCE, Adolphus N. Microfilm production questions & answers: cameras. *AIIM Conference Daily*. April 28, 1987: 12, 30.

SPENCE, Adolphus N. Microfilm production questions & answers: processors. *AIIM Conference Daily*. April 29, 1987: 12.

STILLGER, Josef. The German Patent Office and microfilm integrated retrieval. *INFORM: the Magazine of Information and Image Management.* November 1987: 1(11), 28-30, 43.

STRATFORD, Juri. Public access to government document microforms. *Microform Review.* December 1988: 17(5), 292-294.

SULLIVAN, Robert C. Five decades of microforms at the Library of Congress. *Microform Review.* August 1988: 17(3), 155-158.

SWARTZELL, Ann. Preservation microfilming: in-house initiated microforms. *Conservation Administration News.* July 1988: (34), 6-7.

TERRILL-BREUR, Judith. University publications of America's micropublishing concept for archival material in American history. *Microform Review.* Spring 1987: 16(2), 134-136.

35mm reader seeks manufacturer. *Information Media & Technology.* March 1987: 20(2), 60.

THOMAS, Bill. Archival quality: the test for methylene blue. *INFORM: the Magazine of Information and Image Management.* May 1987: 1(5), 6-7, 46-47.

TIMBERS, Michael J. Microfilm: information management mainstay at IHS. *INFORM: the Magazine of Information and Image Management.* June 1987: 1(6), 30-31.

TIMBERS, Michael J. We are working to solve the problems of paper. *Office.* January 1987: 105(1), 122.

TURNER, Jeffrey H. The suitability of diazo film for long term storage. *Microform Review.* August 1988: 17(3), 142-145.

UNSWORTH, Michael E. Evaluating primary sources on microform. *Microform Review.* May 1988: 17(2), 76-79.

WATSON, Andrew C. Micro-color images: macro economics in color image management. *JIIM: the Journal of Information and Image Management.* December 1986: 19(12), 30-34.

WEHSER, Gary. Quality control: managing process materials. *JIIM: the Journal of Information and Image Management.* December 1986: 19(12), 21-24.

WEILL, Georges. La micrographie et l'archivistique dans la doctrine internationale (1950-1987). *Archives et bibliothèques de Belgique.* 1987: 58(1/2), 331-355.

WHEALAN, Ronald E. Microfilmed records in the John Fitzgerald Kennedy Library. *Microform Review.* October 1988: 17(4), 197-201.

WHEELER, B. A guide by subject to published national and international micrographic standards and technical reports. *Micro-notes.* Spring 1987: 15(2), 19-20.

WHEELER, William D. An introduction to the preservation and storage of microfilm. *Archives et bibliothèques de Belgique.* 1987: 58(1/2), 357-371.

WILSON, Eric. New technologies demand new standards for the quality control of microfilm images of engineering drawings. *IMC Journal.* 1987: 23(3), 15-17.

WISE, Joseph. An American look at micrographics in Japan. *IMC Journal.* 1987: 23(3), 22-23.

WOLF, David K. Update on updatables, 1986: the technologies and role of updatable micrographics records systems; image stability tests today's office microfilm images of engineering drawings. *IMC Journal.* 1987: 23(4), 44-49.

WOOD, Lamont. Computer-assisted retrieval accesses microfilm. *Government Computer News.* 9 October 1987: 6(20), 56-57.

YERBURGH, Mark. Studying all those "tiny little tea leaves": the future of microforms in a complex technological environment. *Microform Review.* Winter 1987: 16(1), 14-20.

ZAGAMI, Robert W. Micrographics management. *Administrative Management*. February 1987: 48(2), 53.

ZAGAMI, Robert W. Record conversion to microfilm safe, stabilized procedure. *Administrative Management*. July 1987: 48(7), 48.

ZAGAMI, Robert W. State-of-the-art report on micrographics and optical disks. *Administrative Management*. April 1987: 48(4), 24-29.

5.2.2 Photography, electrostatic copying, etc. / Photographie, reproduction électrostatique, etc.

BOIS, Jean-Jacques. Reproduction d'une photographie ancienne. *La Gazette des archives*. 1987: (136), 43-49.

COLLINS, Sheldan. *How to photograph works of art*. Nashville, Tennessee: AASLH Press, 1986. 204 p.

EDINGER, J. Raymond. The image analyzer — a tool for the evaluation of electrophotographic text quality. *Journal of Imaging Science*. July/August 1987: 31(4), 177-183.

GWIAZDA, Henry J. Preservation decision-making and archival photocopying. *Restaurator*. 1987: 8(1), 52-62.

NORRIS, Terry O. Photocopying on archival paper. *Restaurator*. 1987: 8(1), 3-8.

REILLY, James M., [et al.]. Stability of black-and-white photographic images, with special reference to microfilm. *Microform Review*. December 1988: 17(5), 270-278.

SARETZKY, Gary D. Photographic conservation: part 1. *Conservation Administration News*. April 1988: (33), 4-5.

SUBT, Sylvia S.Y. Archival quality of xerographic copies. *Restaurator*. 1987: 8(1), 29-39.

TANI, Tadaaki. A study of intensification of latent images in reduction-sensitized emulsions through delayed development...

Journal of Imaging Science. 1986: 30(2), 41-46.

WALKER, Gay. Preservation decision-making and archival photocopying. *Restaurator*. 1987: 8(1), 40-51.

WEBER, Mark. Electrophotography and archiving. *Restaurator*. 1987: 8(1), 9-17.

WHITE, Howard S. Book copiers: past, present, and future. *Restaurator*. 1987: 8(1), 18-28.

WILMAN, Hugh. Copying without damage: the British Library strategy. *Archives: the Journal of the British Records Association*. October 1987: 78, 85-88.

5.3 Restoration / Restauration

AKERS, Robert C. Florence to the eighties: the Data and Archival Damage Control Centre. *Conservation Administration News*. April 1987: (29), 4-5.

APPLEBAUM, Barbara. Criteria for treatment: reversibility. *Journal of the American Institute for Conservation*. Fall 1987: 26(2), 65-73.

BALON, Brett J. and H. Wayne GARDNER. Disaster planning for electronic records. *Records Management Quarterly*. July 1988: 22(3), 20-25, 30.

BANSA, Helmut. Conservation treatment of rare books. *Restaurator*. 1987: 8(2/3), 140-150.

BREDERECK, K. and A. SILLER-GRABENSTEIN. Fixing of ink dyes as a basis for restoration and preservation techniques in archives. *Restaurator*. 1988: 9(3), 113-135.

BUCHANAN, Sally. *Disaster planning: preparedness and recovery for libraries and archives*. Paris: Unesco, 1988. vi, 187 p. (PGI-88/WS/6)

BUTLER, Randall. The Inland Empire Libraries Disaster Response Network. *Conservation Administration News*. July 1988: (34), 8-9.

CALMES, Alan, [et al.]. Theory and practice of paper preservation for archives. *Restaurator*. 1988: 9(2), 97-111.

CIRKOVIC-STANOJLOVIC, Ljiljana. *La restauration mineure des documents sur papier: initiation pratique.* En collaboration avec Robert Chiasson. La Pocatière, Qué.: Documentor, 1987. 127 p.

CLAPP, Anne F. *Curatorial care of works of art on paper: basic procedures for paper preservation.* New York: Nick Lyons Books, 1987. x, 191 p.

COCHRANE, C. Archiving the audiovisual heritage: a joint technical symposium. *Audiovisual Librarian.* November 1987: 13, 231.

Conservazione delle opere d'arte su carta e pergamena: conference report. [Conservation of works of art on paper and parchment]. *Paper Conservation News.* September 1988: (47), 7.

DAHLO, Rolf. Massckonservering — bare et ord? [Mass conservation — only lip service?]. *Synopsis.* April 1987: 18(2), 72-73.

DAINES, Arthur. Des livres remis à neuf. *L'Archiviste.* Juillet/août 1986: 13(4), 16-17.

DAINES, Arthur. New life for old books. *The Archivist.* July/August 1986: 13(4), 16-17.

DEPEW, John N. A statewide disaster preparedness and recovery program for Florida libraries. *Conservation Administration News.* April 1988: (33), 6, 13.

DIXON, Debra. Information salvage: the tobacco connection. *Records Management Quarterly.* January 1988: 22(1), 15-17, 132.

ENGLAND, Claire and Karen EVANS. *Disaster management for libraries planning and process.* [Ottawa]: Canadian Library Association, 1988. xi, 207 p.

FAVIER, Jean. *Les documents graphiques et photographiques: analyse et conservation.* Travaux du Centre de recherche sur la conservation des documents graphiques, 1984-1985. Paris: Archives nationales, 1986. 242 p.

FAVIER, Lucie. Le colmatage des lacunes des papiers anciens aux Archives nationales: automatisation du calcul de la quantité de pâte à papier à utiliser. *Archives et bibliothèques de Belgique.* 1987: 58(1/2), 111-120.

FEINDT, W. Massenrestaurierung. Das beispiel buckeburg und die kunftige entwicklung. *Archives et bibliothèques de Belgique.* 1987: 58(1/2), 121-134.

FLIEDER, Françoise. Méthodes mécaniques utilisées en France pour la restauration du papier. *Archives et bibliothèques de Belgique.* 1987: 58(1/2), 135-144.

FOX, Lisa L. *A core collection in preservation.* Chicago: ALA/RTSD, 1988. 15 p.

HENDERSON, Cathy. Curator or conservator: who decides on what treatment? *Rare Books & Manuscripts Librarianship.* Fall 1987: 2(2), 103-107.

Introducing the conservation information network. *Archival Informatics Newsletter.* Winter 1988/1989: 2(4), 70-73.

JONES, G. William. Nitrate film: dissolving images of the past. *Conservation Administration News.* October 1987: (31), 1-2, 12.

KONRAD, Dietmar. Konservierung von spezialpapieren. *Archives et bibliothèques de Belgique.* 1987: 58(1/2), 183-191.

KUHN, Hermann. *Conservation and restoration of works of art and antiquities.* London: Butterworths, 1986. 262 p.

LA RIE, E. René. Polymer stabilizers. A survey with reference to possible applications in the conservation field. *Studies in Conservation.* February 1988: 33(1), 9-22.

MCCLEARY, John M. *Vacuum freeze-drying, a method used to salvage water-damaged archival and library materials: a RAMP study with guidelines.* Paris: United Nations Educational, Scientific and Cultural Organization, 1987. 75 p.

MCGING, Angela and Anne PICOT. The conservation of building plans project. *Archives and Manuscripts*. November 1988: 16(2), 97-118.

MARSH, F.J. *Problems of archival/book restoration: report prepared for the Government of the Republic of Guyana by the United Nations Educational, Scientific and Cultural Organization.* Paris: Unesco, 1985. i, 24 p.

MERRILL-OLDHAM, Jan. A brief preservation bibliography. *Conservation Administration News*. July 1987: (30), 9.

MONTORI, Carla J. and Karl E. LONGSTRETH. The preservation of library materials, 1987: a review of the literature. *Library Resources and Technical Services*. July 1988: 32(3), 235-247.

PEMBERTON, J. Michael. A video manual for disaster recovery and taking "AIIM" at a useful idea. *Records Management Quarterly*. January 1988: 22(1), 126-129.

PRESLOCK, Karen. Publications. *Conservation Administration News*. July 1987: (30), 16-17.

PRESLOCK, Karen. Publications. *Conservation Administration News*. October 1987: (31), 18-19.

PRESLOCK, Karen. Publications. *Conservation Administration News*. January 1988: (32), 17.

PRESLOCK, Karen. Publications. *Conservation Administration News*. April 1988: (33), 18, 21.

PRESLOCK, Karen. Publications. *Conservation Administration News*. July 1988: (34), 14, 22.

PRESLOCK, Karen. Publications. *Conservation Administration News*. October 1988: (35), 20.

REICHER, Leslie Arden. 9 to 5: the textbook disaster: a case for disaster preparedness. *Conservation Administration News*. July 1986: (26), 6, 10.

RHODES, Barbara J. *Hell and high water: a disaster information sourcebook.* New York: METRO, 1988. 58 p.

SCHNARE, Robert E. and Marilyn D. CURTIS. Fire aftermath and the recovery process. *Conservation Administration News*. October 1988: (35), 1-2, 22.

SCHNARE, Robert E. Publications. *Conservation Administration News*. July 1986: (26), 18-20.

SCHNARE, Robert E. Publications. *Conservation Administration News*. January 1987: (28), 18-21.

SCHNARE, Robert E. Publications. *Conservation Administration News*. April 1987: (29), 24-25, 28.

SCHUR, Susan E. Conservation terminology: a review of past & current nomenclature of materials, part III. *Technology and Conservation*. 1988: 9(3/4), 40-41.

SMITH, Clive. Starting a conservation programme. *Archives and Manuscripts*. May 1987: 15(1), 41-47.

SMITH, Richard D. Reversibility: a questionable philosophy. *Restaurator*. 1988: 9(4), 199-207.

STONER, Joyce Hill. Getty Museum invests in conservation. *Museum News*. April 1986: 64(4), 36-39.

TAYLOR, Hugh A. Strategies for the future: the preservation of archival materials in Canada. *Conservation Administration News*. April 1987: (29), 1-3.

THOMPSON, Michael. Conserving an early map of Canada. *The Archivist*. March/April 1987: 14(2), 16-17.

THOMPSON, Michael. Restauration d'une ancienne carte. *L'Archiviste*. Mars/avril 1987: 14(2), 16-17.

VINAS, V. and R. VINAS. *Las tecnicas tradicionales de restauracion: un estudio del RAMP.* Paris: Unesco, 1988. iii, 72 p. (PGI-88/WS/17)

WACHTER, Wolfgang. Mechanizing restoration work — the Deutsche Bücheri in Leipzig and its role as a regional center for

IFLA. *Restaurator*. 1987: 8(2/3), 129-132.

WALSH, Betty. Salvage of water-damaged archival collections. *ACA Bulletin*. March 1988: 12(4), [17-18].

5.3.1 Examination and analysis: condition reports / Examen et analyse: rapport sur l'état

BERGER, Gustav A. and William H. RUSSELL. An evaluation of the preparation of canvas paintings using stress measurements. *Studies in Conservation*. November 1988: 33(4), 187-204.

CALABRO, Giuseppe, Maria Teresa TANASI and Giancarlo IMPAGLIAZZO. An evaluation method of softening agents for parchment. *Restaurator*. 1986: 7(4), 169-180.

DOYLE, Laurance R., Jean J. LORRE and Eric B. DOYLE. The application of computer image processing techniques to artifact analysis as applied to the shroud of turin study... *Studies in Conservation*. 1986: 31(1), 1-6.

DWAN, Antoinette. Paper complexity and the interpretation of conservation research. *Journal of the American Institute for Conservation*. Spring 1987: 26(1), 1-17.

HANSON, Kenneth M. United States Department of Energy: measurement of microdensitometer wobble. *Journal of Imaging Science*. 1986: 30(6), 274-276.

HANUS, Jozef and Magda KOMORNIKOVA. The application of statistical analysis in evaluation of changes in some properties of aged papers. *Archives et bibliothèques de Belgique*. 1987: 58(1/2), 161-182.

HARLEY, Rosamond. Artists' prepared canvases from Winsor & Newton 1928-1951. *Studies in Conservation*. May 1987: 32(2), 77-85.

HUBENER, Hal. Sunshine state showpieces: alligator-skin bindings in Florida Archives. *Provenance*. Fall 1988: 6(2), 42-43.

KATLAN, Alexander, [et al.]. Some uses of a video cassette recorder in the conservation laboratory. *Journal of the American Institute for Conservation*. Spring 1987: 26(1), 59-63.

KODA, Paul S. Scientific equipment for the examination of rare books, manuscripts, and documents. *Recent Trends in Rare Book Librarianship*. Summer 1987: 39-52.

LAURENCIC, Tamara. *Protective treatments and repair of paper records*. Australia: Library Board of Queensland, 1987. 38 p.

MAGLIANO, Patrizia and Bruno BOESMI. Xeroradiography for paintings on canvas and wood. *Studies in Conservation*. February 1988: 33(1), 41-47.

New security copy paper has implications for archivist [nocopi paper]. *ACA Bulletin*. January 1987: 11(3), 5.

OVERMAN, Linda. Deacidification update. *The Primary Source*. Fall 1987: 9(3), 20-23.

RACELIS, Fernando. The composition of inks. *Conservation Administration News*. April 1987: (29), 6-7, 10, 13.

THOMPSON, Michael. Conserving an early map of Canada. *The Archivist*. March/April 1987: 14(2), 16-17.

THOMPSON, Michael. Restauration d'une ancienne carte. *L'Archiviste*. Mars/avril 1987: 14(2), 16-17.

WHITMORE, Paul M. and Glen R. CASS. The ozone fading of traditional Japanese colorants. *Studies in Conservation*. February 1988: 33(1), 29-40.

WHITMORE, Paul M., [et al.]. The ozone fading of traditional natural organic colorants on paper. *Journal of the American Institute for Conservation*. Spring 1987: 26(1), 45-58.

WOODWARD, David. The Analysis of paper and ink in early maps. *Recent Trends in Rare Book Librarianship*. Summer 1987: 85-118.

WRIGHT, Sandra and Peter YURKIW. The collections survey in the Federal Archives and Manuscript Divisions of the Public Archives of Canada: a progress report on conservation programme planning. *Archivaria*. Summer 1986: (22), 58-74.

5.3.2 Techniques (cleaning, deacidification, etc.) / Techniques (nettoyage, désacidification, etc.)

ALLARD, Danielle and Kenneth B. KATZ. Quantitative study: the effects of sized materials and "drying time" in the use of hascaux 360 HV as a lining adhesive. *Journal of the American Institute for Conservation*. Spring 1987: 26(1), 19-26.

ARNOULT, Jean-Marie. Mass deacidification in France. *Restaurator*. 1987: 8(2/3), 100-105.

BALLARD, Mary W. and Norbert S. BAER. Ethylene oxide fumigation: results and risks. *Restaurator*. December 1986: 7(4), 143-168.

BARGER, M. Susan and Thomas T. HILL. Thiourea and ammonium thiosulfate treatments for the removal of silvering from aged negative materials. *Journal of Imaging Technology*. April 1988: 14(2), 43-46.

BOURBONNAIS, Michel. Un ambitieux projet de conservation. *L'Archiviste*. Mars/avril 1988: 15(2), 9.

BOURBONNAIS, Michel. Disc conservation state of the art. *The Archivist*. March/April 1988: 15(2), 9.

BRANDT, Astrid-Christiane et André-Jean BERTEAUD. Séchage par micro-ondes pour la restauration de documents de papier en feuille ou en cahier. *Studies in Conservation*. February 1987: 32(1), 14-24.

BUTLER, Randall. The Los Angeles Central Library: "nightmare, part II". *Conservation Administration News*. January 1987: (28), 1-2.

CALABRO, Giuseppe, [et al.]. An evaluation method of softening agents for parchment. *Restaurator*. December 1986: 7(4), 169-170.

CLEMENTS, D.W.G. Emerging technologies — paper strengthening. *Restaurator*. 1987: 8(2/3), 124-128.

CRESPO, Carmen. La conservation des documents et son application aux archives d'entreprises. *Conseil international des archives. Comité des archives d'entreprises. Bulletin*. 1988: (11), 27-32.

CRESPO, Carmen. Document conservation and its application to business archives. *International Council on Archives. Committee on Business Archives. Bulletin*. 1988: (11), 23-27.

DE LA RIE, E. Rene. The influence of varnishes on the appearance of paintings. *Studies in Conservation*. February 1987: 32(1), 1-13.

DUHL, Susan and Kathleen BAKER. Considerations in light bleaching art on paper. *Paper Conservation News*. 1986: (40), 5-6.

FLIEDER, Françoise. Méthodes mécaniques utilisées en France pour la restauration du papier. *Archives et bibliothèques de Belgique*. 1987: 58(1/2), 135-144.

FUJII, Etsuo, [et al.]. Evaluation on the stability of light faded images of color reversal films according to color difference in CIELAB. *Journal of Imaging Technology*. April 1988: 14(2), 29-37.

HOOK, John. The use of immiscible solvent combinations for the cleaning of paintings. *Journal of the American Institute for Conservation*. Fall 1988: 27(2), 100-104.

HUMPHREY, Bruce J. Vapor phase consolidation of books with the parylene polymers. *Journal of the American Institute for Conservation*. Spring 1986: 25(1), 15-29.

LAURENCIC, Tamara. *Protective treatments and repair of paper records.* Australia: Library Board of Queensland, 1987. 38 p.

LIENARDY, Anne and Philippe VAN DAMME. A bibliographical survey of the bleaching of paper. *Restaurator.* 1988: 9(4), 178-198.

MCCLEARY, John M. *Vacuum freeze-drying, a method used to salvage water-damaged archival and library materials: a RAMP study with guidelines.* Paris: UNESCO, 1987. 63 p. (PGI-87/WS/7)

MILLER, Deborah R. The challenge of binding music. *Conservation Administration News.* January 1988: (32), 8-9.

NORDSTRAND, Ove K. The conservation treatment of paper. *Restaurator.* 1987: 8(2/3), 133-139.

OVERMAN, Linda. Deacidification update. *The Primary Source.* Fall 1987: 9(3), 20-23.

PAVITT, Rebecca Billings. Non-aqueous adhesives: preparation, use and removal. *Paper Conservation News.* 1987: (41), 3-5.

SCOTT, Marianne. Mass deacidification at the National Library of Canada. *Restaurator.* 1987: 8(2/3), 94-99.

SMITH, Richard D. Deacidifying library collections: myths and realities. *Restaurator.* 1987: 8(2/3), 69-93.

SPARKS, Peter G. Mass deacidification at the Library of Congress. *Restaurator.* 1987: 8(2/3), 106-110.

SPARKS, Peter G. Technology in support of preservation. *Restaurator.* 1987: 8(2/3), 65-68.

STEWART, Eleanore. Freeze disinfection of the McWilliams Collection. *Conservation Administration News.* January 1988: (32), 10-11, 25.

STIRTON, Lavra J. Winterthur water screen bathing. *Paper Conservation News.* June 1987: 42, 3-4.

THOMPSON, Jack C. Mass deacidification: thoughts on the Cunha Report. *Restaurator.* 1988: 9(3), 147-162.

THOMPSON, Michael. Conserving an early map of Canada. *The Archivist.* March/April 1987: 14(2), 16-17.

THOMPSON, Michael. Restauration d'une ancienne carte. *L'Archiviste.* Mars/avril 1987: 14(2), 16-17.

WACHTER, Otto. Paper strengthening: mass conservation of unbound and bound newspapers. *Restaurator.* 1987: 8(2/3), 111-123.

5.3.3 Restoration of photographic records / Restauration des documents photographiques

BRANDT, E.S. Mechanistic studies of image stability: part 3. Oxidation of silver from the vantage point of corrosion theory. *Journal of Imaging Science.* 1987: 31(5), 199-207.

CARTIER-BRESSON, Anne. Approche de quelques problèmes posés par la restauration des collections de photographies historiques. *Science et technologie de la conservation et de la restauration des œuvres d'art et du patrimoine.* Juin 1988: 1, 41-45.

CINLAR, Anne. Preservation of slide libraries. *Conservation Administration News.* October 1988: (35), 7, 23.

MITCHELL, Ann M. On the preservation of dufaycolor transparencies at Sydney Hospital. *Archives and Manuscripts.* May 1986: 14(1), 61-65.

NICKEL, Ulrich. The influence of deamination on the stability of photographic dyes. *Journal of Imaging Technology.* 1986: 12(4), 181-184.

SARETZKY, Gary D. Photographic conservation. Part II. *Conservation Administration News.* July 1988: (34), 4, 9.

SARETZKY, Gary D. Photographic conservation: part III. *Conservation Administration News.* October 1988: (35), 4-5.

SI-YONG, Zhuang. Study of the properties of photographic emulsions with varying iodide content. *Journal of Imaging Science*. 1986: 30(1), 16-21.

5.4 Authentication and forgery / Authentification et falsification

Charles Mount convicted in Boston Federal Court. *SAA Newsletter*. May 1988: 6.

KOOBATIAN, James. *Faking it: an international bibliography of art and literary forgeries, 1949-1986*. 1st ed. Washington, D.C.: Special Libraries Association, c1987. x, 240 p.

RENDELL, Kenneth W. Latter day taints: the Mark Hoffman case. *Manuscripts*. Winter 1988: 40(1), 5-14.

5.5 Future outlook / Pour l'avenir

ALLEN, Marie. Optical character recognition: technology with new relevance for archival automation projects. *The American Archivist*. Winter 1987: 50(1), 88-99.

Archival management: the 1980's and beyond. *Records and Retrieval Report*. October 1986: 2(8), 9-14.

BANKS, Richard L. COM and optical recording — change and challenge. *IMC Journal*. May/June 1988: 24(3), 18-20.

BROWN, J.H.U., Carlos VALLBONA and H. KITASANONO. A new patient record system using the lasercard. *Optical Information Systems*. July/August 1988: 8(4), 156-161.

CINNAMON, Barry. Optical disk applications. *IMC Journal*. July/August 1988: 24(4), 19-22.

DAVIS, Douglas L. Optical archiving: where are we now and where do we go from here? *Optical Information Systems*. January/February 1987: 66-71.

DICKEY, Sam. New directions in micrographics. *Today's Office*. August 1987: 22(3), 34-38.

EDWARDS, Ian C. Optical storage developments — write-once media. *Electronic and Optical Publishing Review*. March 1987: 7(1), 16-20.

FOSTER, Ken. Conserver pour demain. *L'Archiviste*. Mai/juin 1987: 14(3), 14-15.

FOSTER, Ken. New branch dedicated to conservation. *The Archivist*. May/June 1987: 14(3), 14-15.

FRANK, John W. Micrographics and optical disk — friends or foes? *IMC Journal*. July/August 1988: 24(4), 7-9.

GARNETT, Thomas. Development of an authority control system for the Smithsonian Institution Libraries. *Archival Informatics Technical Report*. Summer 1988: 2(2), 21-28.

GELLER, L.D. In-house conservation and the general practice of archival science. *Archivaria*. Summer 1986: (22), 163-167.

GONZALEZ, Pedro. *Des salles de lecture sans papier?* Congrès international des archives (11e: 1988: Paris). Paris, 1988. 4 p.

GRANAT, Burton (Bud). Microfilm service: market savvy for the future. *INFORM: the Magazine of Information and Image Management*. June 1987: 1(6), 14-15.

HALLEEN, Gary. Document retrieval for people who don't care. *IMC Journal*. September/October 1988: 24(5), 9-12.

Imaging. *Records and Retrieval Report*. December 1988: 4(10), 1-14.

KALTHOFF, Robert J. 1987: industry leaders on the outlook for digital document automation (DDA) right decision. *IMC Journal*. 1987: 23(4), 15-19.

KUDNER, James E. Organic materials for optical data storage media: an overview. *Journal of Imaging Technology*. June 1986: 12(3), 140-143.

LANGEMO, Mark. Major trends in the managing of records. *Office*. January 1987: 105(1), 65.

LAROSE, Michèle. Colloque international sur la conservation. *L'Archiviste*. Novembre/décembre 1987: 14(6), 18.

LAROSE, Michèle. International Conservation Symposium in 1988. *The Archivist.* November/December 1987: 14(6), 18.

PTACEK, William P. Microfilm, microfilmers and the future. *INFORM: the Magazine of Information and Image Management.* July/August 1988: 2(7), 8-11.

RAMSAY, Nancy C. Using optical disk in non-image applications. *Optical Information Systems.* July/August 1988: 8(4), 164-168.

Records management for the 1990s. *Records and Retrieval Report.* October 1988: 4(8), 1-14.

TIMBERS, Michael J. We are working to solve the problems of paper. *Office.* January 1987: 105(1), 122.

WILLIAMSON, R. The knowledge warehouse [a national archives of the electronic form of knowledge works, being developed in Great Britain]. *Journal of Information Science.* 1987: 13(4), 253-257.

YU, F.T. *White-light optical information processing and holography (Final rept. 15 Feb 81-14 May 86).* Pennsylvania: Pennsylvania State University, University Park, Department of Electrical Engineering, 1987. 312 p.

6. Auxiliary sciences / Sciences auxiliaires

6.1 Heraldry / Héraldique

BARTHOLDY, Nils G. Rigsarkivet som heraldisk myndighed [The National Archives as heraldic authority]. *Nordisk Arkivnyt.* 1986: 31(2), 36-38.

6.3 Sigillography / Sigillographie

BERTENYI, Ivan. L'utilisation des sceaux dans la chancellerie « judicum curiae regiae » en Hongrie aux XIIIe-XIVe siècles. *Archives et bibliothèques de Belgique.* 1987: 58(1/2), 21-32.

CAUVEREN, Syd. Paraphs and seals — a celebration! Part II: seals. *Manuscripts.* Spring 1987: 39(2), 111-117.

CRESPO, Carmen. El sello en las cancillerias medievales Espanolas segun las partidas de Alfonso x el sabio y las ordenanzas de Pedro iv. *Archives et bibliothèques de Belgique.* 1987: 58(1/2), 45-66.

MAY, Guy. Il avait trouvé le « moulage inoffensif »: à propos de Henri Gomand (1817-1857). *Archives et bibliothèques de Belgique.* 1987: 58(1/2), 285-298.

6.4 Others / Autres

BOWERS, Doris Roney. Genealogical research in the county courthouse. *Illinois Libraries.* September 1988: 70(7), 480-483.

CAUVEREN, Syd. Paraphs and seals — a celebration!. *Manuscripts.* Winter 1987: 39(1), 21-28.

GUYOTJEANNIN, Olivier. Métrologie française d'ancien régime. Guide bibliographique sommaire. *La Gazette des archives.* 1987: (139), 233-247.

KARNS, Kermit B. The care and feeding of genealogists: or what every archivist should know about genealogy. *SAA Newsletter.* March 1987: 12.

POLE, T.A. Sur l'application de la méthode métrique dans la paléographie russe [en russe]. *Sovietskje Arkhivy.* 1987: (1), 45-51.

Author Index / Index des auteurs

BARKER, Kevin, 4.4
BARLEE, Kathleen, 1.6
BARR, Debra, 1.2 / 1.3 / 3.5
BARR, Jean, 2. / 5.2.1
BARR, Robert D., 2.1 / 5.2.1
BARRITT, Marjorie Rabe, 1.6 / 4.1.5
BARTELS, Kerry, 1.6 / 1.7
BARTHOLDY, Nils G., 6.1
BARTZ PETCHENIK, Barbara,
    3.1.4.1
BASSETT, T.D. Seymour, 3.0.1
BATAZZI, David, 2.2 / 4.1.5 / 5.2.1
BATTYE LIBRARY, 4.1.5
BATY, Laurie, 1.6
BAUMANN, Bryan, 2. / 5.1
BAUMANN, Roland M., 1.7 /
    3.0.4.4 / 4.1.4 / 4.4
BAUTSCH, Gail, 2. / 2.5 / 5.1
BAYNES-COPE, A.D, 1.6 / 5.1
BEARMAN, David, 1. / 1.5 / 3.0 /
    3.0.3 / 3.0.5
BEARMAN, T.C., 3.0.4.4
BEATON, Elizabeth, 1.
BEAUD, Marie-Josèphe, 3.6.5 /
    3.8.5
BECHOR, Malvina B., 1.1 / 1.6
BECKLEY, Susan, 3.0.4.2 / 4.1.3
BEECH, Geraldine, 3.1 / 4.1.3
BELANGER, Terry, 1.6
BELL, Mary Margaret, 3.8 / 5.2 /
    5.2.1
BELL, Steven J., 2.1
BELOVA, T.V., 1.1 / 4.1.5
BENDER, Avi, 2. / 2.1 / 3.0.5 / 5.1.4
BENNICK, Ann, 2.1
BENOÎT, Gérard, 5.1.1
BERCHE, Claire, 1.5 / 3.3.2 / 3.3.3 /
    3.5 / 3.7 / 4.1.2
BERGEN, Kathleen, 3.1
BERGER, Gustav A., 5.3.1
BERGERON, Rosemary, 3.3.1
BERNER, Richard C., 1.6
BERNIER, Hélène, 1.5
BERRY, E.K., 1.4 / 4.1.3
BERRY, Elizabeth, 4.1.3
BERTEAUD, André-Jean, 5.3.2
BERTENYI, Ivan, 6.3
BERTIN-MAGHIT, Jean-Pierre,
    4.1.2
BERTRAND, Jean-Wilfrid, 1.7 /4.1.5
BERZINS, Ina, 3.0.4
BEYEA, Marion, 1.5 / 1.6

BIDA, Michael C., 3.0.5 / 5.2.1
BILDFELL, Laurie, 1.5 / 3.0.1
BILLOUX, Claudine, 4.1.2
BIRRELL, A.J., 3.0.5
BLACK, Jeremy, 3.0.3 / 3.0.4.1
BLAIS, Gabrielle, 3.8.1 / 3.8.5
BLANC, Brigitte, 3.7
BLINKHORN, Victoria Kendall,
    3.0.1
BLOODWORTH, J.G., 5.1
BLOOMFIELD, B., 4.1.3
BLOUIN, Francis X., Jr., 1.6 / 4.1.5
BLOUNT, Gail, 2.4
BLUM, Sylvie, 1.1 / 1.7 / 4.1.2
BOAG, P.W., 2.5 / 4.1.5
BOATRIGH, John, 1.5 / 3.0.4.2
BOCKING, Doug, 3.8.1 / 3.8.5
BOESMI, Bruno, 5.3.1
BOGGE, Alfonso, 1.5 / 3.0 / 3.0.5
BOIS, Jean-Jacques, 5.2.2
BOLES, Frank, 3.0.1
BOLNICK, Franklin I., 3.0.5 / 5.2.1
BOLOTENKO, George, 1.6 / 4.1.5
BONNIN, Hélène, 3.4 / 4.1.2
BONVIE, Bill, 2.2
BOOKER, John, 3.0.2 / 4.2
BOOMS, Hans, 3.8.1 / 4.1.5
BORDAS, Richard, 2.1 / 5.2.1
BORSA, Ivan, 3.8.5 / 4.1.5
BOSSE, David, 3.1 / 3.1.4.1
BOTTOMLEY, Michael, 1.1 / 5.2.1
BOUD, R.C., 3.1.4.1
BOUDANOV, O.A., 1.5 / 4.1.5
BOULET-WERNHAM, Monique, 4.5
BOULFATA, Issa J., 4.3 / 4.4
BOURBONNAIS, Michel, 3.7 / 5.3.2
BOURDON, Jérôme, 1.4 / 3.3.4.1 /
    3.3.4.4
BOURKE, Thomas A., 3.0.5 / 5.1.4 /
    5.2.1
BOUVET, Mireille-Bénédicte, 3.3 /
    4.1.2
BOUVIER, Jean-Claude, 3.2 / 3.3 /
    3.5 / 3.7
BOWDEN, Russell, 1.6
BOWEN, Laurel G., 4.1.3 / 4.1.4
BOWERS, Doris Roney, 3.0.4 / 6.4
BOZEVICH, Ken, 2. / 2.1 / 3.0.5 /
    5.1.4
BRACHMANN-TEUBNER,
    Elisabeth, 1.7 / 4.1.5
BRADSHER, Greg, 1.2 / 1.5

CHAPDELAINE, Susan A., 2.1
CHARLAND, Diane, 2.4
CHARMAN, Derek, 2. / 2.4
CHARNEUX, Jacques, 4.5
CHARTRAND, Robert Lee, 1.3 /
   3.0.5
CHEN ZHAO, Wu, 1.6
CHESTAKOVA, I.S., 3.0.3
CHESTERMAN, John, 1.4 / 3.3.4.3 /
   3.4.4.3 / 3.7.4.3
CHESTNUT, Paul, 1.6
CHILD, M.S., 2.4 / 3.0.1
CHIPPIE, Wendy L., 2.
CHMIDT, S.O., 1.6
CHOKHINE, L.I., 3.0.3
CHOMEL, Maïc, 3.7 / 4.1.2
CHOUINARD, Denys, 1.1 / 3.0.1 /
   3.0.2 / 3.0.3
CHRISTENSEN-SKOELD, Beatrice,
   3.7 / 4.1.5
CHRISTIAN, Helen, 3.1
CINLAR, Anne, 5.3.3
CINNAMON, Barry, 3.0.5 / 5.5
CIRKOVIC-STANOJLOVIC,
   Ljiljana, 5.3
CITARELLA, Judith, 2. / 3.0.5 /
   5.1.4
CLAIR, Sylvie, 4.1.2
CLAPP, Anne F., 5.1 / 5.3
CLARK, Ian Christie, 1.4
CLARK, Steve, 2.1
CLARKE, J.A., 3.0.5
CLARKE, Keith C., 3.1.4
CLAUZADE, Sophie de, 1.8 / 3.2 /
   3.3 / 3.5
CLAYSSEN, Dominique, 3.3 / 3.4
CLEMENTS, D.W.G., 1.8 / 4.1.3 /
   5.1 / 5.2.1 / 5.3.2
CLERC, Jean-Pierre, 3.4
CLITES, Lorraine, 2. / 3.0.5 / 5.1.4
CLOUD, Patricia D., 1.5 / 3.0.3 /
   3.0.5 / 4.4
CLUBB, Clare M., 4.1.3 / 4.4
COCHRANE, C., 3.3 / 4.1.3 / 5.3
COCHRANE, Shirley G., 3.8 / 4.1.4
COKER, Kathy Roe, 2.1 / 4.1.4
COLE, Maude D., 3.1 / 4.1.4
COLES, Laura Millar, 1.2 / 3.0.3 /
   3.0.4.2 / 3.0.5 / 3.8.4.2
COLLIER, Rosemary, 1.6 / 2.1 /
   4.1.5
COLLIN, Hubert, 3.0.3

COLLINS, Lori, 3.1.2
COLLINS, Roger, 3.2.4.1
COLLINS, Sheldan, 5.2.2
COLLOQUE ÉNAP/IIAP (6e : 1985 :
   QUÉBEC, QUÉBEC), 1.5
COLMAN, Gould P., 3.0.1
COLQUHOUN, David, 4.1.5
CONCHON, Michèle, 3.4 / 3.4.5 /
   4.1.2
CONNORS, Thomas, 4.2
CONTINI BONACOSSI, Giovanni,
   3.7.4.1
CONWAY, Paul, 1.5 / 1.6 / 3.0.4 /
   4. / 5.2.1
CONYERS, Diann, 2.1 / 5.1
COOK, J. Frank, 1.6
COOK, Michael, 1.2 / 1.5 / 1.6 /
   3.0.3. / 3.0.5
COOK, Terry, 1. / 1.6 / 3.0.1 /
   3.8.1 / 3.8.4.4 / 3.8.5 / 4.1.1
COOKE, Anne, 1.6
COOKE, Donald F., 3.1.5 / 5.1 /
   5.1.4
COONEY, James P., 3.0 / 3.0.5
COOPER, B.J., 3.1.4.1
COOPER, Graham H., 3.1.4.1
COOPER, Sarah, 1.5 / 3.0.1 / 4.5
COPPEJANS-DESMEDT, Hilda,
   3.8.4.1 / 4.2
COPPENS, Chris, 5.1
CORNISH, Graham P., 3. / 3.0 / 3.2 /
   3.3 / 3.5 / 3.7 / 4.1.3 / 4.5
CORTISSOZ, Anne, 2. / 3.0.5
COUEDELO, Rose-Anne, 3.2 / 3.3 /
   3.5 / 4.1.2
COURTOT, Marilyn, 2.5 / 5.2.1
COUTURE, Carol, 1.1 / 1.2 / 1.6 /
   1.7
COUVELIS, Joyce, 2.1 / 5.2.1
COX, Bill, 2.
COX, Richard J., 1.1 / 1.2 / 1.5 /
   1.6 / 1.7 / 3.0.1 / 3.6
CRAIG, Barbara L., 1.6
CRAIG-BULLEN, Catherine, 5.1 /
   5.1.3
CRAVEN, Paul Taylor, 2. / 3.0.5 /
   5.1.4
CRAWFORD, Miriam I., 3.0.1 /
   3.0.2 / 3.0.3
CREIGHTON, Ken, 2. / 3.8.4.1 /
   3.8.4.4 / 4.1.1

CRESPO, Carmen, 4.2 / 5.1.2 /
   5.1.3 / 5.3.2 / 6.3
CREWS, Patricia Cox, 5.1
CRIBBS, Margaret A., 3.5 / 5.1 /
   5.1.3 / 5.1.4
CROCKETT, Margaret A., 4.1.5
CROSADO, Doug, 3.7
CROSS, James Edward, 3.5.1
CROTTS, Joe, 3.1.4.1
CRUSE, Larry, 3.1 / 5.2.1
CRUSH, Peter, 1.6 / 3.0.4.1
CUMMING, Judi, 3.8.1
CUNHA, George M., 5.1
CUNNINGHAM, Roger B., 2. /
   3.0.5 / 5.2.1
CUNNINGHAM, Veronica Colley,
   5.1
CURRIE, Jack, 2.1 / 5.2.1
CURTIS, Marilyn D., 5.1 / 5.3
DAHL, Edward H., 2. / 3.1.1 / 3.1.4.1
DAHLO, Rolf, 5.3
DAINES, Arthur, 5.3
DAJIC, Mirjana, 4.1.5
DALY, John, 4.1.4
DANIELLS, Laurenda, 1.5 / 3.0.5 / 4.
DANIELS, Maygene, 1.7 / 1.8
DANILOV, Victor J., 1.5 / 3.0.4.2
DASCHER, Ottfried, 3.0.4.1 / 4.2
DAUM, Patricia B., 2. / 2.4
DAVENPORT, L., 3.4
DAVID, Andrew C.F., 3.1.4.1
DAVID, Jonathan, 3.0.4.2 / 5.1.1
DAVIES, Stuart, 3.0.1
DAVIES, Vanessa, 4.2
DAVIS, Douglas L., 2. / 3.0.5 / 3.4 /
   5.1.4 / 5.5
DAVIS, James V., 2.1 / 2.5
DAVIS, Susan E., 1.5 / 1.6
DAVIS, Victoria A., 2. / 3.0.5
DAWE, Claire, 1.2 / 1.5
DAY, David A., 4.5
DAYS, D.C., 4.5
DEARSTYNE, Bruce W., 3.0.4.1 /
   3.0.4.2
DE BRUYN, Katherine Aschner, 2.1
DEFRANCE, Jean-Pierre, 3.2 / 3.3 /
   3.5 / 4.1.2
DE GRAFF, Kathryn, 4.4
DELAET, Jean-Louis, 4.5
DELAGE, Gisèle, 1.3
DE LA RIE, E. Rene, 5.3.2
DE LEEUW, G.J.A., 3.1.4.1

DELLER, Howard, 3.1.4.2
DELMAS, Bruno, 1.3 / 1.6 / 3.
DELOTTINVILLE, Peter, 1.6 / 1.7 /
   3.8.1
DELSALLE, Paul, 3.0.4.2
DEMPSEY, Colleen, 1.6
DEMPSEY, Patrick E., 3.1.4.1
DENEL, Francis, 1.3
DENIS, Philippe, 4.5
DENTON, A.W., 4.4
DEPAUW, Claude, 4.2
DEPEW, John N., 4.1.4 / 5.1 / 5.3
DE SILVA, G.P.S.H., 4.1.5 / 4.5
DESLONGCHAMPS, Denis, 1.4 / 2.1
DESMARAIS, Norman, 2. / 3.0.5 /
   5. / 5.1.4
DETHAN, G., 4.1.2
DEVOS, J.-C., 4.1.2
DEWHITT, Benjamin L., 3.4 / 5.1
DIAMOND, Sigmund, 3.0.4 / 3.0.4.4
DIAMONDSTONE, Judith, 3.3.3
DIBBLE, Thomas G., 2. / 4.1.4 / 4.5
DICKEY, Sam, 3.0.5 / 5.2.1 / 5.5
DICKINSON, A. Litchard, 2.1 / 2.5
DIEUZEDE, Geneviève, 1.4 / 3.5.1 /
   3.5.3
DINEL, Guy, 1.5
DINWIDDIE, Robert C., 3.5.1 / 3.5.2
DIXON, Debra, 2.1 / 5.3
DIXON, Diana, 1.1 / 4.2
DJILAS, Hélène, 3.3 / 3.3.4.2
DODD, Sue A., 3.4.3
DODGE, Bernadine, 3.1.2
DOLBEC, Michelle, 4.2
DOLL, John G., 3.1.4.1
DOLLAR, Charles M., 2.5 / 3.0.5 /
   5.1.4
DOOLEY, Jackie M., 3.0.3 / 3.0.5
DORAY, Raymond, 1.4
DOUGLAS, W.A.B., 3.8 / 3.8.4.1
DOWLER, Lawrence, 3.0.3 / 3.0.4 /
   3.0.4.4
DOYLE, Eric B., 5.3.1
DOYLE, Laurance R., 5.3.1
DOZOIS, Paulette, 3.8
DRYDEN, Jean E., 1.3 / 3.0.3 /
   3.8.4.1
DU BOISROUVRAY, Xavier, 3.5 /
   4.1.2
DUCHARME, Jacques, 1.1
DUCHEIN, Michel, 1.4 / 3.0.3 / 3.7 /
   4.1.2

DUCROT, Marie-Odile, 3.0.5
DUFFY, Mark J., 1.5 / 4.3
DUFOUR, Frank, 5.1
DUHL, Susan, 5.3.2
DUKE, David, 2. / 3.0.5
DUMONT, Jacques, 1.5 / 4.1.2
DUNAE, Patrick A., 4.1.1
DUNN, F. Ian, 3.0.4.4
DUNN, Lucia S., 4.4
DUPUIS, Yvon, 1.4
DURANTI, Luciana, 1.6 / 2.5 / 3.4 / 4.1.5
DURR, Theodore W., 3.0.5
DVORIASHINA, Z.P., 5.1 / 5.1.3
DWAN, Antoinette, 5.3.1
EASTWOOD, Terry, 1.4 / 1.5 / 1.6 / 3.0.4 / 4.1.1
ECKER, Ulrich, 4.2
ÉCOLE DES HAUTES ÉTUDES COMMERCIALES. (MONTRÉAL, QUÉBEC). GESTION DES DOCUMENTS, 2.3
EDDISON, Betty, 3.4.4.4
EDINGER, J. Raymond, 5.2.2
EDWARDS, Ian C., 5.2 / 5.5
EELES, Graham, 1.6 / 3.0.4.1
EFIMENKO, R.N., 3.0.5
EGAN, Trevor, 3.1.4.1
ELDER, Sean, 1.6 / 4.1.4
ELKINGTON, Nancy E., 5.1 / 5.2.1
ELLIS, Stephen, 2.4 / 3.0.1 / 4.1.5
ELSHAMI, Ahmed M., 1.1
ELWOOD, Marie, 1.8 / 3.0.1
ENDELMAN, Judith E., 1.6 / 3.0.5 / 3.8.1 / 4.1.4
ENGLAND, Claire, 1.2 / 3.0.4.4 / 5.1 / 5.3
ENGLERT, Marianne, 1.6
ENIN, G.P., 5.2.1
ENSMAN, Richard G., 2.1 / 3.0.5
ERICKSEN, Paul A., 4.3
ERICSON, Timothy L., 1.6
ERLING, Paul A., 3.1.4.1
ERMISSE, Gérard, 3.0.4 / 3.3.4 / 4.1.2 / 4.1.5
ERNST, Volker, 3.0.3 / 4.1.5
ESO, Elizabeth, 1.5 / 3.0.4 / 4.1.1
EVANS, A., 3.3.2
EVANS, Frank B., 1.6 / 1.7 / 1.8
EVANS, Karen, 1.2 / 3.0.4.4 / 5.1 / 5.3

FABIAN, Jurai, 3.8.1
FABREGUETTES, Catherine, 3.0.5 / 5.2.1
FAGAN, Michele L., 3.0.4 / 3.0.4.1 / 4.1.3
FARCIS, Daniel, 4.1.2
FAUVEL-ROUIF, Denise, 4.1.2
FAVIER, Jean, 5.1.3 / 5.3
FAVIER, Lucie, 5.1 / 5.3
FECTEAU, Jean-Marie, 4.1.1
FEINDT, W., 5.1 / 5.3
FELDHAUSEN, Mark, 3.0.5 / 5.2.1
FENSTERMANN, Duane W., 5.1
FIALA, Tomas, 4.1.5
FIELD, Jeffrey, 5.1 / 5.2.1
FIGUEIREDO, Luciano, 3.1.5 / 4.1.5
FILIPOVA, Velicka, 4.1.5
FILLING, Sylvia, 2.2 / 4.1.5 / 5.2.1
FILLION, Chantale, 4.5
FINLAY, Douglas, 1.5 / 3.0.5
FINLAYSON, Brian, 3.1.4.1
FISCHER, Ekkehard, 3.8.1 / 3.8.2 / 4.1.5
FISCHER, Marti, 1.1 / 2.
FISHBEIN, Meyer H., 3.0.1 / 3.0.3 / 3.0.5 / 3.4.1 / 3.8.1
FITZGERALD, S.M.D., 3.0.1 / 3.8.1 / 4.1.3 / 4.5
FLAHERTY, David H., 1.1
FLECKNER, John A., 1.6
FLEIG, Clare, 2. / 3.0.5
FLIEDER, Françoise, 5.1 / 5.3 / 5.3.2
FLINT, Michael F., 1.4
FLUBACHER, F. Shirley, 2. / 3.0.5 / 5.2.1
FLUTY, Steve, 2. / 3.0.5 / 5.1.4 / 5.2.1
FONNES, Ivar, 3.0.5
FONTAINE, Jean-Marc, 3.7
FONTANEL, Francine, 3.0.4.3
FORBES, Jamie, 2.1 / 4.1.1
FOSSIER, Lucie, 3.6.5 / 3.8.5
FOSTER, Ken, 5.1.3 / 5.5
FOTHERINGHAM, Richard, 3.8.4.3 / 4.1.5
FOX, Lisa L., 5.1 / 5.3
FRANCE. MINISTÈRE DE LA CULTURE. DIRECTION DE L'ADMINISTRATION GÉNÉRALE, 3.7.4.3
FRANCIS, James, 2.
FRANK, John W., 5.2.1 / 5.5

HARRIS, Kevin, 3.2.4
HARRISON, Donald Fisher, 1.6 /
　3.4 / 3.4.4.1 / 3.4.4.4
HARRISON, Helen P., 3.3 / 3.7 /
　3.7.1
HART, Beverly, 2.4 / 3.0.1 / 4.1.5
HARTMAN, Hedy A., 1.5
HARTWIG, Robert, 3.1
HARVEY, Charles, 4.1.3 / 4.2
HAWORTH, Kent M., 1.6 / 3.0.3 /
　3.0.5
HAWRY, David A., 3.0.4.1
HAY, Douglas, 3.8 / 3.8.4.1 / 3.8.5
HAYES, Kenneth V., 2. / 2.4
HAYWARD, Robert J., 1.6 / 2. / 2.4
HEAD, Lyndsay, 3.8.4.1
HEALEY, Richard, 3.1.3
HEALY, S, 1.6
HEARN, Terry, 3.0.4.1
HECKROTTE, Warren, 3.1.4.1
HEDLIN, Edie, 1.6 / 3.4
HEDSTROM, Margaret, 3.4
HEFNER, Loretta L., 1.5 / 4.1.4
HEIDENREICH, Conrad E., 3.1.4.1
HELGERSON, Linda W., 2. / 3.0.5 /
　3.8 / 5.1.4
HENDERSON, Cathy, 1.6 / 5.1 / 5.3
HENDLEY, Anthony M., 2.1 / 5.2.1
HENDRICKS, Klaus B., 5.2.1
HENDRICKSON, Gordon O., 1.
HENSEN, Steven L., 3.0.3
HÉON, Gilles, 1. / 1.3 / 3.0.2
HEPP, M.A., 4.1.2
HERBERT, Francis, 3.1.4.1
HEREDIA HERRERA, Antonia,
　3.0.5 / 4.1.5
HEROLD, Wolfgang, 4.1.5 / 4.4
HERSTAD, John, 3.4
HERTHER, N.K., 5.1
HESSLER, David, 3.0.5
HICKERSON, H. Thomas, 3.0.3 /
　3.0.4.1 / 3.0.4.4 / 3.0.5
HIGGINS, Kevin B., 2. / 3.0.5 / 5.2.1
HILDESHEIMER, Françoise, 3.1 /
　3.1.2 / 4.2 / 4.5
HILL, Thomas T., 5.3.2
HILLER, I., 4.5
HILLER, Marc, 1.6 / 3.0.4.1
HIPPOLITO, Maria Regina, 3.1.5 /
　4.1.5
HIRTLE, Peter B., 3.0.5

HIVES, Christopher L., 1.7 / 2. /
　3.0.5 / 4.2
HOBBS, Brenda, 3.0.5 / 4.5
HODGES, Anthony, 2.4
HODGSON, Judith, 3.0.4 / 3.0.4.2
HODSON, Yolande, 3.1
HOFFMAN, Annie, 2. / 5.1
HOHMANN, Judy, 1.5
HOLBERT, Sue E., 1.6
HOLDEN, Harley P., 4.4
HOLDEN, Jill R.J., 1.6 / 5.
HOLDER, Carol, 2. / 5.1.4 / 5.2.1
HOLMAN, H.T., 1.7 / 4.1.1
HOLTON, Mark, 3.1.4.2
HONHART, Frederick L., 3.0.3 /
　3.0.5
HOOD, Annie, 3.1
HOOK, John, 5.3.2
HOOKER, Brian, 3.1.4.1
HOOPER, Patricia, 5.2.1
HOOTEN, Bill, 2. / 3.0.5 / 4.1.4 /
　5.1.4
HOPKINS, Mark, 1.6 / 2.4 / 3.0.5 /
　4.1.1
HOPKINS, Richard, 3.0.4.3
HORNE, Stephen A., 5.1 / 5.1.4
HOSE, John, 5.2.1
HOSTE, Frans E. Ch., 3.1
HOURIEZ, Élisabeth, 4.1.2
HOUTMAN-DE SMEDT, Helma,
　3.8.4.1 / 4.2
HOWARTH, Ken, 3.7
HOWATT-KRAHN, Ann, 5.1
HOWE, Richard D., 1.6
HUBENER, Hal, 4.1.4 / 5.1.4 / 5.3.1
HUDSON, Alice C., 3.1 / 4.1.4
HUDSON, B.J., 2.1
HUMPHREY, Bruce J., 5.3.2
HUNTER, Gregory S., 1.5 / 1.6 / 2. /
　3.0.5 / 5.2.1
HURST, Warwick, 4.1.3
HUSSEY, Harold E., 3.0.5 / 5.2.1
HUTCHISON, Anne, 4.1.5 / 4.5
HYAM, Grace Maurice, 1.4 / 1.6 /
　3.0.1 / 3.0.4.4 / 3.8.4.4 / 4.1 /
　4.1.1
HYE, Franz-Heinz, 4.2
IGUARTUA, José E., 4.2
IMPAGLIAZZO, Giancarlo, 5.3.1
INGEBRETSEN, Dorothy L., 3.0.5
INGRAM, John E., 4.1.4 / 5.1

154

KOJEVNIKOV, E.M., 1.8 / 4.1.1
KOLISH, Evelyn, 4.1.1
KOLOTOV, O.B., 1.5 / 4.1.5
KOMORNIKOVA, Magda, 5.3.1
KONRAD, Dietmar, 5.1 / 5.3
KOOBATIAN, James, 1.1 / 5.4
KOPLOWITZ, Bradford, 2.4
KORCHIA, Robert, 3.5 / 4.1.2
KOUZELENKOV, V.N., 3.0.5
KOUZNETSOVA, T.V., 1.6
KOVAN, Allan, 3.0.4.1
KOWALEWSKI, Anne-Françoise, 3.6 / 4.1.2
KOZINE, Yvan, 3.7
KOZLOV, O.F., 3.0.4.2
KRAEMER, James E., 4.1.1
KRAITCHEVA, Janna S., 5.2.1
KRAMER, C.M., 5.2.1
KRAUSE, Eric, 1.7 / 4.1 / 4.1.1
KRESTOVSKAYA, K.V., 3.0.1
KRIVENKO, M.V., 3.0.4.2
KUBICZEK, Barbara, 4.1.5
KUDER, James E., 5.2
KUDNER, James E., 5.5
KUHN, Hermann, 5.1 / 5.3
KUYK, Robert Egeter van, 1.5 / 5.1
LABERGE, Danielle, 1.4 / 3.8.1 / 3.8.4.1
LACHOWSKI, Michel, 1.6 / 4.1.2
LACROIX, Guylaine, 2.3
LACY, John A., 2. / 3.0.5 / 5.2.1
LADEIRA, Caroline Durant, 1.1
LAINE, Edward W., 1.7 / 4.5
LAING, Josie, 3.1 / 4.1.5
LAJEUNESSE, Marcel, 1.6
LAMPRECHT, Sandra J., 3.1.4.1
LAMUR-DAUDREU, Anne-Claude, 2.1 / 4.1.2
LANCASTER, Wilfrid, 3.0.3 / 3.0.5
LANDON, Richard, 3.0.1
LANGE, Christine, 4.1.2
LANGE, Janet M., 4.3
LANGEMO, Mark, 2. / 3.0.5 / 5.2.1 / 5.5
LANGLOIS, Égide, 3.0.3
LAPOINTE, Richard, 1.7
LA RIE, E. René, 5.3
LARIVIÈRE, Jules, 3.0.4.3
LARNED, Berle E., 2.1
LAROSE, Michèle, 1.8 / 5.1.3 / 5.5
LARSGAARD, Mary Lynette, 3.1.1 / 3.1.2 / 3.1.3 / 3.1.4.1

LARSON, G.W., 5.1.3
LATHROP, Alan K., 3.1.4.3
LAURENCIC, Tamara, 5.1 / 5.3.1 / 5.3.2
LAVOIE, Andrée, 3.8.1
LAW, Susan, 3.0.5 / 5.2.1
LEA, Mary Ann, 2. / 2.4
LEAHY, Lynne, 2. / 3.0.5 / 5.1.4
LEARY, William H., 4.1.3 / 5.2.1
LEBLANC, André, 1.7 / 3.8.1
LEE, F., 2.1
LEESCH, Wolfgang, 1.6
LÉGARÉ, Jacques, 3.0.5
LE MARESQUIER, E., 4.1.2
LENDERS, P., 3.8
LEONARD, Kevin B., 1.1
LEONHIRTH, Janene, 3.5
LEONTIEVA, O.G., 4.1.5
LE PEUTREC, Christian, 4.1.2
LESTER, Robert E., 4.1.3 / 5.2.1
LEUNG, C.K., 3.1.4.1
LEWANDOWSKA, Maria, 4.1.5
L'HUILLIER, Hervé, 3.7 / 4.2
LIENARDY, Anne, 5.3.2
LIENERT, Marina, 3.0.1 / 4.1.5
LI-KUEI, Hsueh, 3.0.5
LILBURN, Rachel, 4.1.5
LINDER, C.E. (Ted), 2. / 3.0.5 / 5.2.1
LIPMAN, Andy, 1.4 / 3.3.4.3 / 3.4.4.3 / 3.7.4.3
LIPPIN, Paula, 5.2
LITALIEN, Raymonde, 3.8.1
LLOYD, Robert, 3.1.4.1
LOBSTEIN, Dominique, Jean, 3.3 / 3.4
LODOLINI, Elio, 1.6
LOMBARDO, Daniel, 3.8 / 5.2 / 5.2.1
LONGSTRETH, Karl E., 5.1 / 5.3
LORRE, Jean J., 5.3.1
LOSIER, Cynthia F., 4.4
LOVE, J.H., 1.3
LOVEGROVE, Terry, 3.0.3 / 3.0.5
LOVELL-SMITH, Brian, 3.1 / 4.1.5 / 4.5
LOWELL, Howard P., 1.5 / 2. / 4.1.4
LUCEY, C.J., 3.1.4.1
LUDWIG, Harry L., 2.
LUEBBE, Mary, 2. / 5.2.1
LUNDGREN, Carol A., 2. / 3.0.5
LUNDGREN, Terry D., 2. / 3.0.5

LYNCH, Clifford A., 2. / 3.0.5 / 3.4.3 / 5.1.4 / 5.2.1
LYNCH, James R., 4.3
MCBAIN, J., 3.3 / 4.1.5
MCCARDLE, Bennett, 3.8.4 / 3.8.4.4 / 4.1.1
MCCARTHY, Paul H., 1.5 / 5.1 / 5.2.1
MCCLEARY, John M., 5.3 / 5.3.2
MCCLELLAN, William M., 5.2.1
MCCLYMONT, Jill, 4.2 / 4.5
MCCORMACK, Ros, 3.8.2 / 3.8.3 / 5.1.1
MCCRANK, Lawrence J., 1.5
MCDONALD, Evelyn, 5.1.4 / 5.2.1
MCDONALD, John, 3.4.4.4
MACDONALD, Kirk, 3.1.2
MCDONALD, Peter, 5.1 / 5.2.1
MACDONALD, R. Malcolm, 2. / 4.1
MACDONALD, Wilma, 4.3
MACE, Angela, 1.7 / 4.5
MACEACHREN, Alan M., 3.1.4.1
MCGING, Angela, 3.1.1 / 5.2.1 / 5.3
MACHOVEC, George S., 3.0.5
MACIEROWSKI, E.M., 3.1
MCINTOSH, Melinda C., 5.1.3
MCINTYRE, John E., 1.2 / 3.0.4.4 / 5.1
MCINTYRE, Katherine, 3.0.1 / 5.1
MCKINNIE, W.G., 4.4
MACLEOD, A., 3.0.4 / 3.0.5
MACLEOD, Donald, 1.7 / 3.0.1 / 4.1.1
MACMILLAN, Bryony, 4.1.5 / 4.5
MCMILLEN, Liz, 1.6
MCMINN, Stuart, 3.1.4.1
MCREYNOLDS, Samuel A., 3.0.1
MCTIERNAN, Miriam, 1.6
MADDEN, Dennis D., 2.5 / 3.0.4.4 / 4.1.4 / 5.1
MADELIN, Patrick, 3.3 / 3.3.4.1
MAEDKE, Wilmer O., 1.2 / 2.1
MAGLIANO, Patrizia, 5.3.1
MAGNUS, Detlef, 4.1.5 / 4.4
MAHER, William J., 1.6 / 4.5
MAKI, John, 2.1 / 5.2.1
MALAVIEILLE, Sophie, 3.7 / 4.1.2
MALING, Derek, 3.1.4.1
MALLINSON, John C., 3.4 / 5.1
MANASSE, P.M., 1.5 / 5.
MARAIS, Anneke, 4.1.5 / 4.4 / 5.1
MARCOTTE, Louise, 3.1.4.1

MARÉCHAL, Michel, 5.1.1
MAREE, Johann, 4.1.5 / 4.4 / 5.1
MARLEY, Carol, 3.1 / 3.1.4.1
MAROTEAUX, Vincent, 3.0.5 / 3.4 / 4.1.2
MARQUARDT, Leigh R., 2. / 5.1.4
MARR, Cathy, 2.1 / 4.1.5
MARSH, F.J., 5.1 / 5.3
MARTIN, Craig, 3.0.5 / 5.1.4
MARTIN, J. Sperling, 3.4.3
MARTIN, Russell, 3.0.3
MARTIN, Wayne, 5.2
MARTIN-MERAS, Luisa, 3.1 / 5.2.1
MARTINEK, Frantisek, 5.1
MATKOVIC, Ivan, 3.1
MATRAS, Hagit, 3.0.2 / 3.0.3 / 4.1.1
MATTERS, Marion, 3.0.3 / 3.0.5
MATTHEWS, Fred W., 2. / 5.1
MAY, Guy, 6.3
MAZIKANA, Peter C., 3.7
MBAYE, Saliou, 1.5 / 3.0.4.1 / 3.3 / 3.7 / 4.1.5
MENIER, Marie-Antoinette, 1.7 / 4.1.2
MENKUS, Belden, 2. / 2.1 / 3.0.5
MENNE-HARITZ, A., 3.0.5
MERKER, Wolfgang, 1.7 / 4.1.5
MEROT, Catherine, 4.1.2
MERRILL-OLDHAM, Jan, 1.1 / 5.1 / 5.3
MERRIN, Geneviève, 3.0.3
MEYER ZU ERPEN, Walter V., 3.0
MICHAUD, Marius, 4.1.5
MICHELS, Fredrick, 3.0.3 / 3.0.5
MICHELSON, Avra, 1.7 / 3.0.3 / 3.0.4.1 / 3.0.5 / 4.5
MIKAERE, Buddy, 3.8.4.1
MILES, Charles S., 5.2.1
MILLER, David, 5.1 / 5.1.4
MILLER, Deborah R., 5.3.2
MILLER, Fredric, 3.0.1 / 3.0.4.1
MILLER, J. Wesley, 3.2.4.4
MILLER, Page Putnam, 1.6 / 4.1.4
MILLER, Peter, 4.2
MILLER, Rosana, 3.1
MILOSEVIC, Milos, 4.1.5
MIMS, Julian L., 2. / 2.1 / 2.3
MINEL, Jean-Luc, 3.6.5 / 3.8.5
MIREAULT, Manon, 3.0.4 / 4.1.5
MITCHELL, Ann M., 1.6 / 5.3.3
MITCHELL, Gary, 1. / 1.4 / 1.5 / 1.6
MOBLEY, Russell L., 2. / 3.0.5

RANDHAWA, Bikkar S., 3.1.4.1
RASCH, M., 3.0.5
RASTAS, Pirkko, 1.6
READER, William A., 2. / 3.0.5
REHKOPF, Charles F., 1.6
REICHER, Leslie Arden, 5.1 / 5.3
REID, Peggy, 2.4
REILLY, James M., 5.1 / 5.2.1 / 5.2.2
REINHARDT, Victor, 5.1.3
RÉMILLARD, Juliette, 4.5
REMINGTON, R.R., 3.2.5
REMOND, René, 3.0.1
RENDELL, Kenneth W., 5.4
RENÉ-BAZIN, Paule, 1. / 1.6 / 1.8 /
    3.0.1 / 4.1.5
RETTER, David C., 4.2
REUBER, A.R., 3.0.4 / 3.0.5
REYNHOUT, Lucien, 3.8
RHOADS, Bert, 1.6
RHOADS, James B., 1.8
RHODES, Barbara J., 1.2 / 5.1 / 5.3
RICCI, I.M., 4.1.5 / 5.1
RICHARDS, Carole, 2.1
RICHARDSON, G., 3.7
RICHARDSON, Lee D., 2.4 / 3.0.5
RICHARDSON, Len, 3.0.4.1
RICHEFORT, Isabelle, 3.0.3 / 4.1 /
    4.1.2
RICKS, Betty R., 2.1
RIKHEIM, Brita, 3.0.4.1 / 4.2
RINALDI MARIANI, Maria-Pia, 1.8
ROADS, Christopher H., 3.3 / 3.7 /
    3.7.5
ROBBINS, Renee M., 3.0.4.4 /
    3.4.4.4
ROBEK, Mary F., 1.2 / 2.1
ROBERGE, Michel, 1.1 / 1.5 / 1.6 /
    2. / 2.1
ROBERTS, David, 1.5
ROBERTS, John W., 1.6
ROBERTS, Kenneth S, 1.8
ROBERTS-MOORE, Judith, 1.7 /
    4.1.1
ROBERTSON, Peter, 1.7 / 4.1.3
RODES, Jean-Michel, 3.7
RODRIGUEZ, Manuel, 3.0.5 / 5.2.1
ROESSLER, Monika, 3.0.4.4 / 4.1.5
ROGERS, Dorothy, 3.0.3 / 3.0.4
ROGERS, Frank, 4.1.5
ROHM, Wendy Goldman, 2. / 5.1
ROLLISON, Jeffrey, 1.3 / 3.0.3 /
    3.0.5

ROLON, Rosalind de, 1.5 / 3.0.4.2
ROOS, Arnold E., 3.2 / 3.2.4.1
ROPER, Michael, 1.1 / 1.6
ROSART, Françoise, 4.5
ROSCHLAU, Gertrud, 3.0.3 / 4.1.5
ROSENBERG, Norma V., 2.
ROSS, Alex, 1.7 / 4.1.1 / 4.2
ROSS, David, 3.5 / 3.5.3
ROSSOL, Erika, 3.0.3
ROSTECKI, Randy R., 3.1.4.1
ROTA, Anthony, 3.8.1
ROTH, Barbara, 1.1
ROUSSEAU, Jean-Yves, 1.2 / 2. / 2.4
ROUX, Lucie, 3.7 / 4.1.2
ROWH, Mark C., 2. / 3.0.5 / 5.2.1
ROWLAND, John, 3.1.4.1
ROY, Madeleine, 2.4
RUBIN, Jack, 5.2.1
RUDELLE, Odile, 3.7 / 3.7.1
RUMM, John C., 4.2
RUMSCHOETTEL, Hermann,
    3.0.5 / 4.1.5
RUSSELL, Bill, 1.7 / 1.8 / 3.8.1
RUSSELL, William H., 5.3.1
RUTH, Janice E., 1.6 / 3.0.4.1
S.L.A. GEOGRAPHY AND MAP
    DIVISION. COMMITTEE ON
    STANDARDS, 3.1.2 / 3.1.3
SABLE, Martin H., 1.1 / 3.1.4.1
SABOURIN, C., 3.7
SACLIER, Michael, 3.0.4.1 / 4.2
SAERGEL, Dagobert, 3.0.5
SAFFADY, William, 2. / 3.0.5 / 3.8 /
    5.1.4
SAINT-PIERRE, Paul, 2.1
SALAUN, Jean-Michel, 1.1 / 1.7 /
    4.1.2
SAMUEL, Jean, 2.1
SAMUELS, Helen Willa, 3.0.1
SANDBERG-FOX, Ann M., 3.4.3
SANDERS, H.A., 1.5 / 5.
SANDERS, Robert L., 2. / 2.1 / 2.4 /
    4.4
SANDFORD, Herbert A., 3.1.4.1
SANFILIPPO, Matteo, 4.3
SANTORO, Corrado A., 1.6
SARETZKY, Gary D., 5.1 / 5.2.2 /
    5.3.3
SARNIA, Lazar, 1.4 / 3.0.4.3
SAULNIER, C., 3.7
SAVAJOLS, R., 4.1 / 4.1.2
SAVARD, Réjean, 1.5 / 3.0.4.2

SOCIETY OF AMERICAN
ARCHIVISTS. COMMITTEE
ON EDUCATION
AND PROFESSIONAL
DEVELOPMENT, 1.6
SOLODOVNIKOVA, L.I., 3.0.4.2 /
4.1.5
SOMINITCH, G.E., 1.7 / 4.1.5 / 5.2.1
SOPKO, Sandra, 5.1 / 5.1.3
SORRELL, Patrick, 3.1
SOURINOV, V.M., 3.8
SOWRY, Clive, 3.3.1
SPADONI, Carl, 4.5
SPANG, Paul, 1.7 / 4.1.5
SPARKS, Peter G., 5.3.2
SPAULDING, George, 2. /3.0.5 /
5.2.1
SPEIDELSBACH, Annelie, 3.0.2
SPEIRS, Brian, 1.6
SPENCE, Adolphus N., 5.2.1
SPENCER, DON, 3.0.5
SPILKER, Chris, 2. / 3.0.5 / 5.1.4
SPORCK, John H., 2. / 5.1
STANGE, Eric, 2. / 5.1 / 5.1.3
STANSFIELD, Geoff, 3.0.4.2
STARK, Peter L., 1.1 / 3.1.4.1
STAROSTINE, E.V., 3.0.2 / 4.1.5
STAZICKER, Elizabeth, 5.1.2
STEHKAEMPER, Hugo, 5.1.3
STEKATCHEVA, E.V., 5.1
STEPHENS, David O., 2.4
STEPPLER, G.A., 3.8
STERETT, Jill Norton, 3.1.4.1
STERN, Gail F., 3.0.4.2
STERN, Teena, 1.6
STEWART, Eleanore, 5.3.2
STICKELLS, Lloyd, 3.7.1 / 3.7.5
STIELOW, Frederick J., 1.2 / 3.7
STILLGER, Josef, 3.0.5 / 5.2.1
STIRTON, Lavra J., 5.3.2
STOCKFORD, Bridget, 3.0.4.2 / 4.2
STOCKSLAGER, Todd, 2. / 3.0.5
STONE, Jeffrey, 3.1
STONER, Joyce Hill, 5.1 / 5.3
STRACHAN, S.R., 1.4 / 1.5 / 4.1.5
STRATFORD, Juri, 2. / 5.2.1
STREIT, Samuel Allen, 1.5 / 4.4
STRICKLAND, Muriel, 3.1.4.2
STRONG, Gary E., 5.1
STUART, Elizabeth A., 1.6 / 3.1.4.1
STUDWELL, William E., 3.1.3
STURGES, P., 3.0.1 / 3.4

SUBT, Sylvia S.Y., 5.2 / 5.2.2
SULLIVAN, Robert C., 5.1 / 5.2.1
SUTHERLAND, Johnnie D., 3.1 /
3.1.2
SUTTON, Cynthia L., 2.
SWARTZELL, Ann, 5.2.1
SWEENEY, Shelley, 1.5 / 4.3
SYLVESTRE, Guy, 1.2
SYMONDSON, B., 2.4 / 4.1.5
SZARY, Richard V., 3.0.3 / 3.0.5
TAIEB, Gilbert, 5.1
TAMMARO, Marie-Françoise, 1.6 /
1.8
TANASI, Maria Teresa, 5.3.1
TANI, Tadaaki, 5.2.2
TAPSCOTT, Bob, 3.0.4.4
TARANOV, I.T., 1.7 / 4.1.5
TATEM, Jill M., 1.3 / 3.0.3 / 3.0.5
TAYLOR, D.S., 3.8.4.1
TAYLOR, Hugh A., 1. / 1.5 / 1.6 /
3.8 / 5.1 / 5.3
TCHERNENKOV, K.G., 1.1 / 4.1.5
TCHIRKOV, S.V., 1.6
TEDDE, Pedro, 2.1 / 4.2
TENER, Jean, 1.5 / 3.0.5
TERRILL-BREUR, Judith, 3.8 / 5.2.1
TESSIER, Marc, 1.7
TESSIER, Yves, 3.1.4.1
TÉTREAULT, Marie-Josée, 2.4
THIAM, Mbaye, 1. / 1.5 / 4.1.5
THIBODEAU, S.G., 4.5
THIEME, B., 3.0.5
THOMA, G., 3.0.5 / 5.1.4
THOMAS, Bettye Collier, 1.7 / 4.5
THOMAS, Bill, 5.2.1
THOMAS, D.L., 3.0.4.4 / 5. / 5.1 /
5.1.3
THOMAS, David, 5.1.1
THOMAS, John B., 3.8.3
THOMAS, John B. III, 1.1
THOMPSON, Jack C., 5.3.2
THOMPSON, Michael, 5.3 / 5.3.1 /
5.3.2
THOMPSON, Robert J., 2. / 5.1
THOMPSON, Terry, 1.6
THORNDALE, William, 3.1.4.1
THORSON, Sandra J., 3.0.4.2
THURSTON, Anne, 4.1.5
TIMBERS, Michael J., 2. / 3.0.5 /
5.2.1 / 5.5
TOMPKINS, Edward, 3.1.4.1
TORTELLA, Teresa, 4.2

TOUCHARD, Jean-Baptiste, 3.3 / 3.4
TOUGH, Alistair, 4.4
TOURTIER-BONAZZI, Chantal de,
    1.5 / 3.0.1 / 3.7 / 4.1.2
TRAUE, J.E., 1.6
TRAUTMAN, Maryellen, 1.1
TREANOR, John J., 4.3
TREVITT-CLARK, Susan, 3.1.4.1
TRUFFER, Bernard, 1.6
TSAPLINE, V.V., 1.5 / 4.1.5
TURKOS, Anne S.K., 1.5 / 3.6
TURNER, Allan, 1.7
TURNER, D. John, 1.1 / 3.3
TURNER, Éric, 3. / 4.1.5
TURNER, James, 3.1 / 3.1.2 / 5.1.3
TURNER, Jeffrey H., 5.1.3 / 5.2.1
TURTON, Alison, 1.1 / 4.2
TUTTLE, William, 2. / 3.0.5 / 5.1.4
TYNDALL, R.M., 3.0.5
UDINA, Federico, 1.7 / 1.8 / 4.1.5
UHL, Bodo, 3. / 3.0.4.4 / 4.1.5
ULATE-SEGURA, Bodil, 3.0.4.4 /
    4.1.5
ULFSPARRE, Anna Christina, 2.1 /
    4.2
UNESCO. GENERAL
    INFORMATION PROGRAMME,
    1.2
UNION OF SOVIET SOCIALIST
    REPUBLICS. MAIN ARCHIVAL
    ADMINISTRATION, 1.2 / 4.1.5
U.S. OFFICE OF MANAGEMENT
    AND BUDGET, 2.1 / 4.1.4
UNIVERSITÉ DE MONTRÉAL.
    SERVICE DES ARCHIVES, 2.3 /
    3.0.2
UNIVERSITÉ DU QUÉBEC À
    MONTRÉAL. SERVICE DES
    ARCHIVES, 2.4
UNSWORTH, Michael E., 3.0.1 /
    5.2.1
USDIN, Steve, 3.0.5 / 5.1
VSA- GILDUNGSAUSSCHUSS,
    3.0.4 / 3.0.4.2 / 5.1 / 5.2
VAGANOV, F.M., 1. / 3. / 4.1.5 / 5.1
VAISEY, David, 5.1
VAISSE, Maurice, 3.7 / 3.7.1
VALERIO, Vladimiro, 3.1.4.1
VALIQUETTE, Diane, 2.1
VALLBONA, Carlos, 2.1 / 5.5
VAN DAMME, Philippe, 5.3.2

VAN DEN BROECKE, Marcel P.R.,
    3.1.1
VAN DER SAAG, Bert J., 3.0.5 /
    4.1.5 / 4.5
VAN DE WIEL, Constant, 4.3
VASSILIEV, N.A., 2.1
VEIT, Fritz, 4.1.4
VERDEBOUT, Luc, 4.5
VERDERY, John D., 1.2 / 1.5
VERNON, John Ed., 3.0.4.2 / 3.2.4.2
VERSCHAFFEL, A., 3.6
VIGNES-DUMAS, Claire, 3.3 / 3.5 /
    3.7 / 4.1.2
VINAS, R., 5.1 / 5.3
VINAS, V., 5.1 / 5.3
VOISIN, Jean-Claude, 3.5.2 / 4.1.2
VOLDMAN, Danièle, 3.7
VOLKOVA, I.V., 3.0.3 / 4.1.5
VOSAHLIKOVA, Dana, 1.7 / 3.8.1 /
    4.1.5
VOSSLER, Janet L., 2. / 5.1
VOYEVODA, Alexandre, 5.1.1
WACHTER, Otto, 5.3.2
WACHTER, Wolfgang, 5.3
WAEGEMANN, C. Peter, 2.1 / 5.1.4
WALCH, Timothy, 3.7
WALCH, Victoria Irons, 1.6
WALFORD, John, 3.0.3 / 3.0.5
WALKER, Cathy, 2.1 / 3.0.5
WALKER, Gay, 5.2.2
WALLACE, Patricia E., 1.2 / 2.1
WALLOT, Jean-Pierre, 1.5 / 1.7 /
    1.8 / 2.1 / 4.1.1 / 4.1.5
WALSH, Betty, 3.0.4.4 / 5.1 / 5.1.4 /
    5.3
WALSH, Jim, 3.1.4
WALSH, Mark, 4.5
WALSH, Steven, 3.3.3
WALTER, Gerry, 3.0.5
WARD, Bob, 3.1.4.1
WARDS, I., 4.1.5
WARNER, Alice Sizer, 1.5 / 3.0.4
WARNER, R.M., 1.6
WARNOW-BLEWETT, Joan, 1.6 /
    3.0.1 / 3.8 / 4.5 / 5.1
WARTIAN, Wayne W., 2.1 / 5.2.1
WATELET-CHERTON, Anne, 4.3
WATERS, N.M., 3.1.4.1
WATSON, Andrew C., 5.2.1
WATT, I., 3.1.3
WEBB, David, 3.1.4.1
WEBER, Dieter, 1.4 / 4.1.5

WEBER, Lisa B., 1.6 / 3.0.3 / 3.0.5
WEBER, Mark, 5.2.2
WEHSER, Gary, 5.2.1
WEIDEMANN, Diethelm, 4.1.5
WEIHS, Jean, 5.1.3
WEIL, Stephen E., 1.4
WEILBRENNER, Bernard, 1.7 /
3.0.4 / 4.1.1
WEILL, Georges, 1.8 / 4.1.4 / 5.1 /
5.2.1
WEINBERG, Gerhard L., 1.2 / 4.1.1
WEIR, Thomas R., 3.1.4.1
WEISE, Carl E., 2.
WELFELE, Odile, 1.6 / 4.1.2
WELLENS, Robert, 4.1.5
WESSMAN, Lars, 3.0.4.1
WESTBROOK, Lynn, 5.1
WESTERBERG, Kermit B., 4.5
WHEALAN, Ronald E., 2. / 4.1.1 /
5.2.1
WHEELER, B., 5.2.1
WHEELER, William D., 5.2.1
WHISTANCE-SMITH, Ron, 3.1.4.1
WHITAKER, Albert H., 4.1.5 / 5.1.1
WHITE, Howard S., 5.2.2
WHITEHEAD, Janet C., 2.1 / 5.1
WHITMORE, Paul M., 5.1.3 / 5.3.1
WHITTICK, Christopher, 1.6 /
3.0.1 / 4.1.5
WHITTICK, Margaret, 1.6 / 3.0.1 /
4.1.5
WHYTE, Doug, 3.8.1 / 3.8.5
WILKINSON, David G., 2. / 3.0.5
WILLIAMS, Anne E., 1.3
WILLIAMS, Bernard, 2. / 3.0.5 /
4.1.3 / 5.1.4
WILLIAMS, Robert V., 2.
WILLIAMSON, R., 3.0.5 / 5.5
WILMAN, Hugh, 5.2.2
WILSON, Bruce, 3.1.4.2 / 3.2.4.2 /
3.8.4.2
WILSON, Don W., 4.1.4
WILSON, Eric, 5.2.1
WILSON, Lofton, 3.0.5
WILSON, Pam, 3.1.4
WILSON, Tony, 3.8.1 / 3.8.4.1
WINN, William, 3.1.4.1
WISE, Donald A., 3.1.4.1
WISE, Joseph, 4.1.5 / 5.2.1
WITTMAN, Elisabeth, 4.3
WOELDERINK, Bernard, 1.6
WOHLFEIL, Rainer, 3.5

WOLCHAK, William H., 2. / 3.0.5
WOLF, David K., 5.2.1
WOLF, Eric W., 1.1 / 3.1.4.1
WOLFSHOERNDL, Vladimir, 1.5 /
4.1.5
WOOD, Denis, 3.1.4.1
WOOD, Lamont, 3.0.5 / 5.2.1
WOOD, Thomas J., 4.4
WOOD LEE, Mary, 5.1 / 5.1.2
WOODWARD, David, 3.1.4.1 / 5.3.1
WOOLGAR, C.M., 3.0.3 / 3.0.5
WORAM, John M., 3.1.4.1
WRATTEN, Nigel, 2.5 / 4.2 / 5.1.1
WRIGHT, Glenn, 1.7
WRIGHT, Sandra, 1.2 / 1.5 / 5.1 /
5.3.1
WURL, Joel, 1.6 / 4.1.4
WURZBURGER, Marilyn, 3.0.4.4 /
4.4
WYTHE, Deborah, 1.2
XIUXIAN, Zhou, 4.2
YASUZAWA, Shuichi, 1.7 / 4.1.5
YATES, Nigel, 3.0.1 / 3.0.4.1
YEE, Martha M., 1.3
YERBURGH, Mark, 3.0.5 / 5.2.1
YOUNG, Rod, 1.1 / 3.8
YU, F.T., 5.5
YURKIW, Peter, 1.5 / 5.1 / 5.3.1
ZAGAMI, Robert W., 2. / 3.0.5 /
5.1.4 / 5.2.1
ZBORAY, Ronald J., 3.0.3 / 3.0.5
ZEIDBERG, David S., 3.0.4.4
ZEITOUN, Jean, 3.3 / 3.4
ZELIS, Guy, 4.5
ZIZHI, Feng, 3. / 4.1.5 / 5.1